ANNALS

of

BATH COUNTY

VIRGINIA

By OREN F. MORTON, B. Lit.

CLEARFIELD

Originally published
Staunton, Virginia, 1917

Reprinted for
Clearfield Company, Inc. by
Genealogical Publishing Co., Inc.
Baltimore, Maryland
1990, 1996, 2000, 2003

International Standard Book Number: 0-8063-4642-6

Made in the United States of America

CONTENTS

Chapter		Page
1.	Geography of Bath	1
II.	Discovery and Settlement	10
III.	The Lewis Land Grant	22
IV.	Areas of Settlement	36
V.	The Mineral Springs	42
VI.	Early Political History	51
VII.	Roads and Road Builders	56
VIII.	Life in the Pioneer Days	62
IX.	Ten years of Indian Wars	79
X.	The Point Pleasant Campaign	88
XI.	Bath During the Revolution	94
XII.	Selim the Algerine	101
XIII.	Efforts Toward a New County	104
XIV.	Organization of Bath	107
XV.	The Surnames of Bath	111
XVI.	A List of Early Marriages	127
XVII.	Seventy Years of Bath History	134
XVIII.	Bath in the War of 1861	143
XIX.	The Bath Squadron	146
XX.	Roster of Confederate Soldiers	152
XXI.	Cloverdale	162
XXII.	The Calfpasture Valley	167
XXIII.	The Bath of Today	172
XXIV.	Alleghany County	176
XXV.	The Families of Greater Bath	186

ANNALS OF BATH COUNTY

I

GEOGRAPHY OF BATH

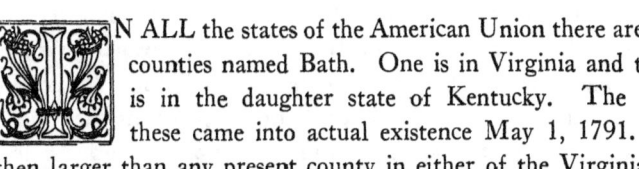N ALL the states of the American Union there are but two counties named Bath. One is in Virginia and the other is in the daughter state of Kentucky. The older of these came into actual existence May 1, 1791. It was then larger than any present county in either of the Virginias. It is still larger than the average of the 155 counties in the two states.

Until West Virginia became a fact, Bath lay near the center of the Old Dominion. It now lies against the western border of the parent state. Near its southwestern angle it is crossed by the thirty-eighth parallel of north latitude and also by the third meridian west from Washington. In outline the county is a fairly regular quadrangle, the four corners pointing very nearly north, east, south, and west. Between the northern and southern corners the diagonal distance is 27 miles, and between the eastern and western corners the distance is 30 miles. The area is placed at 548 square miles, or 352,720 acres. The airline distance from the county seat to the state capital is 135 miles, the direction being a little south of east. The city of Washington is 160 miles away, the direction being northeast.

The western boundary of Bath is the central ridge of the Appalachians, sometimes called the Alleghany Front. It divides the waters coursing toward the Atlantic from those running toward the Mississippi. This massive uplft is a natural boundary. On the eastern side of the county, Walker's Mountain, Sideling Hill, and Mill Mountain take turns in forming the border line. These three elevations run almost precisely in the same direction. From the top of Walter's Mountain the line leaps squarely across a very narrow valley to the top of Sideling Hill. Four miles southward it passes with equal abruptness across a still narrower valley to the summit of Mill Mountain. And yet this complex eastern border opens to the base line only at the one point where Panther Gap provides an easy passage for a railroad and an outlet for the waters of Mill Creek.

On the other hand the northern and southern county lines are entirely artificial. Bath is simply a cross-section of the great valley which extends nearly all the way from New River to the Potomac. The bordering counties are Highland, Augusta, Rockbridge, Alleghany, Greenbrier, and Pocahontas, the last two lying in West Virginia.

The Alleghany Front is lofty throughout, reaching in Paddy Knob at the northern corner of Bath an altitude of 4500 feet. Within the county the most distinctive uplift is the divide running lengthwise through the center, separating Bath into two principal divisions. For more than half the way this divide is Warm Springs Mountain, which enters from the south and terminates near Burnsville. Jack Mountain enters from the north and runs a little past the other ridge, the distance from crest to crest being one mile. From Duncan's Knob, Jack Mountain drops quite suddenly into the lower continuation known as Wilson's Mountain. From the same knob a saddle reaches across to Warm Springs Mountain and thus preserves a continuity of watershed in the central divide. Near the center of the county Warm Springs Mountain forks, the western and lower arm, known as Valley Mountain, running nearly parallel with the eastern, at a distance from summit to summit of two miles, and passing into Alleghany county. The portion lying in Bath is pierced by no fewer than six water-gaps.

Midway between the Alleghany Front and the central divide is a very conspicuous elevation, which to the north of the place where it opens to give passage to Back Creek, is styled Back Creek Mountain. Southward, it is known as Bollar Mountain. Westward of this ridge is Little Mountain, separating the valley of Little Back Creek from that of Back Creek proper. Eastward are Rocky Ridge, Warwick's Mountain, and Callison Ridge. A little east of Warm Springs Mountain is Tower Hill, a continuation of the Bullpasture Mountain of Highland. From the Bullpasture gap on the county line it runs 10 miles southward to a bend in Dry Run. Southward from Thompson's Creek to the line of Alleghany County, the space for five miles east of the crest of Warm Springs Mountain is crowded with a succession of much lower uplifts. Beard's Mountain, the outermost and highest of these, lies in the same axis with Shenandoah Mountain, though separated from it by a long depression. Shenandoah Mountain, after holding for 60 miles an imposing height and breadth, breaks down very abruptly after penetrating Bath only six miles. The Sister Knobs mark the forked southern end. Southward are hill-ridges walling in the basin of Stuart's Creek. Near Millboro Springs begins the higher and ragged uplift of Rough Mountain, which terminates all at once in Griffith Knob at a bend of the Cowpasture on the Alleghany line.

Bath is in fact mainly occupied with mountain ridges, which vary a good deal in heighth, length and contour. To a person following any of the larger watercourses, the river-valley often appears narrower than is truly the case, because of foothill ridges rising sharply from the edge of the bottom land. Sometimes, as on the upper Cowpasture, these heavy bluffs present toward the river abrupt faces of dry, slaty soil, supporting a thin growth of small pines and a little hardwood underbrush.

As is generally the case in Appalachian America, the mountains of Bath occur in long ridges and present outlines of much grace and symmetry. This is particularly true of Walker's Mountain, the skyline of which is almost as horizontal as a house roof. Rough Mountain is quite exceptional in this respect.

The tendency of the Appalachian ridges to run out, or to be interrupted by watergaps, is of much practical importance. Routes of travel were thereby suggested to the white pioneers and to the Indians before them. The breaking down of Shenandoah Mountain offers a line of easy approach from the Valley of Virginia to the Cowpasture at Fort Lewis. Panther Gap and the pass at Griffith Knob presented lines of approach to the settlers who occupied Stuart's Creek and the lower Cowpasture. From the Cowpasture, Thompson's Creek opens a way through a succession of minor ridges to the very foot of Warm Springs Mountain. A depression in the skyline of the latter indicated to the early comers the most advantageous place for crossing that barrier. Then again, the gaps in Valley Mountain offered a choice of routes into the lower lying valley of Jackson's River. In short, physical geography has placed Bath on a through line of travel between the East and the West.

The uplift in the center of the county divides Bath into the two main valleys of Jackson's River and the Cowpasture. The more important sub-valleys of the western division are Warm Springs valley and the valleys of Big and Little Back Creeks. Those of the eastern division are Dry Run, Stuart's Creek, Porter's Mill Creek, and Padd's Creek. In addition to these is the basin of Mill Creek, which drains into the Calfpasture and not into the Cowpasture.

Jackson's River has a course of some 20 miles before touching Bath, and enters this county as a considerable stream. Within Bath it is swollen by Muddy Run, Chimney Run, Warm Springs Run, and Cedar Creek, but most of all by Back Creek. To the point of junction, Back Creek has pursued quite as long a course as the main stream itself but through a narrower valley.

A half mile south of the Highland boundary the Cowpasture is joined by the Bullpasture, which is the longer and larger of the two streams, and is even larger than Jackson's River at the county line. The united waters also pursue a longer course within the confines of Bath. But after passing into Alleghany, and at length reaching the point a little below Clifton Forge where it is joined by the Cowpasture, Jackson's River gains upon its companion both in length and volume. It is therefore regarded as the head branch of the James, which is the title the waters assume below the confluence. In colonial days this section of the James was known as the Fluvanna. The chief tributaries of the Cowpasture are the five mentioned in a preceding paragraph. None of these, except Stuart's Creek, is ordinarily of much size. Dry Run is so named because in its lower course there is no visible water except in a wet season.

The running waters of Bath are nearly always rapid as well as clear. In the sandstone areas are excellent springs of cool freestone water. The caverns which underlie the limestone belts attract the rainfall into underground channels. Near the base level of the valleys in which these belts occur, the waters reappear as powerful, never-failing springs. Except in times of flood, fordable places occur in all the rivers, although bridges sometimes obviate the need of taking the rocky bed.

Rock formations are called stratified, when they are due to the marl, sand, clay, or gravel which has been deposited by water, especially that of tidal streams. Because of the pressure of newer deposits above, these soft materials finally solidify into hard rock. The internal heat of the earth assists in this process, and when intense it works a change in structure, causing the rock to be of the kind known as metamorphic. Of this latter nature is the flinty sandstone, layers of which, bent into an almost vertical position, may be seen in some of the watergaps. The stratified rocks of Bath are among the oldest known to geology. On the eastern and western borders they are of the Devonian series. There are also small areas of these in the intervening ridges. Elsewhere, the greater portion of the county is covered by the older Silurian series. Older yet is the narrow rim of Ordovician rocks in the Warm Springs valley. This rim incloses a large, oval-shaped area of the yet older Cambro-Ordovician rocks. Since all these formations are older than the Carboniferous beds, it is scarcely worth while to look for coal, unless on the extreme western border. But the deposits of iron ore and building stones are of much extent and value, although as yet undeveloped. There is also some manganese.

Layers of hard sandstone form the cores of the steeper ridges and tell us why these mountains exist. They protect the adjacent softer layers, which are more susceptible to wear and tear. It is mainly in the valleys and on the broad-topped elevations that we find the flaky slates and the limestones. The former blister from the action of frost and sun. The latter dissolve under the honeycombing effect of rainwater charged with carbonic and vegetable acids. Caverns, which are underground waterways, are thus eaten into the limestone beds, the presence of which is shown by the sinkholes on the surface above. But the limestone areas in Bath are not extensive. They occur chiefly in the Warm Springs valley and around Burnsville. Shale, more commonly termed slate, is a characteristic feature of the sterile bluffs which sometimes hem in the fertile bottoms of alluvial origin.

The soils of Bath differ very much in quality. First in value is the deep, dark loam of the river bottoms. The soil of the limestone belts is likewise superor and is particularly suited to grass. Much of the upland soil elsewhere is light in color and sandy in texture. Tight or loose stones, sometimes waterworn, occur everywhere, but in varying frequency. It is only the bottoms, the bench lands, and limited portions of the higher levels that have been in demand for tillage. A belt of bench and bottom is sometimes a mile from side to side. Yet such a strip is not continuous, bold heights sometimes coming close to the river on either side, as in the case of Jackson's River above Fort Dinwiddie. Furthermore, the bottoms are confined to the two rivers and the lower courses of their larger affluents.

With respect to the climate, Bath is highly favored. The elevation gives it a more temperate air than is found in the same latitude on the Atlantic or the plains of the West. The Alleghany Front breaks the force of the northwesters that have such free play throughout the Mississippi basin. It also causes a lower degree of humidity on the eastern side than on the western. Shenandoah Mountain scatters the east wind that is so trying along the seacoast. Bath has not the damp air that one would expect in a mountain region. It has not the close summer atmosphere and the winter keenness of the seashore, nor the accentuated extremes of heat and cold that are a well known feature of the Western climate. The air movement is less than in either of the other sections, high winds being rare. The winters are not usually of a severe type, the summers and falls are particularly delightful, and the air is pure, healthful and invigorating. There is, in fact, a fine climate at all seasons.

To be more precise, the climate of Warm Springs valley, with its altitude of 2200 feet, is but slightly below the average for the county. In this locality the mean temperatures for winter, spring, summer, and fall are 31, 51, 69, and 53 degrees. The yearly average, which is 51 degrees, is about the same as at Harrisburg in Pennsylvania, or Lincoln in Nebraska, although the climate of this valley is more regular than that of the other places. The yearly rainfall is 42 inches, including the snow, which in an unmelted form amounts to 26 inches. Along the two rivers, especally the Cowpasture, the climate is perceptibly warmer, the altitudes being less by from 500 to 1000 feet.

In the old-time solitudes of Bath there was a great deal of animal life. The buffalo and the elk have been gone much more than a century. The wolf, once a great scourge to the young livestock, is locally extinct, thanks to the large bounty that was maintained so long as he was here. The name of Panther Gap keeps us from forgetting that the puma, called "painter" by the pioneer, was once a co-tenant with the wolf. The fox and the wildcat, and an occasional black bear still linger, and now and then an eagle disports himself in the air. A very few deer remain in the more extensive woodlands, yet even the gray squirrel and cottontail are now comparative rare. Other small mammals are the raccoon, the opossum, the woodchuck, the skunk, the muskrat, the chipmunk, and the bat. Turkeys, pheasants, quails, and other game birds are now rather few, and the small migrants that appear in the spring are not so numerous as the true interests of the farmer demand. Rattlesnakes and copperheads are few, unless in their regular haunts. The clear streams contain some trout, bass, perch, suckers, and eels. The former abundance of wild game is reflected in the following rhyme, written of William Wilson of Bolar Run:

> Old Wilson could sit at his door,
> And count buffalo, elk, and deer by the score.

As is true in all Appalachia, the hills and valleys of Bath take naturally to a forest covering. The deciduous trees, such as maples, chestnuts, hickories, sycamores, willows, and oaks, heavily preponderate. Small pines cling to the dry soil of certain river-hills. The larger specimens on the mountain sides are mostly killed about fifteen years before the date of this book, by an insect pest, but many of their barkless trunks are yet standing. A varied undergrowth of shrubs and small trees is now more in evidence than in the time of the pioneer. Some of the more conspicuous wild fruits are the blackberry, the huckleberry, the teaberry, and the common and mountain raspberries. The wild grapevine grows to large dimensions.

Outside of the bottoms and the small lime stone area, the soils of Bath are not so favorable to making a good grass sod as in the more elevated county of Highland. Hence tillage farming is more conspicuous than there. The leading field crops are corn, grain, and hay, and large yields are obtained on the bottoms. The Fort Lewis farm has produced 2340 bushels of wheat in a single season. Orchard fruits, particularly apples, have always been grown for home use, but only of late has there been much attention to the producing of either large or small fruits on a commercial scale. The county is well suited to this branch of agriculture. An apple tree just over the Highland line was set out in 1765 by William Wilson, and in 1908 was still yielding 35 bushels of good spitzenbergs.

The scenic beauty of Appalachia is at once recognized by the observant traveler. There is an absence of monotony, because the prospect distinctly varies from mile to mile. When the woods are in summer foliage, the contour of the numerous ridges assumes the most graceful appearance. The emerald verdure of the meadows and pastures then renders the open ground more pleasing to the eye than in regions where grass is not spontaneous.

The view from Flag Rock, on the crest-line of Warm Springs Mountain, can scarcely be surpassed with respect to scenic loveliness and interest. Looking southeastward, the eye passes over the succession of comparatively low ridges on the nearer side of the Cowpasture. Turning nearly to the east one gazes through a low gap into the valley of Thompson's Creek, and has distant glimpses of the Millboro turnpike among the fields around Fairview and Bath Alum. Beyond the winding course of the unseen Cowpasture there comes into view, for its entire length, the irregular summit and fluted slope of Rough Mountain. Beyond is the far smoother outline of Mill Mountain. Still further beyond, and of a pearly hue from the effect of distance, are the two House Mountains toward Lexington. Their short, straight summits and their abrupt endings loom well above the deeper-hued crest-level of the prominence in front. Yet the final sky-line in the east is not reached until one makes out the pale Blue Ridge, 40 miles away, and dominated by the towering Peaks of Otter. Looking more nearly east, and in a line with the view down Thompson's Creek, the observer peers into the deep notch of Panther Gap. In front of and to the right of this opening are the two uplifts on either side of Stuart's Creek. Beyond is Sideling Hill and then comes the remarkable horizontal crest of Walker's Mountain. A dozen miles away in the northeast are the Sister Knobs, marking the south end of Shenandoah Mountain and standing like sentinels above the low expanse in front. In the same direction, but at more than twice the distance, is Elliott's Knob, one of the loftiest peaks in Virginia. Turning about and facing the point of sunset, we behold another rapid alternation of forested heights, the Alleghany Front occupying the horizon. In the foreground is an exquisite panorama of Warm Springs valley, which lies a thousand feet below. Whether one is looking eastward or westward, mountain rises behind mountain at intervals that are seemingly short. Because these heights are forest-clad, and thus screen the open lands between them, the outlook is almost as primeval to us as it was to the pathfinder of nearly two centuries ago. And when the whole prospect is bathed in the clear, bright atmosphere of a Virginia sky, the picture receives a touch of completeness.

Among the natural curiosities of Bath is Ebbing Spring, three miles south of Williamsville. Intermittent springs are usually quite regular as to ebb and flow. But this one is so abnormal that the McClintic family, whose mansion lies within a few rods, have never been so fortunate as to see the waters at the exact moment of high tide. The rush comes with a considerable noise, yet during the times of ebb there is still considerable outflow. The stream once ran a mill, and so important was then the period of high water that when it came in the night, the miller would get up and set his burrs in motion. Two miles north is Meadow Lake, covering more than an acre of the Cowpasture bottom. It is fed by a powerful spring, and is the source of Spring Branch, which is capable of turning a very large overshot wheel. It is thought that the spring is simply a reappearance of Cowpasture waters. At all events, the Cowpasture at ordinary stages is nearly dry for several miles above the mouth of the Bullpasture. Near Wallawhatoola Spring the Cowpasture seems again to lose a share of its visible volume, recovering it in a large spring near Nimrod Hall.

In a bluff on this river, near Windy Cove church, is Blowing Cave, mentioned in Jefferson's *Notes on Virginia*. The cavern has been explored a considerable distance and seems to have a second opening. There is a strong outward draft in hot weather and a strong inward draft in cold weather. The explanation is simple. Any deep cave has a uniform temperature the year round. This temperature is practically the same as the yearly average of the surface above. Such a cave in Bath would have a constant temperature, day and night, winter and summer, of from 50 to 52 degrees. So when the outer air is warmer than that of the cave, the heavy cold air rushes out, giving place to an equal weight of the lighter warm air. In winter the outer air is the colder, and it displaces the warmer air within.

II

DISCOVERY AND SETTLEMENT

T IS an established fact that in 1671 a party sent out from Fort Henry—now Petersburg—penetrated to the Falls of New River and found on the way several letters cut into the bark of the trees. These markings were by still earlier prospectors of whom nothing else is known. But the journal kept by this party, and the journal written about the same time by John Lederer, were scarcely supplemented during the next half century by any further authentic information as to the country west of the Blue Ridge. That mountain barrier presents from the east a rather rugged and lofty outline. It was thought impassible. The country on the farther side was uninhabited by Indians and was believed to be very uninviting.

During the first century after the settlement at Jamestown, the eight original counties grew into 25, yet they were tenanted by only a fifth of the half million inhabitants of the English colonies in America. In Virginia the area of actual settlement had not spread two-thirds of the way from the Atlantic coast to the Blue Ridge.

In 1716 the governor of Virginia was Alexander Spottswood, a man of energy and foresight. He believed in making good the claim of the British to the region beyond the mountains. Geographical knowledge concerning the interior of the American continent was very foggy, and the governor believed the Blue Ridge to lie much nearer the Great Lakes than is really the case. He wished to find a way to those lakes, so that forts might be established on them, these forts to be linked with the coast settlements by a line of fortified stations. He thus thought the French on the St. Lawrence might be checkmated in their ambition to occupy the region south of the lakes.

So the governor headed a party of exploration. The start was from Williamsburg, then the capital of Virginia. Above Fredericksburg there was no road. The Blue Ridge was crossed through or near Swift Run Gap, and near where Elkton now stands the South Fork of the Shenandoah was reached. It was named the Euphrates and was thought to flow into the Great Lakes. On the west bank

Spottswood and his gay companions uncorked the large variety of liquors they had brought along and indulged in a grand spree. Probably not enough firewater remained for a second big drunk, and the "gentlemen" of the party seem to have been in no mood for farther adventure. But the rangers who had guided Spottswood were left behind to continue the exploration.

The governor did not half accomplish his declared purpose, and yet his trip was of much significance. The lowlands of the Valley of Virginia were found to be a grassy prairie with a soil more fertile than that of the tidewater region. No Indians were living here and the country was stocked with game. The land beyond the Blue Ridge was now officially discovered, and the news was published on both sides of the Atlantic. Exploration in detail now went forward with some rapidity.

Yet the new region would not have been occupied very soon,—in fact, not for a long while,—had it waited on the advance of settlement from Tidewater Virginia. That district was a land of tobacco plantations. Nearly every estate was within easy reach of some river always navigable by seagoing vessels. The planter had no wish to make a new home 150 miles beyond the heads of navigation. The immigration from Britain was no longer large, and the district east of the Blue Ridge was by no means fully occupied.

About 1725 there set in a new and very large stream of American immigration. It came from the north of Ireland and the valley of the upper Rhine. Nearly all these people landed at Philadelphia, because the Pennsylvania government had in Europe the reputation of being more liberal than in the case of the other colonies. But the Germans were scarcely represented at all among the earlier settlers of Bath.

A little more than a century before Spottswood's trip the province of Ulster in the north of Ireland had been conquered and almost depopulated. The British government confiscated several million acres of its lands and colonized them with people from the southwest of Scotland and the north of England. Among them were many of the Highland Scotch and a few Huguenots from France. The settlers were plain, hardy, and industrious, and they soon redeemed Ulster from its sorry appearance at the close of the conquest. Yet with the exception of a few breathing spells, there was a nagging persecution of the Ulster people. This persecution was partly religious and partly industrial, and did not cease until 1782. The spirit of that age was very intolerant. It had not yet outgrown the opinion that a state should permit no difference in church organization within its confines. The immigrants were Presbyterians, while the native Irish were Catholics. England placed under civil disabilities those who did not adhere to the Church of England. The Presbyterian ministers were not permitted to perform the marriage ceremony, and at times their congregations could not meet in public. The industrial persecution was because of the thrift and industry of the Ulster people. Vexatious restrictions were thrown upon their manufactures with a view to strangling the competition from them.

To get away from this harsh and illiberal treatment the people of Ulster began flocking to America. Here they were called Irish. The term Scotch-Irish is of recent coinage and is inexact. They were a blend of Scotch, English, Celtic Irish, and French Hugenots, the first element being the largest. In the settled southeast corner of Pennsylvania there was little room or welcome for the strangers. They were therefore constrained to press inland, and in doing so they pushed westward the colonial frontier. Within fifty years the Ulster people and the colonial Americans who joined them had occupied a broad belt of mountain and piedmont country extending from New York to Georgia. They made good pioneers, because they were a resolute folk, accustomed to a simple life. They took kindly to the mountains for the reason that they came from a country of hills. They were overcomers by nature, and in Appalachian America they proceeded to subdue the forest, the beasts of prey, the Indians, the French, and the British.

The Blue Ridge is nearer the seaboard in Pennsylvania than in Virginia. The broad Cumberland Valley is but a continuation of the Valley of Virginia. Nature, aided by Indian paths, had thus provided an easy line of travel to the South. Many of the immigrants poured into the hitherto uninhabited district made known by Spottswood. They reached Virginia by a side entrance, and without coming into close touch with the people of Tidewater, who were almost wholly of English origin.

Between the two sections of Virginia sundered by the natural boundary of the Blue Ridge, there has remained since the dawn of settlement a very perceptible difference. Their populations are of diverse origin, and consequently their manners and customs have never been the same. Nevertheless, the laws and institutions of the colony began at once to exert a unifying influence.

We are now brought to the threshold of the settlement of Bath. Eleven years after Spottswood's revel on the bank of South River, we find a petition to the governor and council that speaks of the Cowpasture by its present name. The signers were Beverly Robinson, Robert Brooke, William Lynn, and Robert and William Lewis. These men were not themselves explorers, but were influential planters of Tidewater. The two Lewises were not of the family that became so conspicuous in the annals of Augusta and her daughter counties. John, the father of the Lewises of Augusta, had not yet come from Ireland. But William Lynn was his brother-in-law. The paper is dated in 1727 and reads as follows:

"Your Petitioners have been at great Trouble and Charges in making Discoveries of Lands among the Mountains, and are desirous of taking up some of these Lands they have discovered; whereupon your petitioners humbly pray your Honours to grant him an order to take up Fifty Thousand Acres in one or more tracts of the head branches of James River to the West and Northwestward of the Cow Pasture, on seating thereon one family for every Thousand Acres, and as the said Lands are very remote and lying among the great North Mountains, being about Two Hundred Miles at least from any landing—Your Petitioners humbly pray Your Honours will grant them six years time to seat the same."

The above petition does not seem to have been acted upon. But an attempt to colonize the valleys of Bath even before there was a settler at Staunton or within 30 miles of it looks rather curious. However, it must be remembered that the Ulstermen were not used to the sight of wild land uncovered with wood. The prairies of the Shenandoah were not so inviting to them as we might suppose. A tract of good soil might not have a spring because of the limestone formation. Some of the best lands of the Valley are not among the first that were reduced to private ownership.

How the Calfpasture, Cowpasture, and Bullpasture rivers came to acquire such unusual names is not clearly known. The legend that some early hunters killed a buffalo calf on the first stream, a cow on the second, and a bull on the third is too much of the nature of stories that are told to children, and has the earmark of being an afterthought. There is good evidence that in all these valleys there was much open land. This was covered with grass and attracted the buffalo, an animal that does not live in the woods. These natural pastures had been created by the Indians, and were perpetuated by burning the grass at the close of each hunting season. Thus the valleys watered by the three streams came to be known as "the Pastures." The names the rivers now bear were first applied to the valleys and not to the streams. The colonial deeds relating to the most eastern of the pastures speak uniformly of "the Great River of the Calf Pasture" and "the Little River of the Calf Pasture." The Cowpasture river in 1743 was better known as Clover Creek, and until 1760 the Bullpasture was generally called Newfoundland Creek. For some years the valley of the Bullpasture was more generally called the "New Found Land," probably because it is so walled in by mountains that it may not have been found for several years after the main Cowpasture was explored.

The red men called the Cowpasture the Walatoola (Wah-lah-too-lah). This musical name was corrupted by the white people into Wallawhatoola, which now survives only as the designation of an alum spring above Nimrod Hall. It has been supposed to mean "the river that bends," or "winding river," and such a meaning is indeed very appropriate to so crooked a river as the Cowpasture. But the real meaning is "fine white cedar." The only other stream in this region, of which the Indian name does not seem to be totally lost, is Dunlap Creek. The natives called it the Escataba, meaning "wild rushing water."

Speaking of the Indian place-names, the authors of the "Heart of the Alleghanies" makes this very just observation: "There is a meaning in their euphony, and a suggestiveness in their melody. It is a grievous fault, the more grievous because irreparable, that so many of the bold streams which thunder down forest slopes and through echoing canyons have lost those designations whose syllables glide from the tongue in harmony with the music of the crystal currents."

In the summer of 1732 John Lewis settled a mile north from where Staunton soon arose. He was a person of means and leadership and was accompanied by about 30 of his Ulster followers. A more prominent comer was James Patton, who was unwearied in soliciting immigration to the Augusta colony. By the end of a dozen years there were several hundred Ulster families scattered over the present counties of Augusta, Rockingham, and Rockbridge, and even into the Valley counties lying nearer the Tennessee line. The first county to include any portion of the Valley of Virginia was Spottsylvania, organized in 1720. It took in only that small strip lying wholly east of South River and between lines meeting it a little below Port Republic and a little above Front Royal. In 1734, Orange was carved out of Spottsylvania. It was defined, however, as covering the entire region west of the Blue Ridge, so far as it lay within the boundaries claimed by Virginia. So when John Lewis appeared in the vicinty of Staunton, he had come to a "no man's land."

In 1738 that portion of Orange west of the Blue Ridge was divided into the counties of Frederick and Augusta by a line running from where is now the northwest corner of Greene County, to the Fairfax Stone at the southern extremity of the western line of Maryland. But until there should be more settlers west of the mountains, the two new counties were left under the jurisdiction of Orange. It was not until December, 1745, that Augusta was organized. It is for this reason that the early records of Orange have something to do with the district west of Shenandoah Mountain. When it was set off, Augusta contained about 4000 people, but they were scattered over a wide area.

Lewis and his companions were regarded as squatters on the public domain. To make them feel the authority of the state, two immense tracts of choice land were given to William Beverly and Benjamin Borden. The grant of 118,491 acres to Beverly lay around Staunton. It was known as Beverly Manor and also as Irish Tract.

Lewis was of middle age when he came to Virginia. His sons, Thomas, Andrew, and William were then minors but became more prominent than himself. Thomas was the first county surveyor of Augusta. Andrew assisted in surveying and both brothers were very energetic as land prospectors.

Under the date of October 29, 1743, an order of council for 30,-000 acres was issued in favor of James and Henry Robinson, James Wood, and Thomas and Andrew Lewis. The grant was located in the basin of the James River above the mouth of the Cowpasture. Thomas and Andrew Lewis, now 25 and 23 years old, seem to have been the only active members of the syndicate, although Wood, of Frederick County, was also a surveyor. The Robinsons were aristocrats of Tidewater and their names were enough to give prestige to the enterprise.

If, as is probable, no settlers had appeared in the Bath area before 1743, this will explain why the surveying did not begin in earnest until nearly two years had elapsed. September 26, 1745*, the Lewises appeared on the Cowpasture, just above Nimrod Hall, and surveyed 1080 acres for Adam Dickenson. This tract was the most northern in a chain of four. During the next two days the others were run off for Alexander Millroy, John Donally, and Hugh Coffey. The fourth day was Sunday, and after the manner of good Presbyterians the surveyors reported no work. During the first half of the following week they were moving northward, adding seven more links to the chain. These surveys were in favor of James Waddell, Ralph Laverty, James Stuart, James McCay, John Mitchell, John Cartmill, and James Hughart. Those of Stuart, McCay, and Mitchell were on Stuart's Creek.

The last day in March, 1746, the date falling on Monday, the surveyors returned to the Cowpasture, and below Coffey they laid off parcels for Joseph Watson, Andrew Muldrock, and William Daugherty. On the first of "Aprile," they continued down the river to the vicinity of Griffith Knob, surveying for John Walker, James Mayse, and Robert Crockett. Meanwhile a detachment of the surveying party was at work far above, laying off selections for James Scott, John McCreery, William Gillespie, William Lewis, James Jackson, James Simpson, William Black, Robert Abercrombie, Thomas Gillespie, Thomas Fitzpatrick, Hugh Edwards, William Warwick, and James Hall. The surveys already mentioned took in nearly all the choice morsels of Cowpasture bottom that lie within the present limits of Bath and also the more desirable land on Stuart's Creek.

During the last week in April the surveyors were busy on Jackson's River. Their largest tract was for William Jackson. Immediately

---

*According to the Old Style Calendar, which was 11 days behind the true time. The correct date is therefore October 7. The New Style calendar, was put into force in 1752. To correct the error, 11 days were taken out of the September of that year. Until then, the English began the new year with March 25. For example, all dates in 1746 coming prior to March 25 were counted as belonging to 1745, but were often written as in this illustration: March 1, 1745-6.

below was a second large tract for Adam Dickenson, who took a third a little lower down. The lands of James Ewing, William Jameson, and Archibald Elliott were still farther below. The surveying continued at intervals until October 4. Meanwhile the Lewises did not fail to look out for Number One. The Fort Lewis survey of 950 acres was run off September 5 in the name of John Lewis. William Lewis took a tract immediately below Bullpasture Gap. Thomas Lewis took two tracts on Jackson's River, at and just below the Highland line, and four on Back Creek. Of the long list of surveys four remained for a while in the hands of the syndicate.

It is not to be assumed that every given acreage, as put down in the suryevor's book, is very close to the actual amount. The Lewises understood how to survey, but their work was done too rapidly for precise results. The wilderness was broad and the methods they used were slapdash. The length of a course was sometimes paced off or guessed at. An open line was occasionally drawn. But it is significant that in nearly or quite every instance the true area is found to overrun the surveyor's figure, sometimes to a very considerable extent. The loose way in which the courses were often run appears in the frequency with which the phrase, "containing by estimation," occurs in the deeds based on these surveys.

In the surveys not held until a purchaser should appear, the surveyor entered this clause in his report: "Now in possession of ————————." This does not necessarily imply that the person named was already living on his land. Millroy, Coffey, and Daugherty are indeed mentioned as having houses on their selections. The same was doubtless true of several other settlers. But in some instances the expression means no more than that purchase had been made. Several claimants lived on the Beverly or Borden grants, and not here. Sometimes an actual settler would take a second and perhaps a third tract, possibly at a considerable distance from his homestead.

On Jackson's River, and within the Bath area*, it is doubtful

---

*By "Bath area," we mean Bath County within its present lines, just as if these limits had always existed. By "Greater Bath," whenever the term is used in this book, we mean Bath as it stood from 1790 to 1822.

whether there was any settler as early as 1746, unless it were William Jackson.

How long had the settlers been on their lands? Dickenson, the foremost man in the Cowpasture settlement, calls himself a resident of Maryland in 1742. As to the other settlers, there is no evidence that any of them came sooner than 1744. Carpenter, Mayse, and Wright did not appear until 1746. Had the settlements generally been prior to 1745, the surveyors would have come sooner than they did. In his list of surveys in Augusta between the dates, January 29 and June 15, 1745, Thomas Lewis mentions none west of Shenandoah Mountain. Again, if there had been settlers here for some length of time, the court records should disclose some indication of the fact. The first constable for the Cowpasture was James Mayse, appointed in February, 1745. And as the head tax was closely looked after, the pioneers could not have escaped the attention of the county court. The first recognition by that body of tithables beyond Shenandoah Mountain occurs May 23, 1745. The justices of Orange, in describing precincts to the various tithe-takers, then instruct John Lewis to list "all the Inhabitants of the Cow and Calf Pastures and the Settlers back of the same." The expression, "back of the same," is not quite conclusive that any man had as yet located beyond Warm Springs Mountain. It seems worded to cover a possible and perhaps probable contingency. Once again, the muster rolls of the militia for 1742 do not include the names that were soon to appear in the region covered by the Lewis grant.

The county surveyor did not come again for four years. In 1750 and 1751 he surveyed 37 tracts, which, however, aggregate not quite 2000 acres. Those of above 100 acres number only four. Several are of 10 to 20 acres only. Twelve were taken by men already here. Some others were seemingly taken by junior members of the pioneer families. During the next four years, which interval brings us to the outbreak of the Indian war, there are only five new surveys which seem to belong to the Bath area.

This abrupt falling off in the amount of land surveyed between 1746 and 1755 tells a very plain story. All the more desirable lands had now been taken; the early settlers, who seldom chose tracts of less than 200 acres, were a substantial class of men and the little surveys of 1750-51, so far as associated with the names of later comers, generally indicate men of less stability and more limited means.

DISCOVERY AND SETTLEMENT

We close this chapter with a tradition bearng on the early settlement of Bath. The story was put into print quite a while ago, and was related by a man whose personal recollection must have begun nearly a century since. It runs as follows:

Peter Francisco settled near the eastern foot of the Blue Ridge. With the help of the men who located around him, he blazed a path to the summit of the mountain wall. John Lewis, Robert Clark, and James Mayse joined him in the decision to explore the country lying westward, and late in a September the four men set out afoot. Once on the mountan top they were struck with the broad expanse of desirable country in full view. They went forward a considerable distance, and on their return they marked out a trail for packhorses.

In the spring they set forth again, this time with horses, and reached the Cowpasture at Fort Lewis. Selecting a hollow lying against a high cliff, they built a hut of three rooms and fenced it in with a barracade of felled trees. They planted corn, potatoes, and turnips, and in the fall stored away their little crop, burying the vegetables under the floor of the hut. Then they returned, no Indians having been seen.

The second spring there were about 20 men to go to the Cowpasture several being accompanied by their families. The hut was undisturbed, except that squirrels had eaten much of the corn and the foxes had looked out for the venison and bear meat. More land was cleared and individual huts were to be built in the fall. After the growing corn was "laid by," several of the men went back for additional supplies. There were left behind four women, a man lamed by an axe-cut in his foot, and a boy named Joseph Mayse.

The third morning afterward, a party of Indians captured the four women and the small store of eatables and fired the hut. The boy who was hoeing corn barefoot, was also taken. The man had hobbled some distance up the river and was fishing. Hearing the yells and seeing the smoke, he crawled up a bluff to get a better view. Some Indians with the boy and two of the women passed below without seeing him. He supposed the other women killed, but feared to fire, since it might lead to the death of the captives. The company passed on, and he was about to descend the bluff, when the other women came in sight, urged along by a switch in the hand of a solitary Indian.

Their condition made it impossible for them to travel as fast as the others. Enraged by the spectacle, the lame man shot the driver dead, but the report of his gun did not cause the other Indians to return.

The red men and their prisoners camped that night in a cave a mile above Bath Alum. When they had reached Beaver Run on Gauley they were overtaken by the men of the settlement, who, upon seeing the smoke from a mountain summit, at once turned back in pursuit. The Indians, though taken by surprise, made their escape, but the captives tried to follow, thinking the assailants were other Indians. They had reached and swum the Gauley, before the rescuers could overtake them and tell them to go back to camp and live on the venison that was there. The men resumed the pursuit. The women and the boy missed the trail in the darkness and followed a deerpath, which took them to a river that ran the wrong way to be the Gauley. This stream was broad and shoal and they easily got across. On the farther side they saw many buffalos and other grazing animals, some of them drinking from a spring. The fugitives were hungry and tired. The boy picked up a knife that had been dropped by an Indian and killed a buffalo calf, although for a while its cries maddened the herd and compelled the boy and women to keep out of its way. After the animals dispersed he cut out a ham. While searching for the women he fell into the spring, and its salty water made his feet smart.

In two days they reached the source of the river, which was the Elk. From the mountain they were now on, they thought they could recognize the ridge east of the Greenbrier. Their meat had become tainted, but the resourceful boy caught fish in the Elk, using a string of hickory bark as a fishing line. When they reached the Greenbrier they recognized the point where they had crossed. The waters were too deep for wading, their firsh were spoiled, and they could get no more in the muddy river. But the men, who were mounted, presently came along and they had plenty of venison captured from the Indians. What had happened to the latter the men could not be induced to tell. In two more days they reached the home on the Cowpasture, where the lame man had saved from the fire a building of green logs intended for a stable. This he had made comfortable for the women, and in a few days the little colony was increased by two infant boys.

This legend of the discovery of the mineral springs of Webster county cannot be accepted at face value. Like some other narratives of the old frontier, it appears to confuse names and events belonging to different periods of time. John Lewis never lived east of the Blue Ridge, and the elder Joseph Mayse did not settle on the Cowpasture before 1746. Peter Francisco lived in Bedford County and was a soldier of the Revolution. He was a giant in size and strength and wielded a broad-sword five feet long? With this terrible weapon he cut down eleven British soldiers in the battle of Guilford. The younger Joseph Mayse was not taken by the Indians until nearly 20 years after the settlement of the Cowpasture. His experience, as told by himself, has little agreement with this narrative. And if the four captives could swim the Gauley, why could they not swim the Greenbrier?

The only chronological place for the story is in the year 1743, at which time the Augusta people had some trouble with the red men, though it was not of very serious nature. It is probable that the legend includes some facts, otherwise lost sight of, which concern the original settlement around Fort Lewis. That settlement may have begun in 1743, in which case the legend would be partially correct.

III

THE LEWIS LAND GRANT

IN COLONIAL times an immigrant to Virginia who was of age and could prove he had paid the cost of his passage from Europe could claim a "headright," which entitled him to 50 acres of the public domain. He could also take up 50 acres for each adult male member of his household. The man availing himself of the headright privilege was required to settle on the land, to improve at least six per cent of the acreage, and to pay each year a quitrent of one shilling (17 cents) for each 5 acres. The tendency of this system was to fill Virginia with a good class of citizens. The principle on which it is based is the same as in the case of the present homestead law of the national government. Fifty acres was also the amount of public land which might be taken up by the private soldier of the Indian wars, by virtue of a proclamation of the royal governor of 1763. In Bath the headright was not permitted to cut any figure. As for the corn right and tomahawk right, which are one and the same thing, they did not acquire a recognized status until 1766, and consequently have no actual bearing on the settlement of this county.

Another system was the order of council. The governor, with the concurrence of his council, a body of men corresponding to the present state senate, would grant a huge block of land to an individual, or to a group of men acting as a company. In theory the purpose of the order of council was to settle a minimum number of families on the grant within a stated time. The grantee was supposed to be prohibited from charging more than a specified price per acre. He issued deeds, just as though the grant was owned by himself in fee simple. In modern usage the order of council would be defined as a method of colonization. But in practice there was created a non-resident proprietorship, enabling influential men in favor with the powers-that-were to levy for their personal benefit a plump tax on a body of settlers, and without rendering a corresponding benefit in return. Such a way of doing things was a graft. It discriminated against the small landseeker. It cornered the desirable land in a region where the proportion of rough land is very large. Unless the settler was able to pay a comparatively high price for such choice land, he had to go on to the very verge of settlement. Many persons did so and in this way a thin fringe of settlement was pushed forward too rapidly for comfort or safety. Furthermore, the colonial government is said to have been very lenient toward its favorites in the matter of enforcing forfeiture where there was a failure to comply with the settlement condition. Sometimes the grantee did not charge the full minimum price per acre. At other times he exacted more than was his due.

The headright method was equitable. It assumed that the settler was capable of choosing land for himself. The other method was monopolistic. It assumed that the immigrant was too much like a child to select for himself, and that it was fair and proper to allow some self-constituted agency to charge him a high price for a comparatively small service.

The following paragraph, taken from a petition presented to the Legislature by Botetourt citizens in 1779, doubtless voiced a very prevalent feeling:

> A few artful monopolizers, possessed of immense sums of money, which they have accumulated by taking advantage of the necessities of individuals, have it in their power to engross the greatest part of the public lands on this side of the Ohio, whilst the brave soldier is limited to a small portion and the virtuous citizen is implicitly debarred from getting any at all.

As we have already seen, a syndicate which included Thomas and Andrew Lewis was given in 1743 an order of council for 30,000 acres. We recognize as portions of this grant 91 separate tracts, covering about 27,000 acres, and surveyed in 1745-6. The Lewis brothers were good judges of land and they scarcely overlooked any section of riverbottom that was of first desirability. Neither did they fail to take notice of the limestone uplands of Warm Springs. These they seem to have covered by entries, probably as early as 1743. The surveys based upon such entries are of considerably later date than the 91 we are about to consider.

These original surveys average about 300 acres. Several of the more choice tracts were reserved by the Lewises for personal ownership or for speculation. Of the others all but seven had been taken by individual landseekers before the surveyors came around. The further progress of private ownership in this basin of the upper James may be read in the lists of patents for the remaining fragments of river-bottom and the more desirable tracts of upland. Much of this later patenting went to the enlargement of the original estates. These later surveys may be classed as culls. Many of them were not made into new farms and their history is of far less interest than that of the primary surveys.

We therefore append to this chapter a list and description of these primary surveys. Where we find conveyances of title during the first 50 years of settlement, we include in the record all but the least important of these transactions. Yet here and there an item is missing which we have not been able to find. In a few other instances there is an element of uncertainty. Now and then an entry seems not to have found its way into the record books.

The holdings under the Lewis grant constituted the key to the early history of the upper basin of the James. The lands esteemed choice by the settlers cover only one-twentieth of this area. This fraction was taken up by men of enterprise and resource; men capable of carrying on a plantation rather than a common farm. Now and then a settler dropped out of the race, usually because of Indian raids or financial embarrassment. Other men, feeling cramped by the narrow valleys, or impelled by sheer restlessness, moved at length to the Carolina uplands or into the smooth country of the Mississippi Valley. If the pioneer did not himself migrate, his son or his grandson was quite certain to do so. If his surname has not utterly disappeared during the seventeen decades of settlement, the outflow has in most instances been of such volume as to leave behind only a small representation of his posterity.

Since Greater Bath covered nearly all the upper valley of the James, we have thought it best to include the Lewis surveys in Highland and Alleghany.

Beginning with the most eastern of the sources of the Bullpasture, that valley, as far down as the Lockridge neighborhood, was parcelled off into the surveys claimed by Elliot, De la Montony, syndicate (224 acres), Armstrong (112), Carlile (204), McCreery (208), Holman, Largent, syndicate (175), Harper, Miller (250), Bodkin, Estill, Carlile (304), Carlile (284), and Lewis (348).

On the Cowpasture, immediately above the mouth of the Bullpasture, was Black. Just above him was Knox (254) and across the

Cowpasture was Jackson (340). Above Knox was Hall (212), and beyond him were Rainey, Jackson (163), and syndicate (286), these four not forming an altogether connected series. For about nine miles below the mouth of the Bullpasture the order was as follows: Lewis (390), McCreery (520), Lewis (430), Lewis (950), and Mayse (182). Southward to the mouth of Stuart's Creek the order is approximately this: Cartmill, Knox (93), Moore, Clendennin (195), Clendennin (130). Knox and Moore were separated by the river. Abercrombie lay on Cromby's Run, now Thompson's Creek. Laverty was at the mouth of Stuart's Creek. Just above him on that stream was Stuart. Beyond was first McCay and then Mitchell. Some distance higher up were Gillespie (300), Edwards, Hall (150), and Fitzpatrick. Just below Laverty and nearly opposite was Waddell. Thence, until we come into the great bend of the Cowpasture beginning at Griffith's Knob, the succession is as follows: Dickenson (1080), Millroy, Donally, Coffey, Watson, Muldrock (130), Duagherty, Walker, Mayse (415), Crockett (246), Scott, Simpson, Gillespie (320). Muldrock had a small survey near the mouth of the Cowpasture, and in the bend above was Gannt's.

In the pocket of bottom on Jackson's River, beginning just above the Highland line, there came, successively, Miller (487), Mayse (234), Lewis (304), and Lewis (489). Below the defile above Fort Dinwiddie were the very long surveys of Jackson (1100) and Dickenson (870). Thence along the river to the mouth of Dunlap—first called Carpenter's Creek, Peter's Creek, and Meadow Creek—the succession is about as follows: Crockett (283), Davis, Jameson, Armstrong (270), Ewing, Crockett (195), Elliot (163), Wilson, Montgomery, and Dunlap, together with three syndicate surveys. On the lower portion of the site of Covington was Wright, and in the river-loop below was Carpenter.

About the source of Falling Spring was a Dickenson survey. Well up on Dunlap was a large Lewis survey and another held by the syndicate. On Back Creek was a Lewis survey and four syndicate surveys, three of the latter lying at the mouth of Little Back Creek.

The surveys in the Lewis grant were patented by the first occupants or by their successors. The certificates of survey were transferable by law, and were given to the settlers in return for the purchase money of 10 cents per acre.

It would seem as though most of the settlers were either unable or unwilling to pay for their lands, or that they wished to worry the Lewis syndicate into granting patents for a nominal consideration. At any rate, many suits were brought against them by Robinson and Lewis between 1747 and 1752. The defendants in these suits include an undue proportion of the leading men of the settlements. The suit of Mays v. Lewis, 1746, throws considerable light on the early settlement of Bath. Joseph Mayse states that he agreed to purchase of John Lewis 500 acres in one or more blocks. Lewis was to survey at his own cost, and give perfect title in fee simple whenever so required. Mayse was to pay three pounds per 100 acres and paid down two pounds. A 200-acre tract was laid off on the Cowpasture and Lewis promised to lay off the other 300 acres when asked to do so. Mayse paid the surveyor one pistole ($3.61) and decided to take the other 300 acres on Jackson's River, adjoining William Wilson. James Trimble, alias Turnbull, there ran off for him 234 acres. In the fall Mayse built a cabin on it, paid 40 shillings, and always stood ready to pay the residue in cash, but Lewis demanded a bond, which Mayse refused to give, as he expected interest would be required. Mayse understands that Lewis has sold the 234 acres to a stranger.

In his reply, Lewis states that the bargaining was in June, 1746. Mayse lives on the Cowpasture survey. Lewis denies that Mayse paid him 40 shillings or any smaller sum on the same, but admits that Mayse let him have a tweed hat and some other trifles, which he understands were not to apply on the purchase. Lewis says Mayse never paid 40 shillings on the Jackson's River land, but on the contrary owed him 43 shillings, which he could not get till he threatened suit. Mayse had money in the hands of John Brown. The latter made over to Lewis a doubloon, out of which Lewis paid to himself the 43 shillings and was ready to pay Mayse what was left. He confessed selling the 234 acres and being paid in cash for it. He gave Mayse notice to settle and either pay down or give bond for the purchase money for both tracts, the bond to bear interest from the end of August, 1747. Mayse flatly refused to do either and demanded a patent in his own name. Lewis declares he has always been ready to give deed or patent for the 200-acre tract, provided Mayse took 500 acres in all, either paying in specie or giving his bond. In his rejoinder, Mayse reaffirms his previous statement.

THE LEWIS LAND GRANT 27

In McCreery v. Justice, we find this memorandum by James Trimble, dated August 7, 1750: "Surveyed for Wm. Warrick 224 Acres in Newfound Land between Saml De La Matonye & Carlile." Thomas Lewis says John McCreery paid him $6.54 for the surveying, which was done for Warrick. In 1749 a charge of $10.75 was added to the foregoing. John Justice gave bond to pay McCreery $22.50 "for my right of a piece in the bull paster," also the purchase money to John Lewis, and the charges for the surveying and the "patton."

The name of the person for whom the tract was surveyed is mentioned first. Then follow, in regular succession, the acreage, the location, the date of patent, and finally the conveyances, if any, which ensued. When no name immediately follows the year of patent, it is to be understood that the patent was issued in the name of the person for whom the survey was made. Otherwise, the name of the new owner is mentioned. A star following the acreage—as 100*—means that the survey was in 1745. All other surveys were in 1746. The Virignia pound of $3.33 is represented by "p". Therefore, to reduce pounds to dollars, add one cipher and divide by 3. Other special abbreviations are these:

CP—Cowpasture; BP—Bullpasture; JR—Jackson's River; BC—Back Creek; SC—Stuart's Creek; FS—Falling Spring Run; DC—Dunlap Creek; A—acres: P—patent; br—branch; n—near; opp—opposite; adj—adjoining; cor—cornering on; mo—mouth of.

Abercrombie, Robert—425—Cromby's Run, CP—P, 1760, James Gay—336 A sold, 1773, to John Gay for 100p—the same sold by Jas. and Jno. Gay to Henry Rockey, of Pennsylvania for 3500p (depreciated paper money).

Armstrong, Robert—270—JR, below Bath line—P, 1760.

Armstrong, Robert—112—BP, below Doe Hill—P, 1760, William Wilson—sold, 1768, to Abraham Hempenstall for 46p.

Black, Alexander—250—CP at mo. BP—P, 1750—125 A sold to Alexander Black, Jr., 1765, for 40p—whole P plus later P of 34 A sold by pioneer's sons, 1792, to Thomas Houston for 400p—sold by Houston, 1796, to John Lewis for 1000 p—sold by Lewis, 1798, to Charles Cameron for 1000p.

Bodkin, Richard—339—BP above Pullin—P, 1750—sold, 1762, to Samuel Given for 158p—100 A sold, 1765, to James Burnside for 40p—239 A sold 1768, to John Hicklin for 150p.

Carlile, Robert and John—304—BP below Estill—P 1765—divided equally 1773. between Robert and John.

Carlile, Robert and John—204—W side BP below Armstrong's 112—P, 1759—sold, 1786, by George Carlile to William Erwin for 10p. Sold, 1793, by William and Susanna Erwin to James Hutchinson for 140p.

Carlile, Robert and John—300—P, 1759—CP, E side Indian Draft—sold to John Carlile, Jr., 1773 for 70p.

Carlile, John—281—BP below Carlile's 304—P, 1750, William Wilson—sold 1761, by Matthew Wilson (brother and heir) to Robert Graham for 67½p.

Carpenter, Joseph—782—JR below Wright—P, 1750—230 A sold, 1762, to John Mann for 700—464 A divided equally, 1765, between Joseph and Solomon Carpenter (sons), each paying father 10p—160 A of Solomon's share purchased at public sale, 1772, by William Hughart for 90p, and sold by him, 1786, to Wallace Estill, Jr. for 260p. However, Solomon Carpenter and Sutney his wife sold to John Mann, 1773, 160 A for 130p.

Cartmill, John—300*—CP touching Indian Draft—P, 1760—245 A sold, 1774, to Samuel Cartmill for 100p, and by him, 1787, to Nathan Crawford.

Clendennin, Archibald—195—CP n mo SC—P 1750, Thomas Thompson,
Clendennin, Archibald—130—adj his other tract—P, 1750, Thomas Thompson.

Coffey, Hugh—220*—CP below Donally—P 1750—Sold 1766, by John Coffey (son) to John Ramsey for 40p, and by him, 1794, to Samuel McDannald for 150p. John McDannald then a neighbor.

Crockett, Robert—195—JR mo Cedar Creek—P, 1760, John Dickenson—sold 1762, to James Fitzpatrick for 30p—sold, 1793, by Fitzpatrick to Paul Harpole for 225p.

Crockett, Robert—246—CP below James Mayse—P, 1750, John and Archibald (sons)—sold, 1776, to James Beard and by him to Richard Mayse, 1794, for 385p.

Crockett, Robert—283—JR above mo FS—P 1750,Samuel (son)—sold, 1762, to Alexander Hamilton for 40p—sold by Hamilton, 1765, to William Hamilton for 100p—sold by latter, 1771, to Samuel Kincaid for 50p—sold by Kincaid, 1780, to Andrew Kincaid for 400p—76 A sold by Andrew Kincaid, of Greenbrier, to John Kincaid, 1795, for 35p.

Davis, David—320—E side JR, mo FS—P, 1760, Robert Abercrombie—sold, 1761, to John Stuart for 150p—sold by Stuart, 1761, to William Mann for 152p—sold by Mann, 1784, to John Robinson for 60p.

De La Montony, Samuel—200—CP below Elliott—P, John McCreery—sold, 1760 to John Bodkin for 25p—sold by Bodkin, 1762, to Robert Duffield for 21½p—sold by Duffield, 1794, to William Armstrong for 300p.

Dickenson, Adam—1080*—CP between Waddell and Millroy—P, 1750—311 A sold, 1754, to Alexander Craighead for 150p, and by Craighead, 1765, to Andrew Sitlington for 200p.

Dickenson, Adam—870—JR below Jackson's 1100 A—P 1750—215 A (upper end) sold, 1754, to John Byrd for 25p—377 A (middle) sold, 1754, to James Bourland for 75p—317 A (lower end) sold, 1754, to William Dean for 75p. Dean sold to John Dean (brother), 1765, for 100p—Bourland sold 175 A, 1774 to Robert McClentic for 154p. Note:—The sales by Dickenson show an excess of acreage.

Dickenson, Adam—546—FS valley—P, 1750—sold, 1767, by John Dickenson and Benjamin Estill (mortgagee) to Gabriel Jones for 250p—sold by

Jones, 1792, together with P's of 217 and 82 A to Thomas Massie for 500p. At same time, Jones sold to Elisha Williams 3 other tracts in WS, 910 A, for 150p.

Donally John—277*—CP above Coffey—P, 1751.

Daugherty, William—285*—CP between Muldrock and Walker—P, 1750 —sold by heirs, 1791, to Robert Sitlington for 330p.

Dunlap, Arthur—270—JR mo Dunlap Creek—P, 1750, William Jackson— sold, 1772, to Richard Morris for 100p.

Edwards, Hugh—174—SC, cor Thomas Gillespie—P, 1763, Charles Lewis sold, 1769, to John McCausland—sold by latter, 1791, to Andrew McCausland (son).

Elliott, Archibald—364—sources of BP and Blackthorn—P, 1756, James Trimble—sold, 1757, to George Wilson for 55p—200 A sold by Wilson to Samuel Wilson for 40p—164 A (remainder of survey?) sold by Samuel Wilson, 1773, to John McCoy for 150p.

Elliott, Archibald—163—JR—P (?)—sold, 1758, to John Johnson—sold, 1759, by James Clark and William Elliott (through power of attorney from Archibald Elliott) to William Johnson, assignee of John Johnson, for 60p— sold by William Johnson, 1762, to John Bollar for 50p.

Estill, Wallace—344—BP at Clover Creek mill—P, 1750—131 A sold, 1761, to Boude Estill (son) for 40p, and by latter, 1774, to James Carlile for 108p—213 A sold by Wallace Estill, 1774, to John Pebbles for 200p, and sold by Pebbles' heirs, 1805, to David Gwin for $1500.

Ewing, James—254—JR at Muddy Run—P, 1760, Archibald Armstrong— sold, 1793, by Armstrong to John Sumwalt for 105p.

Fitzpatrick, Thomas—190—SC—P, 1761, John Stephenson—sold to John Gillespie, 1767, for 30p.

Gannt, Robert—40—CP—P, 1770, John Ramsay (?)

Gillespie, William—320—CP opp Griffith Knob—P, 1761—sold, 1780, to Aaron Hughes for 10,000p (depreciated money).

Gillespie, Thomas—300—SC—P, 1760—150 A sold, 1795, to John Edwards for 110p, and by him, 1779, to Jacob Rodecap for 180p.

Hall, James—150—SC—P, 1750—sold, 1770, to Andrew Donally, and by him, 1779 to Leonard Bell. Seems to have been sold, 1797, by Samuel Gillespie to John Edwards for 110p.

Hall, James—212—CP above Laurel Gap—P, 1750—sold to Robert Hall, 1760, for 10p, and by him to Joseph Gwin, 1772, for 100p.

Harper, Matthew—220—BP above Miller—P, 1758—sold, 1764, to Hugh Martin for 80p—sold by Martin to John Miller, of Rockingham,—sold by Miller, 1789, to Charles Callahan.

Holman, William—265—BP above Largent—P (?)—probably acquired by Edward Hynes, who died about 1778.

Hughart, James—590—E side CP adj Cartmill and Indian Draft—P. 1750 —sold, 1772, by Thomas Hughart (son) to James Hughart, Jr., (son)—112 A sold by Thomas and James, 1784, to Nathan Crawford for 40p—110 A sold by James Hughart, Jr., 1793 to John Hughart (son) for 5p.

Jackson, William—1100—JR at Fort Dinwiddie—P, 1750—Repatented, 1784, by Robert Hall, who in 1780 purchased for 5 shillings 320 A of John Oliver—100 A sold by Hall (1783?) to William Allen—1000 A sold, 1788, to Jacob Warrick for 1500p—261¾ A sold, 1795, by Warrick to Charles Cameron.

Jackson, James—340—CP opp mo BP—P, 1750, John Jackson—170 A sold 1765, by William Jackson to Francis Jackson for 30p, and by latter, 1769, to William Renick for 42p—sold by Renick, 1776, to George Benson for 65p—the other 170 sold, by William Jackson, Jr., to Robert Hall for 600p.

Jackson, James—168—CP—P, 1759, William Sprowl—sold to William Steuart, 1761, for 30p.

Jameson, William—280—E side JR cor Ewing—P, 1760, John Jameson (son)—sold, 1765, to Archibald Armstrong, Sr., for 50p, and by the latter, 1767, to Robert Armstrong, Sr., for 100p—145 A sold, 1780, to Benjamin Tallman—James Kirk, a neighbor, 1780. But in 1795, Robert Armstrong, Sr., sold 196 to James Sttele for 200p.

Knox, James—254—CP above Black—P, 1760—100 A sold, 1765, to Robert Knox for 20 p, and by latter, 1776, to Thomas Nickell—160 A sold, 1769, to Patrick Miller for 70p.

Knox, James—93—CP adj John Moore—P, 1760—sold, 1761, to Edward Thompson for 31½p, and by him, 1763, to Joseph McClung for 30p.

Largent, James—212—BP below Holman and on a small br—P (?)—sold, 1762, by William Johnson to Thomas Hamilton for 16½p, and by Hamilton, 1773, to Joseph Beathe.

Laverty, Ralph—300—CP mo SC—P, 1750—conveyed to Mrs. Rebecca Hamilton (daughter), 1786.

Lewis, John—950—CP at Fort Lewis—P, 1750, Charles Lewis.

Lewis, John—304—JR at "great lick" (Bolar Run)—P, 1760, William Wilson.

Lewis, Andrew—348—BP below Carlile's 281 A—P. 1750—sold, 1756, to Thomas Hicklin for 60p—217 sold by latter, 1761, to John Hicklin (son) for 50p, and by Samuel Given, of Botetourt, 1776, to Andrew Lockridge for 270p—131 A sold, 1770, by Thomas Hicklin to Thomas Hicklin, Jr., (son) and sold, 1793, by James Lockridge to Alexander Wiley for 230p—this sold by Wiley to John Steuart 1797.

Lewis, William—390—CP and BP below Black—P, 1750—sold, 1752, to Thomas Feamster for 37½p—100 A sold, 1764, by Feamster to John Montgomery for 48p, and by latter, 1792, to Alexander Taylor for 180p.

Lewis, Thomas—304, 210, and 150—mo of little BC—P as one tract, 1759, by Robert Abercrombie—sold, 1760, to Robert Gay—364 A sold, 1765, by Gay to Samuel Vance and William Hutchinson for 60p—183 A sold, 1766, to Samuel Vance for 50p—133 A sold, 1766, to John Vance for 50p.

Lewis, Thomas—489—JR below Bolar Run—P, 1764, Robert Bratton and Ralph Laverty—sold, 1769, by Bratton and Laverty, 244½ A to William Given for 70p and 244½ to Adam Bratton, 1770, for 150p—Given sold, 1792, 98½ A to Robert Given for 10p. But in 1753, Thomas patented his survey here of 489 acres and sold it the same year to James Gay for 115p.

THE LEWIS LAND GRANT 31

Lewis, Thomas—560—BC—P, 1761—sold, 1761 to James and Robert Allen for 80p—280 A sold by the Allens, 1763, to John Young for 45p—sold by Young, 1766, to John Davis for 67p, and by latter to James Gregory, 1768 for 75p—280 A sold by Robert Allen, 1763, to John Davis for 100p, and 85 A sold by Davis, 1768, to David Tate for 17p, and by latter to John Sprowl, 1770, for 20p.

Lewis, Thomas—95—BC—P (?)

Lewis, George—430—CP below McCreerys 520 A—P, 1752—215 sold, 1755, to John Lewis (son) for 120p, and by him to Charles Lewis, 1772, for 100p—215 sold, 1775, to Benjamin Lewis (son) for 90p, and by him to David Frame, 1772, for 150p.

Mayse, James—415—CP below Walker—P, 1760, William Mayse (son).

Mayse, Joseph—182—CP below Lewis' 950 A—P, 1761.

Mayse, Joseph—234—JR below Miller—P, 1760, Stephen Wilson—sold, 1797, to David Gwin for 1600p.

McCay, James—290—SC above Stuart—P, 1759—sold, 1784, by Jane McCay of Greenbrier (widow) to Andrew and Charles Donally—sold, 1795 by Charles Donally to Benedict Ailshe for 300p—150 sold by Aishe, 1798, to James Graham.

McCreery, John—520—CP below Lewis' 390 A—P, 1751—260 A sold, 1765, to Robert McCreery (son) for 120p, and by him, 1790, plus 30 A to Thomas Wallace for 500p—260 A plus later P of 16 A sold, 1787, by John McCreery Jr (son) to John Bourland for 500p.

McCreery, John—280—BP below Carlile's 204 A—P, 1760, 1773, sold, 1763, to Richard Bodkin for 45p—sold (with mill) by Bodkin to Joseph Malcom for 50p.

Miller, John—487—JR above Mayse's 234 A—P, 1760—243 A sold, 1770, to David Gwin for 100p—244 A sold, 1767, by Robert Miller, of Albemarle, to George Skillern for 250p.

Miller, James—250—BP above Bodkins'—P, 1760, James Burnside—sold plus 100 A of Bodkin land, to John Hicklin, 1786, for 300p—196 A sold, 1789, by Andrew Lockridge to James Lockridge.

Millroy, Alexander—200*—CP below Dickenson's 1080 A—P, 1751—sold 1762, to William Sprowl for 200p, and by Sprowl, 1772, to Hugh Hicklin for 132p—178 A sold by Hicklin, 1794, to George Whiteman for 250p and 22 A 1794, to John Dickenson.

Mitchell, John—234*—SC above McCay—P, 1759—sold to George Wilson for 80p—sold by Wilson, 1768, to Charles Donally for 90p, and by latter, 1791, to James Graham for 250p.

Montgomery, James—220—JR above Wright—P, 1750, Charles Walker.

Moore, John—220*—CP below Mayse's 182—P, 1759.

Muldrock, Andrew—130—CP between Watson and Daugherty—P, 1761 —sold by Hugh Muldrock, 1781, to Casper Faught for 140p and by him, 1785, to Robert Sitlington for 80p.

Muldrock, Andrew—40—mo of CP—P, 1761.

Pullen, Loftus—321—BP between Estill and Bodkin—P, 1758.

Raney, Michael—216—CP adj Hall's 212 A—P, 1760, Charles Gilham—sold, 1763, to James Bodkin for 41p, and by him to Robert Carlile, 1767, for 50p.

Scott, James—490—CP below Crockett's 246 A—P, 1751—sold, 1781, to Joseph Surber for 400p.

Simpson, James—300*—CP below Scott—P, 1761—sold to James Handley 1762—58 A sold, 1772, to John Henry Insminger for 55p.

Stuart, James—300—SC Laverty—P, 1750—sold, 1800, by Robert Stuart to Richard Mathews and by him, 1802, to Joseph Kincaid.

Syndicate—875—DC—P, 1750, Adam Dickenson.

Syndicate—490—DC—P, 1760, John Dickenson—sold, 1766, to William Hughart for 80p, and by him, 1768, to Andrew and Thomas Lewis for 120p —sold 1768 by Andrew Lewis to James Blair.

Syndicate—286—CP above Knox's 254 A—P, 1760, John Miller—sold, to John Kincaid for 80p.

Syndicate—175—BP between Largent and Harper—P, 1750, John Brown —sold to Hance Harper, 1753, for 20p, and by him, 1768, to Samuel Black— 63 A sold, 1787, by John Black (son) to James Curry for 10p.

Syndicate—224—BP below De La Montony—P, 1750, John McCreery— sold 1753, to John Justice for 13¼p, and by him, 1754, to Michael Harper for 30p—sold by Harper, 1760, to William Shannon for 35p, and by him, 1765, to Robert Scott for 29p—sold by Scott, 1768, to James Burnside for 42p, and by him, 1772, to William McCandless for 42p—sold by McCandless, 1775, to Robert Hestent, of Dunmore, (Shenandoah) county for 170p, and by him, 1779, to Paul Summers for 700p (depreciated money). This place was by this time known as the Burdie house.

Syndicate—196 (169?)—JR mo Cedar Creek—P (?)

Syndicate—94—JR—P, 1771, William Lewis

Waddell, James—224*—CP between Laverty and Dickenson's 1890 A—P, 1750, Ralph Laverty—sold, 1770, to William Laverty (son) for 25p, and by him, 1774 to John Sitlington for 112½p—deeded by Sitlington, 1790, to James Kelso (son-in-law).

Walker, John—340—CP below Daugherty—P, 1759, John and Archibald Clendennin.

Warrick, William—216—br of CP—P, 1759, Henry Gay—98 A sold by Martha Gay (widow), 1780, to Andrew Moody for 1000p (depreciated money).

Watson, Joseph—200 CP between Coffey and Muldrock—P, 1760, by heirs who sold, 1769, to James Scott for 22½p.

Wilson, George—175—JR n Cedar Creek—P, 1759 (?) James Callison— sold, 1760, to James Bourland for 30p, and by him to Rowland Madison— sold by Madison, 1787, to James Elliot for 100p and by James Elliot, 1791, to Moses Mann for 250p. Note:—George Wilson, 1758, patented on the CP or Shaw's Fork an unlisted survey of 316 A. From this he appears to have sold in 1759 105 A to William Steuart for 20p, and 100 A to James Shaw for

10p. In 1762 he sold James Clements 100 A for $15.46. Shaw sold to James Bodkin, 1766, for 25p, and he to James Steuart, 1794 for 109p. Clements sold, 1776, to Jared Erwin, of Rockingham, for 200p.

Wright, Peter—286—JR at Covington—P, 1750—divided between Peter, Jr., and John (sons).

SURVEYS OF 1750-1754

Clendennin, Thomas—1754—68—Warm Springs Run—P, 1757—sold, 1797, by Thomas, Jr., (son) to Anthony Mustoe and William Chambers for 150p.

Cochran, Patrick—1750—24—JR—P, 1765, James Scott—sold, 1768, to Patrick Corrigan for 20p.

Cochran, Patrick—1750—18—CP—P, 1765, James Scott.

Crockett, John—1750—24—CP.

Davis, Patrick—1750—44—CP below Robert Crockett—P, 1767—sold, 1770, to James Milligan for 30p, and by him to William Griffith, 1776, for 103p.

Dickenson, Adam—1750—135—JR, P, 1761, Zopher Carpenter—sold to Michael Mallow, 1789, for 275p.

Dickinson, Adam—1751—33—DC—P, 1763, John Dickenson.

Seely, Jeremiah—1754—100—Dry Run of JR—P, 1761, Peter Wright.

Thompson, Edward—1751—42—CP adj Knox's 93 A—P, 1770, William McClung.

Warwick, William—1750—50—JR—P, 1761, William Gillispie.

Wilson, William—1754—100—JR—P, 1765.

Wilson, Hercules—1754—74—head of CP—P, 1774, George Wilson.

Wilson, George—1750—90—br of SC—P, 1761, James McCay—sold, 1793, by William McCay to Charles Donally for 25p.

Other patents for this region, in the period 1741-1769 inclusive, are these, the acreage, date and descriptions being given consecutively:

Adams, Thomas—340—1767—adjoining Hot Springs survey.
Arbuckle, James—400—1749—north side James below Island Ford.
Boggs, James—235—1766—JR—between Jackson and William Hamilton.
Clark, John—210—1769—BC of James.
Davis, John—45—1769—JR.
Dunlap, William—100—1750—mo BC.
Fulton, Thomas—115—1759—west side JR.
Gellispie, Hugh—85—1769—west side SC.
Grove, John—400—1741—including fork at mo of CP.
Hanly, Archibald—58—1765—northwest side of CP.
Hardin, Benjamin—44—1775—head of JR.
Hanley, Archibald—58—1765—northwest side CP.
Hardin, Benjamin—44—1755—head of JR.
Henry, William—120—1759—main branch James opp. mo. of CP.
Hicklin, Hugh: (1) 130—1769—CP (2) 100—1758—on a draft of BP.

Hicklin, Thomas—68—1761—BP—adj. Andrew Lewis land on southwest.
Lewis, Thomas—1300—1763—"the valley" of BC.
Lewis William—six surveys on BC, in 1763, of 110, 148, 172, 220, 187, and 100 A. and one at Vanderpool of 270.
Hugart, Thomas—65—1760—JR.
Mann, William—49—1765—JR below BC.
Mathews, Sampson and George—69—1769—head SC.
McCallister, James—100—1760—JR.
McCay, James—90—1761—SC.
McClenahan, William—50—1769—BC below Davis.
McCutchen, William—166—1760 (?)—mo of Cedar of JR.
McIlwain, Alexander—190—1761—branch of Cedar.
McMurray, William—20—1761—McMurray Creek of CP.
McSherry, Luke—186—1761—BC of James.
Miller, Robert—150—1762—JR.
Montgomery, John—30—1769—BP.
Montgomery, James—54—1757—northwest side JR.
Moore, David—200—1763—Bolar Run.
Muldrock, Jean: (1) 30—1769—fork of James at CP (2) 33—1769—James River adj. homestead.
Preston, William—130—1763—small branch of BP. William Preston in 1769 took 6 surveys on Pott's Creek of 250, 200, 150, 300, and 95 A.
Simpson, James—45—1761—BC of CP.
Switchard, Henry—85—1755—BC of James.
Wade, Dawson—125—1767—branch of BP.
Wright, Peter—100—1767—Pott's Creek.
Young, James—98—1769—head branch of CP.

The foregoing surveys do not include all the individual patents in Warm Springs Valley by the Lewises, Bullitts, etc.

The new names occurring among the patentees for the remainder of the eighteenth century are but few. The following are all we are reasonably sure of:

Adams, Robert	Dowden, Michael	Persinger, Jacob
Alley, William	Evans, Evan	Poage, John
Baxter, John	Hosaw, Andrew	Putnam, John
Berry, John	Hume, William	Rhea, William
Boggs, James	Logue, Samuel	Richardson, Robert
Bullitt, Thomas	Mason, Joseph	Rockey, Henry
Bullitt, Cuthbert	McColgan, Edward	Satchell, William, Jr.
Clark, Samuel	McDonald, Samuel	Sloan, James
Coole, Richard	Morrison, Hugh	Sydnor, Richard
Cowardson, John	O'Hara, Daniel	Wildridge, William
Dickey, John	Oliver, John	Wooten, William
Dixon, William	Park, Benjamin	

THE LEWIS LAND GRANT

We now mention several early purchasers, which in some instances seem to relate to the original patents.

Dennis Callahan of John Dickenson—76 of tract of 195 acres—Ugly Creek—5p—1793.

Christopher Clark of Peter Wright—96—JR—50p—1791.

Jacob Cleek of Alexander McFarland—213—JR below Given—400p—1792.

Henry Dill of Peter Hubbard—285 of 600 deeded, 1767, by John Wilson to William Rhea—Mill Cretk—130p—1792.

John Gillespie of Martha McCroskey, sole daughter and heir of Hugh Gillespie, of Greenbrier—85—SC—20p—P, 1769—1795.

James Harris of John Cartmill—140—CP between James Hughart and Nathan Crawford and corner Samuel Cartmill—100p—1733—sold by Harris, 1792, to Isaac Mayse for 120p.

James Johnson of Robert Armstrong, Jr.,—100—JR both sides Robert's Run—50p—1793.

Thomas and Joseph Kincaid of John Eddy—158—237p—1797.

Robert and James McAvoy of Joseph Carpenter—134—Little Valley—100p—1799.

Richard McCallister of John Dickenson—113—Ugly—15p—1793

John McCorkle of Patrick Miller—17—CP adj William Dickey—3p—1794.

John McCorkle of John and William Dickey—231 (2 surveys)—CP—100p—1794.

Thomas Milhollen of Thomas Fitzpatrick—32—Cedar Creek—30p—P, 1779—1792.

Hugh Tiffany of James Blake—13—SC—11p—1793.

Alexander Simpson of Charles Donally—75—SC—50p—1792.

William Smythe of Peter Wright—176—JR—50p—1791.

Stephen Wanless of Hugh Morrison—95—SC at forks of road above James Morrow—40p—1792.

Jacob Warrick of William Lewis—400—Clover Lick on Greenbrier—600p—1797.

The last mentioned sale looks like a high figure, considering the situation.

IV

AREAS OF SETTLEMENT

SINCE only a very minor portion of Bath was covered by the early holdings of the pioneer families, it is possible to group these holdings into several tolerably well defined areas of settlement. The names we aportion among these areas are not presented as an exhaustive list or as one that is free from error, even so far as it goes.

The Dickenson settlement may be considered as extending along the Cowpasture from the gorge below Fort Lewis into the bend at Griffith's Knob, and as including the lower course of Stuart's Creek and the occupied part of Porter's Mill Creek. The more conspicuous of the earlier names associated with this belt are Abercrombie, Beard, Clendennin, Coffey, Crockett, Daugherty, Dickenson, Donally, Douglass, Gay, Gillispie, Graham, Hicklin, Insminger, Kelso, Kincaid, Laverty, Madison, Mayse, McCay, McClung, McDannald, Millroy, Mitchell, Muldrock, O'Hara, Porter, Ramsey, Scott, Simpson, Sitlington, Sloan, Stuart, Thompson, Waddell, Walker, Watson.

The Fort Lewis settlement began a little above the mouth of Thompson's Creek and extended up the Cowpasture to Laurel Gap. Here we find the names, Benson, Black, Cartmill, Cowardin, Dickey, Feamster, Francisco, Frame, Hall, Hughart, Jackson, Knox, Lewis, Mayse, McCreery, Miller, Montgomery, Moody, Moore, Wallace.

The upper Cowpasture settlement included the bottoms on that river between Laurel Gap and the mouth of Shaw's Fork and on the lower course of the latter stream. Here were the Devericks, Erwin, Gwin, Johns, Shaw, and Steuart families.

The upper Mill Creek settlement occupied the basin of that stream above Panther Gap. Names associated with this somewhat limited space are Bratton, McDonald, Putnam, Rhea, Swearingen.

The Green Valley settlement embraced the upper basin of Stuart's Creek and is connected with the following names: Bell, Crawford, Eddy, Hall, Hepler, Fitzpatrick, McCausland, Morrow, and Warrick.

The Bullpasture settlement stretched along the entire course of that stream from its source nearly to the Bullpasture Gap. Here the names are Beathe, Black, Bodkin, Bradshaw, Burnside, Carlile, Curry, Davis, Duffield, Erwin, Estill, Ferguson, Graham, Harper, Hempenstall, Hicklin, Hiner, Hynes, Jones, Justice, Lockridge, Malcom, McCoy, Peebles, Pullin, Siron, Summers, Wiley.

Adjacent to the Bullpasture valley, and just within the Bath line, is the Red Holes, or Burnsville, settlement. The earlier name is derived either from the reddish loam exposed to view in the sinkholes, or from the artificial licks, made by driving stakes into the ground, withdrawing them, and then filling the holes with salt. Here David Frame patented a tract that nominally covered 1150 acres. But when sold in 1792 to Elisha Williams, John Burns, and James and Daniel Monroe, the lines proved so elastic as to include 1363 acres.

The bottoms on Jackson's River are less continuous than those of the Cowpasture. The "pockets" in which they occur were mainly gathered into a few large surveys. The northernmost of these pockets begins beyond the Highland line and may be called the Wilson settlement. The names found here are Bratton, Cleek, Given, Gwin, McFarland, Wilson.

For several miles below the Wilson settlement Jackson's River is closely confined between lofty hills. Then comes the Fort Dinwiddie settlement, comprising two very long surveys by William Jackson and Adam Dickenson. Here are the names Bourland, Byrd, Cameron, Davis, Dean, Jackson, McClintic.

A short distance east of the Wilson settlement is Little Valley, where the early names are Carpenter, McAvoy, and Pritt.

Beginning below the Fort Dinwiddie settlement, reaching nearly to Covington, and extending up the valley of Cedar Creek was the Fort Mann settlement, where these names occur: Armstrong, Bollar, Elliot, Kincaid, Kirk, Mann, McGuffin, Montgomery, Morris, Robinson, Walker.

Around and just below Covington was the Fort Young settlement, occupied by the Carpenters, Mallows, Seelys, and Wrights.

On Great Back Creek, stretching some distance above and below the mouth of Little Back Creek, was the Vance or Mountain Grove settlement where lived the Baxters, Gregorys, Hamiltons, Kellys, and Vances.

On the lower course of Potts Creek were the Potts and Persinger families.

On the Cowpasture, below the pass at Griffith Knob, were several pioneers, but our knowledge of their names is quite unsatisfactory.

The Warm Springs basin and the upper valley of Falling Spring Run may be termed the Warm Springs settlement. But so closely were the lands in this locality monopolized by wealthy non-residents, that most of the people living here in the early days were tenants, and we know little as to who they were. This was not quite so much the case at the Falling Springs end, which is associated with the Chambers, Massie, and Mustoe families. The three tracts held by Gabriel Jones of Port Republic begin at Healing Springs and run a long way to the north. North, east, and south of him were the lands of Thomas and Cuthbert Bullitt. John Bollar had 400 acres alongside Jones. Against the present Alleghany line were the holdings of Oliver and Thompson. Immediately to the south was Thomas Massie's tract of 3329 acres. The John Lewis survey ran north from Warm Springs itself, and one owned by John Cowardin ran in the direction of Warm Springs gap.

Adam Dickenson, the leading pioneer on the lower Cowpasture, was in 1733 living at Hanover, New Jersey. In 1742 he was an ironworker in Lancaster County, Pennsylvania, but seems to have moved in the same year to Prince George County, Maryland. It was at this date that he entered into a bond in favor of Thomas Lindsay, whereby he was to patent 1,000 acres on Clover Creek, "otherwise ye Cow Pasture"; and place two families on the tract. Four years later, he brought suit against Roger Hunt, Lindsay's assignee, for a failure to comply with the contract. He must have come to the Cowpasture himself by 1744. When Augusta was organized, at the close of 1745, he alone, of the 21 justices in the first county court, represented the portion of the county west of Shenandoah Mountain. His grist-mill was evidently the first in this region, and the church built on his homestead was undoubtedly the first house of worship among the southern Alleghanies. Dickenson acquired at least 3321 acres of choice land. He died intestate about 1760. His personal property was appraised by his neighbors, James Gillespie, James McCay, John Young, and Andrew Sitlington, at almost $1,000, easily the equivalent of $5,000 today. The estate included two slaves, 33 cattle, and a wagon valued at $23.33. The only book was a large Bible. Abigail, a daughter, married William McClung. Another daughter was Mary Davis.

John, the only son of Adams Dickenson, was almost an exact contemporary to George Washington. He was born in 1731 and died in 1799. At the age of 22 he was a captain of horse, and during the next 25 years he saw very much military service on the frontier. After being wounded in at least two skirmishes with the Indians, he received a severe hurt in the shoulder at the battle of Point Pleasant. For this injury he was granted a pension of 50 pounds ($166.67) a year. In 1777, with the rank of colonel, he returned to Point Pleasant at the head of a regiment of militia. In 1757 he was a justice of Augusta, but in 1779 he declined further service. Although appointed a member of the first county court of Bath, he refused the honor. Colonel Dickenson was a large holder of real estate, owning land on the Greenbrier and even in North Carolina. He was of positive convictions and was influenced by high motives. His generous impulse appears in his kindness to the unfortunate Selim, and in his refusal to deliver up some converted Indians whom the governor assumed to be spies of the French. By a clause in his will, no liquor was to be served at his interment, and in this matter he stood against a very pernicious custom of his day.

His children were Mary, Martha, Nancy, Adam, Jean, and John. Mary and Martha married, in order of mention, Samuel and John Shrewsbury, who, after being prominent in Bath, migrated to West Virginia. The only grandson in the male line to finish his days in Bath was John Usher Dickenson, who returned about 1850 and was the first proprietor of the hotel at Millboro.

William Jackson gave his name to the river which runs more than three miles through the land he took up. He may have been the first settler on its upper course, although he could not have been living in this valley in 1740, when he succeeded James Pickett as constable. His home on Jackson's River was probably near the site of Fort Dinwiddie. Jane and William were children. The former married Archibald Bourland, his executor. The son, and probably the son-in-law also, went to North Carolina. Whether the early Jacksons of the Cowpasture were related to this family we do not know. William Jackson died June 1, 1750, and his suits against

Robert Abercrombie and Jacob Marlin were thereby abated. His personality of $1106.07 ranked him among the nabobs of early Bath. The appraisement by Ralph Laverty, George Wilson, and Archibald Elliot mentions 23 horses, 18 cattle, and some timothy seed. A lancet, and the instrument of torture styled a "tooth drawers" would appear to indicate that he made some pretensions to the healing art. It took seven gallons of liquor to lubricate the sale of the personal effects. Archibald Bourland, the executor, named the following persons at the "vandue": James Bourland, James Brown, Thomas Bryan, John Carlile, John Crockett, William Davis, Robert Duffield, Andrew Dunlap, Charles Dunlap, Archibald Elliot, Samuel Ferguson, Alexander Gillespie, John Graham, Napthalim Gregory, William Hamilton, John Harden, Michael Harper, George Lewis, James Lockridge, Joseph Mayse, Samuel McAlvery, Alexander Millroy, Nathan Patterson, David Stanley, John Warrick, John Williamson, George Wilson, and Alexander Wright. A number of these persons lived more than 20 miles away.

According to C. K. Bolton, the following Ulster immigrants came from county Antrim. The Arbuckles, Campbells, Clarks, Crawfords, Givens, Harpers, Jacksons, Jamesons, McCays; from Derry, the Grahams, Lockridges, Pattons, Rheas; from Down, the Carliles, Dunlaps, Mathews, Steuarts; from Donegal, the Brattons, Hamiltons; from Londonderry, the Kincaids; from Tyrone, the Burnsides, Knoxes, and Walkups.

Certain of the families who have migrated from this country include names of considerable prominence. Thus James B. McCreery and his cousin, Thomas C. McCreery, of Kentucky, are great grandsons of Robert, son of John McCreery, of the Cowpasture. Both these men have served in the United States Senate, and the former has twice been governor of his state. Dr. Charles McCreery, the first physician to remove the collar-bone in a surgical operation, which was done in 1813, was a son of Robert. By way of North Carolina we are told that Zebulon B., Robert B., and Robert E. Vance of North Carolina, are of the Vance family of Back Creek. All three served in Congress. The first was also a famous governor of North Carolina, and the second was a brigadier general in the Confederate army. Meigs County, Tennessee, is named for Return Jonathan Meigs, a descendent of the Clendennins. C. C. O'Hara, an eminent geologist, appears to be a descendant of the O'Hara who once lived on the Cowpasture. William Bratton, one of the picked men of the Lewis and Clarke expedition of 1803, was a grandson of Robert Bratton of the Calfpasture. A monument stands over his grave in Indiana giving his services in that famous expedition. Colonels Robert and John McFarland, early pioneers of Jefferson county, Tennesse, are descendants of Duncan McFarland, as was also William McFarland, a congressman from that state.

V

THE MINERAL SPRINGS

ISTILLED water is chemically pure, but is tasteless and therefore insipid. The "pure, cool spring water" we hear about is pure only with respect to its harmlessness. After the water from the clouds has had time to soak through the ground it has become charged with various mineral ingredients, and is thereby rendered palatable. Water that has been much in contact with limestone or calcareous earth is called "hard." If, on the other hand, there had been a filtering through deposits containing little lime, we call the water "soft." But when ground water is unfit to drink, it is rarely because of the minerals it has taken up. The harmfulness is usually due to organic matter, either of vegetable or animal tissue.

But while the water from wells and springs is mineral water in the strict sense of the term, it is customary to regard as mineral waters only those which have distinct medicinal effect. The character of such waters varies with the chemical composition of the rock and earth from which they issue. Beds of slate often contain the bright yellow particles known as iron pyrites, or "fool's gold." The yellow color is due to the sulphur in the pyrites. On exposure to the air, these particles decompose into the sulphates of iron and alumina, and give rise to springs of alum, sulphur, or chalybeate waters. The valley of the Cowpasture abounds in slate formations, and hence the mineral springs, particularly of alum and sulphur waters, which there occur.

The mineral springs of the Cowpasture are cool, while those of Warm Springs valley are warm. This difference is because of the geological structure of that valley.

In the very deepest mines the temperature is so constantly and oppressively hot that the miners can work only in short shifts and with very little clothing. We can thus understand that if surface waters sink to very great depths, and thus come well within the influnece of the internal heat of the earth, they reappear with much higher temperature than are found in ordinary springs. They are also more heavily loaded with mineral, because heated water has a greater dissolving power than cold water, and is more energetic in absorbing gases from the rocks through which it forces its way. The chemical action of this process tends to further increase the heat of the water. Let us suppose that a section of pipe is bent into two arms of unequal length, and then placed in a vertical position, the elbow being embedded in redhot coals. If water is steadily poured into the upper arm, it will as steadily come out of the lower opening because water seeks to maintain a level. But it will issue at a higher temperature, because of the coals. This illustration will help to explain the thermal springs of Bath County. The Warm Springs Valley has the form of a canoe, but the mountain wall on the east is higher than the one on the west. It is also significant that all the thermal springs lie on the western side of the valley. In the first chapter of this book it was observed that the basin within this mountain rampart is largely occupied by an oval-shaped area of very early geologic origin. Surrounding this rock formation, and appearing next the surface as an oval ring, is a more recent stratum. If, now, this last-named deposit passed underneath the other, and to a great depth, and if it were impervious to water, we would have a very easy explanation of the heated waters. However, the rock strata in this valley-floor are convex and not concave. Nevertheless, the rainwater falling on the sharp western slope of Warm Springs Mountain and reappearing as warm mineral water in the depression below, behaves in about the same manner as the water which in our illustration is poured into the upper end of the bent tube.

The several springs differ in temperature, and this would indicate that their waters do not rise from an equal depth. It is also worthy of notice that the basin is cross-sectioned into sub-valleys, each, with one exception, having a thermal spring of its own. Each spring, or group of springs, lies near the upper entrance to a watergap in Valley Mountain. And as the mineral elements in the several springs differ in number and also in proportion, it would indicate that the rock structure below the suface is not uniform.

Lying mostly in Highland, but crossing into the northern confine of Bath is another canoe-shaped basin drained by Bolar Run. It presents the same peculiarities as Warm Springs Valley, and has a group of thermal springs lying a little above its solitary watergap.

Certain plants have medicinal qualities of one kind or another. To supplement them, certain mineral springs have great curative powers, by reason of the gases and the solid ingredients which their waters hold in solution. And as it is an error of judgment to use any vegetable drug in a random manner, it is no less an error to use a given mineral water without regard to expert knowledge of its effects on the human system. The various springs of these two valleys differ in their healing qualities, one reaching one class of ailments, and another reaching to a certain extent a different class. The peculiarities of the individual patient are also to be taken into account.

The Hot Springs of Bath are primarily a group of six flowing fountains of great volume. The leading one has a temperature of 106 degrees and contains of mineral salts 43 grains to the gallon. The minerals held in solution are mainly calcium, magnesium, sodium, and potassium. Calcium, which is the basis of lime, is by far the most important. The large proportion of it in all the springs of this valley is indeed what we might expect, since the entire floor of this basin consists of limestone strata. The Hot Springs also contain sulphuric and carbonic acids, and chlorine. These make various combinations with the four minerals already named. The waters are particularly beneficial in rheumatic ailments. They are also useful in nervous and dyspeptic disorders, and in liver, kidney, and female diseases. There are springs of soda, sulphur, and magnesia waters close by, and alum waters at a little greater distance. The magnesia water, issuing at a temperature of 100 degrees, acts as a mild alterative. The soda waters, which have a temperature of 74 degrees, are serviceable in urinary complaints. The alum water is an excellent tonic and a mild yet certain astringent. The very great depth from which all these springs rise, and the force with which they come to the surface, render them free from organic impurities. Otherwise, their medicinal value would be impaired, and they would be unfit for bottling.

The Warm Springs, five miles northeast of the Hot Springs, have a temperature of 98 degrees and an outflow of 1200 gallons a minute. To style them warm rather than hot is incorrect. In temperature they are of the same class as the Hot Springs, and they contain a larger variety of mineral elements. The principal ones which do not appear to be found in the other are carbonate of iron, sodium sulphate, and silicic acid. Taken as a beverage, the water is tonic, aperient, and diuretic. It is useful in nearly the same class of ailments as the waters of the Hot Springs, and is very advantageous in dyspepsia.

The Healing Springs are about three miles southward from the Hot Springs. They are likewise of strong volume and their temperature is 84 degrees. They are more varied in composition than the Hot Springs. They may be said to possess about the same elements that occur in the Warm Springs, but in differing proportions. A few ingredients do not appear to be found at either of the other places. As the name would indicate, these waters constitute a powerful healing agent, and are bottled in large quantities. They are very good in affections of the skin, but are also used in rheumatism, in bronchial complaints, and in disorders of the urinary and digestive organs.

The Rubino Spring lies within a mile of the Healing Springs and is of the same character.

Bolar Spring in Great Valley has a temperature of 74 degrees and an outflow of 1600 gallons a minute. Like the other thermal waters, it is highly charged with gases. Iodine and arsenic are present, but there has been no complete analysis. Taken internally, the water is diuretic and alterative, and mildly aperient. Taken externally, it enjoys much repute in ailments of the skin and in nasal catarrh. One mile northward is the Burns Spring, 79 degrees warm and somewhat stronger in mineral qualities though of the same general nature.

In the valley of the Cowpasture the best known of its mineral waters are the sulphur fountains at Millboro Springs and All Healing Springs, and the alum waters of Bath Alum and Wallawhatoola.

The red men of America have a natural aptitude for the healing art. That the thermal waters of Bath had been known to them from time immemorial may be taken for granted. An attractive legend, published in 1838 in the *Southern Literary Messenger,* relates that a young brave was making his first journey across the Alleghanies in order to carry a message from his powerful tribe to the council fire kindling on the shore of the Great Water. The shades of night overtook him in Warm Springs Valley. The darkness was profound, and the wind was moaning dismally among the tree-tops. On the sodden ground he could find no comfortable place to sleep, and he was too weary to climb the mountain lying across his path. But continuing to search, he came upon an opening in a laurel thicket. Here was a pool in which he could see the reflection of the evening star. The waters were so clear that the pebbly bottom could be made out. The warm vapor that rose to his nostrils tempted him into the pool so that he might bathe his aching limbs. To his surprise and delight the temperature was of blood warmth. By the strong current issuing from the basin, he knew he had found a spring. He laid himself down, and the Spirit of Strength gave him new life and hope. At dawn the Young Panther strode with easy step up the bold mountain wall. At the council fire on the eve of that day, no other warrior was more graceful in address, more commanding in manner, or more sagacious in council.

But this legend of a poetic race, seemingly adapted to the time of arrival of the first English settlers, is not to be taken as a precise fact of history. It is an expression in symbolic form of the virtues of these health-giving waters, as they had been experienced during centuries upon centuries by the wild men of the forest.

A family tradition relates that Andrew Lewis came accidentally upon the Hot Springs while escaping from hostile Indians. On the other hand, it is alleged that a knowledge of them had been carried to the capital of Virginia before the expedition under Spottswood in 1716. That white explorers were told of these thermal waters by the Indians is very probable. Be this as it may, Lewis was very matter of fact, and seems to have been more deeply impressed with the limestone lands of Warm Springs Valley than with the hygienic value of its remarkable fountains.

In 1750, which was during the early infancy of the settlement of Bath, the springs were already well known. Thomas Walker, on his return from a prospecting tour into the southwest extremity of Virginia, makes this entry in his journal, the date being July 9, 1750:

"We went to the hot Springs and found Six Invalides there. The Spring Water is very Clear & Warmer than new Milk, an there is a Spring of cold Water within 20 feet of the Warm one."

Between 1763 and 1767, Andrew Lewis surveyed in his own name 884 acres in Warm Springs Valley. Meanwhile, Thomas Bullitt, a fellow soldier who in one instance acted in partnership with Lewis, surveyed 1120 acres. These tracts do not include the lands they surveyed along the course of Falling Springs Run. No more surveys are recorded for quite a while, for the evident reason that Lewis, Bullitt, and Dickenson had taken the cream of the agricultural lands in the valley. It is to be noted that the entry of a tract of public land usually took place some years before the actual survey.

The Lewises reduced to patent 1886 acres, and Bullitt 1248. Gabriel Jones is credited with 720 acres and John Dickenson with 250. And as in the case of the surveys, these patents do not include the tracts on the upper course of Falling Springs Run. Thus a few influential non-residents monopolized the valley.

A patent of 1764, calling for 300 acres, and including the Hot Springs, was taken by Thomas Bullitt and Andrew and Thomas Lewis. These men entered into an agreement to build a hotel and stock it with the distilled and fermented liquors which in their day as in ours were deemed by many persons to be superior to the beverage prepared by Dame Nature. So far as the Lewises were concerned this plan was not carried out. They made an arrangement with Bullitt whereby access to the springs was secured to each party. Bullitt erected a hotel about 1764, portions of which remained until destroyed, together with a newer building, in the fire of 1901. In 1790, Bullitt authorized John Oliver to grant twenty-year leases on his lands in Warm Springs Valley. But the Hot Springs tract was excepted, and so was another supposed to contain an undeveloped mine.

As early a 1778, Cuthbert Bullitt, then a resident of this valley, petitioned the assembly that 50 acres of his land be laid off into lots and a town established at "Little Warm Springs," this being the early name for the Hot Springs. He remarks that it was extremely difficult to procure building materials.

In 1793 the owners of this property were Nathaniel Wilkenson, John Littlepage, and John Oliver. They petitioned the Assembly, under the date of October 23, "That they have laid off a town of one hundred half-acre Lotts with convenient Streets on this land at Hot Springs in the County of Bath, and that the benefit of those Waters (especially Scorbutick and Rheumatick Complaints) may be enjoyed by all who may have occasion to visit those springs, they pray the said Town may be established by an act to be passed for that purpose."

The Act was at once passed. The trustees named in the charter were Sampson Mathews, Samuel Vance, Thomas Hughart, Charles Cameron, George Poage, John Montgomery, John White, John

Lewis, John Bollar, Anthony Mustoe, and Samuel Shrewsbury. They were authorized to make such rules and orders concerning the building of houses as they might think best. They were also empowered to settle all disputes relating to the boundaries of lots. Whenever the purchaser of a lot had built a house at least 16 feet square, and provided it with a chimney of brick or stone, he was to be entitled to all the rights and privileges which were enjoyed by the freehold inhabitants of unincorporated towns.

The lot drawing was held in Staunton, July 14, 1794. William Forbes who drew ticket 51, purchased a one-half acre lot at "Hott Bath" for 10 pounds ($33.33).

In 1820 the mail came only three times a week to the resorts in this valley, and the ordinary postage was 18¾ cents.

But as a resort for health or pleasure, Hot Springs languished until the hotel was purchased in 1832 by Doctor Thomas Goode. Under his régime the hotel was 200 feet long and two stories high. It was well filled during the summer season, because the resort was now swiftly coming into a wide-reaching repute. In the summer of 1838, Hot Springs and the other resorts within a radius of 40 miles were visited by about 6000 people. The guests had to come by stage coach or private conveyance. To arrive from Philadelphia in four days, the traveler had to make prompt connections among the various stage lines, and to submit to being jolted in a coach for 16 hours a day. And yet from the far more distant lowlands of the Gulf States came many cotton planters and their families. It is hardly necessary to add that no such journeys could be made by weak invalids.

P. H. Nicklin, writing of Hot Springs in 1835, says that "at first sight, appearances do not invite a long sojourn." He speaks of the old frame hotel and bath houses and several rows of cabins. But the table fare was very good, and "the scenery grows into your affection the deeper the longer you remain."

Doctor Goode died in 1858 and there were more changes in ownership. Finally, in 1890, the Virginia Hot Springs Company came into control. This corporation also acquired title to the Warm and the Healing Springs.

The tract of 140 acres which includes the Warm Springs was surveyed in 1751 for John Lewis, Sr., and John Lewis, Jr. The younger

John settled on the land, dying here in 1788. The same year he sold to William Bowyer of Staunton two one-half acre lots for $200, these being on "a line with the large dwelling house and store house now built."

In the summer of 1781, the Virginia Assembly, which had adjourned from Charlottesville to Staunton, voted to adjourn again to Warm Springs, and thus would have made this hamlet a third temporary state capital, had the British cavalry made good their threatened raid into the Shenandoah Valley. A writer of 1792 remarks that it lay "on a great leading road from Richmond to the Illinois and Kentucky and several of the western countys"; that it was the "numerous resort of all ranks of people." But he adds that the real estate was owned by minors, and that rent was under such restrictions as nearly to forbid population.

Enjoying the prestige of being the county seat, Warm Springs was, during the stage-coach era, as widely and favorably known as its nearby rival. In fact, Hot Springs is sometimes mentioned in the early surveys as Little Warm Springs. Prior to the purchase of the springs and hotel by the corporation which also controls the other resorts of the valley, the owner was the late Colonel John L. Eubank, secretary of the Virginia Secession Convention of 1861.

Healing Springs, like the "Hot" and the "Warm," as the others are popularly known in the county, has attracted to its neighborhood a considerable village. But in a social point of view this resort is much less conspicuous. Until about 1850 it was quite undeveloped.

Five miles east of Warm Springs, and a little beyond the foot of the intervening mountain, is Bath Alum. During the many years when the pike leading toward Staunton was the only entrance to Bath from the east, Bath Alum was a well known summer resort. But no village grew up around it, and the brick hotel was at length closed by an owner who was indifferent to the tourist business. It is now unvisited and stands in quiet loneliness amid fields and forests.

The hotel at Millboro Springs was opened by John U. Dickenson a few years before the war of 1861, and being within three miles of a railroad station, it enjoys a good patronage. Wallawhatoola Spring, a mile down the Cowpasture, is a private resort only. Nimrod Hall, three miles still farther below, is without the adjunct of an important mineral spring. Panther Spring in Panther Gap is controlled by the Alleghany Inn, at Goshen. All Healing Spring, at the south end of Shenandoah Mountain, is little developed as a resort.

The hotels of Warm Spring Valley heavily preponderate in drawing visitors to Bath. As a field for health and pleasure, this upland is exceptionally favored. In the matter of climate it has advantages over the outside portion of the county. The towering mountain wall shields it from storms. The several watergaps on the west side, the absence of any stream coursing lengthwise through the valley, and the considerable elevation of its floor above the level of Jackson's River, combine to exempt this locality from the morning fogs which hover over the river bottoms during the warm season. In consequence the air is more than usually dry for a mountain valley, and even in the winter season many a day is mild and sunny.

General David H. Strother*, better known as Porte Crayon, speaks of "the matchless gift of beauty with which Heaven has endowed this happy region, its beautiful and invigorating atmosphere, its abundance even to superfluity in all the good things that make it a desirable residence for man. It is a picture, soft and luxuriant, of rolling plains and rich woodlands, watered by crystal streams, enriched with rare and curious gems wrought by the plastic hand of Nature, all superbly set in an azure frame of mountains, beautiful always, and sometimes rising into sublimity."

In 1856, the three leading resorts in Bath paid the following in license fees: Warm Springs, $114.59; Hot Springs, $100.84; Bath Alum, $87.09.

The corporation now owning the resorts has at a large outlay supplemented the advantages bestowed by nature. Among the improvments is first the railroad spur of 25 miles which connects Hot Springs with the main line of the Chesapeake & Ohio at Covington. The present very modern hotel, with accommodations for 700 guests, more than equals the combined capacity of the hostelries at Warm Springs and Healing Springs. Roadways totalling 15 miles are owned and controlled by the management. A large share of this mileage is macadamized. Bridle-paths and foot-paths have been cut through the woods to the mountain summits on either side, particularly to Flag Rock on Warm Springs Mountain.

---

*Nephew to Doctor Archer P. Strother, a highly respected citizen who lived between Hot Springs and Warm Springs and died in 1856.

VI

EARLY POLITICAL HISTORY

HE pioneer history of the Bath area starts with the beginning of white settlement about 1745, and comes to a close with the organization of the county in 1791. By the end of the half-century the region had become well populated, according to the standard which then and for many years later prevailed in the Southland.

But not until after Bath had become a county was there any group of houses large enough to be termed a village. There were a few stores and gristmills, and a few dwelling houses were licensed as taverns. Only in one instance was there a sufficient nucleus to be called a hamlet. This exception was Warm Springs. At Hot Springs there could have been no more than a primitive hotel with its accessory buildings.

The earliest tavern licenses we know of were those granted to George Wilson in 1758, to James Ward in 1759, and to John Dickenson in 1763. The rates which the tavern-keeper might not exceed were minutely prescribed by the county court, and had to be posted in the public room. By a ruling of the court of Botetourt in 1775, the charge for a "warm diet with good meat" was one shilling, or 16 2-3 cents. For a cold meal it was 10½ cents. If the guest slept alone, his lodging cost him half a shilling. If two or more slept in the same bed, the charge to each was a third of a shilling. Pasturage or hay for 24 hours cost 10½ cents. All hostelries kept intoxicants in variety, and the drinking habit must have been very general. The charge at this time for rum, whiskey, or peach brandy was one dollar a gallon. For three pints of toddy made with half a pint of rum and "single refined sugar" the charge was 21 cents. The books of William Crow, who was a merchant of Staunton in 1760-70, show few very long accounts, yet scarcely a day passed without several charges for drinks. A petition of 1754 condemns the selling by ordinaries of large quantities of liquor at extravagant rates, whereby money is drained out of the country. The signers express their intention of making their own liquor so as to keep their money in the home neighborhood. Among the 91 signers who "felt the smart" of this state of things were Archibald Armstrong, John Allen, Joseph Bell, John Carlile, James Gay, Matthew Harper, James Knox, James Montgomery, Loftus Pullin, and James Scott.

The first definite mention of a store is that of Sampson and George Mathews at Cloverdale. It was built about 1775. The first store we read of at Warm Springs was that of White, Kirk and Company in 1787. Until local stores, began to appear, the merchants of Staunton had a monopoly of the Bath trade, except so far as they had to compete with traveling pedlers. This competition must have been considerable. The pedler went everywhere and was a welcome visitor.

The earliest mill license seems to be the one issued to Adam Dickenson February 12, 1747. It must have been a new mill that was built on the Dickenson plantation by William Hamilton about 1763. In that year the labor that had been put into the new building was pronounced by David Davis and Samuel Vance as worth four pounds cash, or $13.33. The Hamilton mill was doubtless to replace one burned by the Indians. The second mill license is that in favor of George Wilson in August, 1747. In 1750 John Justice built for William Wilson on Bolar Run a tubmill at the contract price of $20. It was to have been completed by May 1, but the builder was much behind time. Wilson sued for 20 pounds damages, and Patrick Martin, William Hamilton, and David Davis, ordered by the court to view the mill, reported it insufficient. In the spring of 1753 John McCreery put in a mill on the Cowpasture, just below Ebbing Spring. The first mention of a sawmill is in 1761. The owner was George Wilson, and the site is probably on the upper course of Stuart's Creek.

Until 1852, the county court in Virginia was a close corporation and had extensive powers. For a long time there was no higher tribunal than the Governor's Council, a body corresponding to the present state senate. When a new county was created, its justices were nominated by the court of the parent county. Whenever a county court was to be enlarged, or when vacancies were to be filled, the court made its own nominations. In either case, the nominations were passed upon by the governor and the appointments were made by him. He also chose the sheriff and the commissioned officers of the militia from the men nominated by the court. But it was the court itself that appointed the county clerk, the constables, and the overseers of the roads. It passed judgment on all offenses except felonies and high treason, and in the case of such criminals as were negro slaves it could decree the death penalty and order the sheriff to execute it.

Under British rule the highest county official was the county lieutenant. He was a sort of deputy governor, and when the militia were called out he held the rank of colonel. The coroner was a conservator of the peace, and his office was much more important than it is now.

There was a property qualification for voters, and a considerable number of men were thus deprived of the use of the elective franchise. Yet the only dignitaries the colonial voter had a regular opportunity to elect were members of the House of Burgesses. Until 1776 the governor was sent from England under appointment by the British crown, and he acted as its personal representative. His salary was large and it was paid by the colony. He lived in much pomp and wielded a great influence. At the close of his term he usually returned to Britain.

Until local government was organized in Augusta, which was not until the close of 1745, its settlers had to go to Orange to attend court, a distance from Fort Lewis of over 100 miles. The first justices from its own territory were John Lewis and James Patton. The former seems to have been commissioned in 1739. There was no resident justice in the Bath area until Adam Dickenson was appointed in 1745. John Dickenson was chosen in 1756. Whether the William Wilson who was serving in the same year was the man of that name living on Jackson's River, we cannot determine. Charles Lewis was appointed in 1763, but declined to serve. Jacob Warwick was on the court in 1778, and John McCreery, Jr., in 1781, but in the year following both these men declined further service because of the distance to the courthouse.

The first local coroner we read of was John McCreery, Jr., who was serving in 1779. The first constable was James Mayse, appointed by Orange, February 28, 1745. The June court of the same year ordered him to qualify at its next meeting. Wallace Estill and James Hughart succeeded Mayse in 1747. Later constables whom we can identify as belonging to Greater Bath were these:

Ralph Laverty—1748	Thomas Thompson—1763
Archibald Elliott—1749	Alexander Black—1763
James Stuart—1751	Thomas Cartmill—1767
William Daugherty—1752	Joseph McClung—1763
Henry Gay—1753	Richard Mayse—1768
John Byrd—1755	Thomas Wright—1770
James Bourland—1756	Andrew Hamilton—1770
Andrew Muldrock—1756	Andrew McCausland—1780

Wright and Hamilton were appointed by the Botetourt court. Both represented Jackson's River, the former from that section of the valley above the "bent."

Another close corporation within each county was the vestry. It had charge of the local interests of the Church of England. This was the established church in Virginia and was supported by public taxation. The taxes for this purpose were levied by the vestry, which had also the care of the poor, and it bound out the children of illegitimate birth. When a new county was formed, the members of its first vestry were chosen by the qualified voters. But with a curious inconsistency, the board was thenceforward self-perpetuating. It filled its own vacancies and was a close corporation like the county court. The executive officers of the vestry were the two church-wardens chosen from its own membership.

The laws were harsh, although a lax administration of severe laws was often winked at. Under British rule, Virginia recognized 27 offenses as punishable by death. Imprisonment for debt continued until the middle of the nineteenth century. Lashes at the public whipping-post, on the bare back and "well laid on," were frequently ordered, 39 being the limit at any one time. Women were thus punished as well as men.

The first lawsuit pertaining to the Bath area and recorded in Augusta, was that of Adam Dickenson against John Potts, called February 11, 1746. A gray mare was ordered sold to satisfy a debt of five pounds ($16.67).

Until 1769 the county of Augusta had for its eastern boundary the crest of the Blue Ridge from the Tennessee line to a point nearly east of Port Republic. Westward it was understood as extending far enough to cover all the territory in that direction that was claimed by Virginia. But in practical sense, the actual county was never larger than the area that was occupied. As population extended the real county grew in size. After it had become unwieldy it was subdivided. The first curtailment was in 1769, when Botetourt was authorized. The line between the old county and the new ran in a southeast and northwest direction, crossing the present county of Bath in the vicinity of Dunn's Gap between Hot Springs and Warm Springs. The Cowpasture was crossed at the Donally farm and Jackson's River at the John Davis place. James Trimble surveyed this line in 1770, so far as it lay between the Blue Ridge and the Alleghany Front. To reimburse him for the fees and expenses the court of Botetourt voted $53.88. Four years later the same court ordered that application be made to Augusta to have the line extended to the Ohio River. It does not appear that this was ever carried into effect.

During 21 years the south of Bath and all of Alleghany lay under the jurisdiction of Botetourt. Until after 1776, however, there is no mention of justices or grandjurors from the Bath area. In 1770 William Christian was directed to list the tithables on "James River and the Pastures from the mouth of Craig up to and including the Greenbrier settlement." Three years later Matthew Arbuckle took the list from the mouth of Craig up the James and Cowpasture to the county line, and up Jackson's River to William Hughart's. The rest of Jackson's River was assigned to John Robinson. In 1775, Richard Mayse had Arbuckle's district enlarged by being extended to Sweet Springs. The next official was William McClenahan, whose district comprised Arbuckle's and Robinson's.

In 1772 Botetourt had 2202 tithables. Perhaps less than one-eighth of these were in the space now included in Bath, Alleghany, Greenbrier, and Monroe. For her first county buildings the sum of $1280 was voted. In 1772 Richard Mayse was appointed to look after putting up an office building for the use of the court. In 1770, 169 wolf-heads were brought in, the bounty being $5.00 for a grown animal and $2.50 for a cub.

VII

ROADS AND ROAD BUILDERS

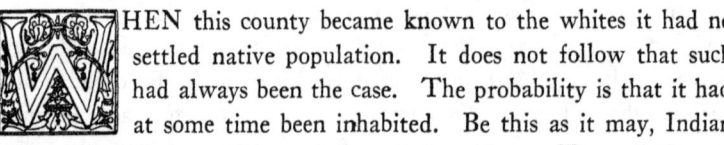HEN this county became known to the whites it had no settled native population. It does not follow that such had always been the case. The probability is that it had at some time been inhabited. Be this as it may, Indian paths followed the valleys and crossed the ridges. These trails certainly existed but are now forgotten. The settler was quick to use them whenever they could serve his purpose. Some portions of the aboriginal highways may still exist in the form of county roads. In fact the Indian road was sometimes broad enough to admit a wagon, and often it was deep on account of long continued use. A stream was ordinarily crossed at the mouth of a branch, because a bar will occur at such a place.

The buffalo was also a maker of paths. This animal lives in herds, and when the grazing gives out at one place, the whole herd moves to another, taking a very straight course. There is no doubt that the Indian appropriated some of the buffalo paths for his own use. At first sight, it would look as though the buffalo and not the Indian was the first road-builder in Bath. The contrary is almost certainly the case. The buffalo lived only in open, grassy country, and never in the dense forest. The whole Alleghany country is by nature an unbroken forest. The large expanses of open ground seen by the early explorers were caused by the Indians, so as to develop an ample supply of large game. So the buffalo herds crept farther and farther eastward from their native western plains, and as a consequence the mound-building ancestors of the historic Indian tribes fell away from their agricultural habits.

A remnant of a buffalo trail is said to be still visible on a Cowpasture bluff, about a mile northward from the crossing of the Harrisonburg and Warm Springs turnpike, and on the east side of the river.

The roads of the early period of white settlement were rough and ready affairs. With a small population, and but little money passing from hand to hand, it was out of the question to build what we would now consider a good highway. The pioneer acted quite literally on the belief that a straight line is the shortest distance between two points. He was more inclined to go directly over a ridge than to wind through a hollow, and there contend with side-cutting, laurel thickets, and ledges of rock. He had no time for grading, and a road through a narrow pass offered too good an opportunity for Indians to lay in ambush. But the woods had less underbrush than now, and it was comparatively easy to open a tolerable wagon way. As for bridges, it was seldom that they were seriously thought of.

The earliest roads were used almost wholly as bridle-paths, the usual mode of travel being horseback and the packsaddle being the usual mode of transporting goods. Nevertheless, there was now and then a pioneer, even among the earliest, who had a wagon, and the more important roads had to be wide enough to permit a vehicle to be used. Wherever the road forked, the colonial law required an index to be set up for the information of the traveler. Crude, stumpy, rocky, and innocent of grading as the first roads must have been, the public opinion of the day required a certain standard of excellence. Many a road overseer was presented by the grand jury for failing to keep his road in order.

Two classes of highways received very early attention. A road was needed along each river, for it was directly upon the watercourses that almost all the early comers located. In these valleys were the forts for their protection and the indipensable gristmills. Other roads ran over the mountains, or if possible, around them, so as to reach the neighboring valleys. The most important of such roads were those leading toward the courthouse, which was the chief commercial point for a wide radius.

Thus it is easy to see why the first road leading to the Cowpasture should come from Staunton, and that it should pass around the end of Shenandoah Mountain. That it should strike the Cowpasture at Fort Lewis is because here was the choicest of the surveys taken by the influential Lewis family. So it was ordered by the court of Augusta, May 12, 1746, that "a road be laid off and marked from the great lick in the Cow Pasture adjoining Col. Lewis Land to Andrew Hamilton in the Calf Pasture, and that Andrew Lewis and George Lewis mark out and lay off the same and make report to the next court."

Two years later there was an order for a road from Jackson's River to the above mentioned land of Colonel Lewis on the Cowpastur, William Jackson being apponted to lay off the same. A year later still, the matter was again taken up, for we find the court reiterating its order, May 18, 1749. William Jackson and James Mayse were appointed overseers, the latter taking the portion of road "already marked" from the Fort Lewis survey to William Hamilton's on the Cowpasture. All the tithables on the Cowpasture above James Hughart's were ordered to turn out and build the highway.

Meanwhile, the Dickenson settlement was moving for an outlet. A petition by Adam Dickenson, for a road from the "lower end of the Cowpasture to Carter's mill" on the Calfpasture was rejected in February, 1748, but granted a month later. The signers were John Cartmill, Hugh Coffey, Adam Dickenson, John Donally, William Daugherty, William Gillespie, James Mayse, William Hugh (?) Ralph Laverty, Alexander Millroy, James McCay, John Mitchell, John Moore, Andrew Muldrock, James Scott, James Simpson, and James Stuart. These people were living above and below Fort Dickenson, and on Stuart's Creek. Whether this road was to go through "Painter's Gap" is not clear. We do not find definite mention of that passage in road orders until 1762.

In 1748, also, a view was ordered from Peter Wright's to Adam Dickenson's. Wright lived where Covington now stands. An order of 1751 calls for a road from Wright's mill to the Cowpasture near Hughart or Knox. This would bring it up the river to the vicinity of the bridge on the Harrisonburg pike. The work was entrusted to Adam Dickenson, David Davis, Peter Wright and Joseph Carpenter. On the same date, a road, apparently below the Bath line, was ordered from the Cowpasture to Borden's grant. The builders designated were James Frame, William Gillespie, Hugh McDonald, Robert and James Montgomery, William McMurray, James and John Scott, and James Simpson.

Just a year later, a petition by Cowpasture settlers led to an order for another eastward road. This was to go from "Patrick Davis to the road leading to Beverly's big meadows." Adam Dickenson was to lay off the precincts for the two overseers, John Dickenson and James Mayse.

By this time the dwellers on the Cowpasture were quite well accommodated with roads. During the next ten years there was a slowing up in road-building throughout the Bath area, largely a result of the long war with the Indians. In 1762, Ralph Laverty, James McCay, and John Dickenson were to view a route from Davis's to Dickenson's. The same year, Laverty and James Gay were to survey a road through Panther Gap to Dickenson's. It is in 1763 that we find the first mention of a public road to Warm Springs. The other terminus was Walker's place on the Cowpasture. The overseers were Thomas Feamster, from Walker's to Charles Lewis's, and John Lewis, from the latter point to Warm Springs.

In 1766, William Gillespie and James Beard were overseers for a road down the river from Dickenson's to a point eight miles from "Pedlar foard." John Dickenson and William Hughart were to divide their precincts. A year earlier there was an order for a road from Estill's mill (now McClung's) on the Bullpasture to the George Lewis place on the Cowpasture. The overseers were William Black, John Hicklin, and John Estill. But in 1767 a petition for a road over a part of this same course was rejected. The 18 petitioners, all or almost all of whom lived on the Bullpasture, asked for a road from John Hicklin's to Feamster's mill. In the same year, however, a view was ordered from William Wilson's mill on Bolar Run "into the New Layed out Road at the foot of the Bull Pastures and thence into the Branch near Feamster's." The petitioners were Robert Bratton, Robert Barnett, John Davis, David Frame, William Given, Ralph and William Laverty, Thomas Lewis, Duncan and Alexander McFarland, George Skillern, and Stephen Wilson. Skillern was a non-resident land-holder.

We have seen that the first mention of an authorized road to Warm Springs is in 1763. But in both English and French maps of 1755, a road is drawn all the way to the Hot Springs from the mouth of the South Branch of the Potomac. Its course inside the Bath area begins near the mouth of the Bullpasture. In 1769 a view was ordered from "Little Warm (Hot) Springs" to the forks of the road on Dunlap Creek. The viewers were Robert Armstrong and John Bollar. For a time wagons were unloaded at the east foot of Warm Springs Mountain where Brinkley's tavern was afterward built.

Goods could be moved farther west only by packsaddle. Until after 1774 there was no wagon route beyond Warm Springs. But in 1779, and probably as early as 1774, there were mileposts all the way to this point from Staunton.

The Revolution, with its domestic turmoil, high taxation, and depreciated paper money, was not favorable to the building of new roads or the improvement of old ones. In 1785 Robert McCreery, William Dickey, and Patrick Miller were delegated to view a road from Feamster's mill to the Bullpasture ford next above John Montgomery. This would locate the ford at Williamsville. In 1790 a road was established from Ralph Laverty's to Thompson's mill by way of Windy Cove. To build it the tithables were summoned from Thomas Thompson's to Patrick Davis's, and the call included those on Jackson's River who lived within convenient reach.

In 1770 the first county court of Botetourt named and described 39 road precincts. One of these lay partly in the Bath area, and its first overseer was James Montgomery. In 1772 the court of Botetourt ordered Peter Wright and Robert Armstrong to survey a road from Wright's to Sweet Springs.

We have now given all we know as to the steps taken to build public roads within the present limits of Bath and previous to its organization. The reader has already noticed that an order by the county court was not always promptly followed by actual construction.

We next mention the road overseers under Augusta, and also their precincts, where the latter are described:

James Mayse—1748.
Ralph Laverty—1753.
John Dickenson—1754.
William Gillespie—1765—Pedler Ford to Dickenson's.
John Miller vice Loftus Pullin—1767—Estill's to Feamster's.
John McCreery—1768—from Charles Lewis' to where the Dickenson road joins the Staunton and Warm Springs road.
John Hamilton—1768—Warm Springs to forks of road leading to John Dickenson's.
John Dean—1769—same precinct as Hamilton's.
Charles Donally and John McCreery—1769.
John Byrd vice John Lewis—1773—Cowpasture to Warm Springs.
William Black and George Bratton—1777.
David Frame—1778—from Frame's to William Black's and from Fort

Lewis to Colonel Mathews' on the Calfpasture. Next year, his precinct is "from the forks of the road leading to Warm Springs and Cowpasture, and to the new store."

Stephen Wilson—1778—John Wilson's to Warm Springs, and from William Wilson's to the Bullpasture road over the mountain.

John Oliver—1780—Warm Springs to Cowpasture.

Edward Thompson—1780—Cowpasture to Leonard Bell's.

Hugh Hicklin—1780—from the county (Botetourt) line to the schoolhouse on Indian Draft.

Charles Donally—1780—from the above named schoolhouse to Leonard Bell's.

John Montgomery—1781—William Black's to David Frame's.

John Rucker—1781—Thomas Cartmill's to Samuel Vance's.

James Young—1783—Cloverdale to big hill above Andrew Hamilton's.

Osborn Hamilton vice Adam Blackman—1786—Samuel Vance's to Fort Dinwiddie.

Robert Kirk vice John Oliver—1788—Warm Springs to Cowpasture. Jacob Warrick succeeded Kirk.

VIII

LIFE IN THE PIONEER DAYS

IN NEARLY every instance, the parents of the early pioneer were born on the other side of the ocean, landed at Philadelphia, and proceeded with little delay to the settlements in Augusta. Occasionally, however, they lived some years in Pennslyvania. The journey was by wagon. It led through the towns of Lancaster and Frederick, across the Potomac at Shepherd's Ferry, and up the Shenandoah Valley to Staunton by what was at first an Indian trail. The route was styled the "Pennsylvania Road." This side the Potomac it rather closely followed the course of the present Valley Turnpike. From Staunton they continued as best they could over rough paths to the Cowpasture and Jackson's River.

Doctor Walker, writing in 1750, during the infancy of Bath settlement, makes these entries in his diary:

"July 9—Having a Path (from Hot Springs) We rode 20 miles and lodged at Captain Jemysons below the Panther Gap. Two of my Company went to a Smith to get their Horses Shod.

"July 11—Our way mending We travelled 30 miles to Augusta Court House."

As a rule, men are slow to adopt a radical change in their manner of living. After once choosing his piece of land in the wilderness, the pioneer sought to feed, clothe, and house himself as he had done in the native land. But Europe was an old country, comparatively well peopled. America had only a few wild Indians, and the frontier looked to the new comer as though it had never been peopled at all. So the environment led to some departure from the old mode. The modification was not hard to accept, because the plain ways of the immigrants made them adaptable to new conditions. For example, they had lived in stone dwellings. It was now more convenient to build a log cabin. Indian corn was to them a new food and fodder plant, yet it was accepted at once. The potato, however, was not well known in Scotland before 1760. A cradle could be made of peeled hickory bark.

The climate was found to be more sunny than the European, but in general temperature not greatly different. The soil was unworn. Yet the small seaports of America were 200 miles away, and in the intervening distance there was almost no town population whatever. Nearly every man was a producer and not a consumer. These were disadvantages, but the Ulstermen were bent on escaping the vexations they had undergone in Ireland. In some instances the settler brought with him a considerable stock of hard cash. But in the wilderness itself there was no money, and there were few commodities which would bring money. All manufactured goods and such necessities as salt and ammunition had to be brought from the seacoast and were expensive. The pioneer was thus constrained to be as independent as possible of the outside world.

Where there are handicaps on travel and trade, a frontier community tends to lag behind in the march of civilization. In some of the more isolated valleys of Appalachian America the people still live very much as their grandparents lived a century ago. It has been different in Bath, because this county lies on a natural line of travel. But in the abundance of game there is a novelty. Walker remarks that during his summer expedition to Cumberland Gap, his party killed 13 buffaloes, 53 bears, and about 150 turkeys, to say nothing of other game, and could have killed three times as much if there had been the need. Slumbering instincts, inherited from remote ancestors, began at once to assert themselves. Some of the newcomers almost literally took to the woods. They neglected the soil and made hunting a business. The skins they did not need as articles of clothing could be sent to the seaports. The bounty on the destructive wolf put some additional coin into their pockets. Nearly every pioneer seems to have yielded in some degree to this "call of the wild."

On the other hand, it is a great error to assume that coonskin caps and deerskin hunting shirts were generally worn in this region, or that the pioneer lived within doors in almost as primitive a fashion as the Indian himself. This was true of some persons, but it was not the recognized standard of living. The dress suit of the person who by the usage of the time was styled either a gentleman or a yeoman was more elaborate than in our day. The colors were brighter and more diversfiied. We read of green and plum colored broadcloths and of bright red fabrics. George Wilson's coat was valued by himself at $13.33, and it would have taken two of his cows to pay for it. James Burnside was charged $10 for three beaver hats. William Jackson lived on the verge of settlement, yet he wore a wig and a stock and buckle. In presenting a bill of $1003.52 against his father's estate, John Dickenson mentions broadcloth at $3 a yard, and calico at 75 cents. A pair of silver knee buckles is listed at $3.33, a lawn handkerchief at $1.25, a silk bonnet at $11.33, a set of silver breeches buttons at $3.33, and a pair of men's stockings at 83 cents. There was a tailor's bill in favor of James Stuart of $7.67. And Adam Dickenson was the founder of the settlement on the lower Cowpasture. Robert Armstrong was a hunter, but wore silver buckles. The statute of Andrew Lewis, at Richmond, represents that general as attired in hunting shirt and leggings. Such was not his ordinary apparel, for he is known to have been particular in the matter of dress. His brother, Charles, was equally particular and left a brown suit inventoried at $50.

The person acquiring 100 or more acres in the Augusta colony was usually a yeoman, his class constituting the backbone of British society. Of the very much smaller class known as gentlemen, there were very few among the Augustans, although a prominent man would be given that title by courtesy. The gentleman, according to the aristocratic meaning of the word, was a man who claimed that his ancestors had never been serfs. He had a coat of arms and could wear a sword.

In deeds and other documents it was customary, if the grantor or grantee were a yeoman, to state the fact, or to name his occupation. This was a means of defining his social standing. Bound white servants were numerous in Augusta. Some of these were orphans or of illegitimate parentage. In the early days of the colony they were chiefly young persons brought from Europe under indenture. To pay their passage across the Atlantic they were sold into servitude for the average term of five years. At the end of this time the servant became free. But while his servitude continued, he was virtually a slave. If he ran away and was retaken he was made to serve his master an extra period, the length of which was proportioned to the cost of recovery. Some of the servants made as good citizens as any other people. Some others had a record as petty criminals, or were of loose moral character. If, as frequently occurred, the woman servant had bastard children by another man than her master, her term of servitude was lengthened. But immoral behavior was not confined to the servant class.

Until after the Indian war of 1754, negro slaves were very scarce in Augusta.

White male adults were enrolled in militia companies, of which the commissioned officers were captains, lieutenants, and ensigns. But the frontiersmen were little amenable to restraint, and only the officer with a strong inborn power of leadership could control his men. The day of general muster was the fourth Tuesday in September. There was a company muster every three months.

The "processioning" of lands was a colonial custom. It began in 1751 and was to be repeated every four years. It consisted in remarking the corners of the surveys, and was done by men appointed for that purpose by the vestry. The purpose was to keep the lines from being lost sight of, and to prevent unlawful hunting and ranging. In 1755, James Hughart processioned in John Dickenson's militia company of the Cowpasture, and Stephen Wilson and Joseph Carpenter in Jeremiah Seely's company on Jackson's River. The following document is dated October 12, 1765:

"As it has pleased your Worships to send an order to nominate Four Persons in the Cow Pasture to mark the lines of the Several plantations there, we the subscribers hereof have gone from the Forks at Jackson's River upward to Joseph Mayse, and Thomas Feamster and William Black from there to the head of the waters. There is many places that there is no livers in and others that doth not know their lines. The names of such as have f'd their lines are as follows.

James McCay
James Scott."

McCay and Scott marked for themselves and for William Gillespie, John Handley, William McMurray, James Beard, John Dickenson, James Hamilton, Ralph Laverty, John Cartmill, James Hughart, Robert Stuart, Charles Donally, and Thomas Gillespie. Feamster and Black marked for themselves and James Mayse, John McCreery, James Knox, James Shaw, George Lewis, James Clements, Hugh Hicklin, Charles Lewis, John Kinkead, Robert Hall, Boude Estill, William Jackson, and James Bodkin.

About 1768, Samuel Hamilton marked for the following men between his house and James Beard's: Andrew Sitlington, John Dickenson, William Sprowl, John Donally, Hugh Coffey, Joseph Watson, Andrew Muldrock, William Daugherty, John Clendennin, and William Mayse.

The first dwelling houses were small round-log cabins. The roof was of long riven shingles held down by weight-poles. The floor was of puncheons, or even the natural earth. But larger and better houses of hewn logs soon made their appearance. That of William Jameson, of the Calfpasture, built in 1752, was 18 by 24 feet in the clear, and one and one-half stories high. James Carlile did the work for $22.50. Jameson brought suit on the ground that the house was badly put together, some of the logs being but four inches thick instead of the six inches required by the agreement, and that some rows of shingles lay 20 inches to the weather.

In many an instance the settler had learned some handicraft. On the frontier he could still follow his trade to some extent, making it a side-line to his farming. One man was a weaver, another a millwright, another a cooper, and still another a carpenter or cabinetmaker. A very important man was the blacksmith. He did not limit himself to repair work, but was really an iron-worker. He manufactured nails, horeshoes, edged tools, and copper-glazed bells. He also made farm implements, except such as were wholly of wood.

The tilled acreage was small, because the pioneer grew little more than the supplies consumed on his place. The farming tools were few and simple. Almost the only horse implements were the wooden plow and the brush harrow. Wagons were scarce at first, but were fairly common during the Revolution. Indian corn, unknown in the British Isles, was the only staple the pioneer had to learn how to grow. The Ulster people were proficient in linen weaving, and the flax patch was seen on every frontier farm. Only the well-to-do could wear clothes made of imported cloth. Others wore homespun made of flax fiber or wool, or a mixture of the two. Hemp was peculiarly a money crop and was encouraged by the Virginia government. It was suited to the deep black soil of the river bottoms. The price was $5 a hundredweight, and there was also a bounty of $1. Charles Lewis, the champion hemp grower of Bath, had a crop of 2374 pounds in 1773. Few planters produced so much as 1000 pounds.

Bath has been a grazing region from the very first, and the pioneer farm was well stocked with horses, sheep, and hogs. The smaller domestic animals needed protection from the bears, panthers, and wolves. The grown animals were not so large as those of the present day.

The frequency with which the colonial will begins with a long pious preamble, would seem to indicate that the pioneers were usually attendants on religious service. And yet profanity was very prevalent, not to mention coarseness of speech. Gambling was also common. Complaint was made of one Bath magistrate for visiting a gaming house and violating his official duty by failing to report it.

The pioneers of this county were Presbyterians. Their first minister was John Craig, who preached on the Cowpasture at least as early as 1749. He was followed by Alexander Craighead, who came to Augusta in 1752 and two years later purchased a part of the Dickenson homestead. Whether he lived here or on the farm he owned in the Borden grant, we do not know. At this time the Church of England was also the established church in Virginia. No one except a minister of that communion might marry a couple, and there was no resident clergyman in Augusta until 1760. The Indian war broke out shortly after Craighead's arrival. He thought it too great a hardship for the frontier people to bear the brunt of this bitter conflict, and at the same time be subject to religious disabilities. In 1755 he went to North Carolina, where the laws were more liberal. In that colony he was the only Presbyterian minister between the Yadkin and the Catawba. Craigheard was followed by so many of his congregation on the Cowpasture that for a while it was almost broken up. One effect of the Indian war was greatly to loosen the application of the laws against dissenters, and one result of American independence was full religious liberty in Virginia. It may be open to question whether Craighead chose the better course in quitting his field and not helping in the fight for toleration. But in North Carolina, where he died in 1768, he did good service in preparing his flock for the inevitable conflict with England. It was his adopted county—Mecklenberg—that was a year ahead of the Continental Congress in declaring for the independence of America.

Windy Cove is the mother church of all the Presbyterian organizations in Greater Bath. The original church building, a little round-log structure with a large fireplace, stood on Craighhead's farm. According to the memorial slab that marks the spot, it was erected in 1760. This is an error. At that date the Indian war had not ceased, there was no resident minister, and the congregation was nearly broken up because of the exodus to North Carolina. The real date is probably not later than 1752. The church seems to have been burned by the Indians between 1753 and 1763. About 1756, Laverty and Millroy employed William Gillespie to reroof the church for $10, but they brought suit on the ground that his work did not sufficiently turn the rain and snow. A second and smaller church was built about 1766 near the site of the present Windy Cove. This was succeeded by a church and a session house of hewed logs, and these in 1837 by the present brick buildings. The second resident minister was John Montgomery. His ministry was from 1789 to 1804.

The first of the offshoots from Windy Cove used as a house of worship was a log building on the Dean homestead on Jackson's River. This gave place to a church at Warm Springs.

The first elders of Windy Cove were William Gillespie, John Sitlington, Nathaniel Crawford, and Joseph Surber.

The names given below are those of the communicants at Windy Cove in 1833:

Avis, Margaret	Dickenson, Emily	Jameson, Rachel
Bell, Thomas A.	Dickenson, Harriet	Kelso, Hugh
Bell, Joseph W. G.	Dickenson, John U.	Kelso, John
Bratton, Andrew	Dickenson, Samuel	Lyle, Isabella
Bratton, John	Feamster, Margaret	Lyle, James
Bratton, Lewis	Francisco, Elizabeth	McCland, Andrew
Bratton, Mary, Sr.	Francisco, George	McCland, Frances
Bratton, Mary, Jr.	Frasier, James	McClung, John
Bratton, Mary	Frasier, Jane G.	McClung, Rachel
Bratton, Rebecca	Frasier, Martha	McClung, Sarah
Burger, Martha	Frasier, Martha G.	McDannald, Adam
Carlile, Jane	Gillespie, Peggy	McDannald, Harriett
Crawford, Martha	Gilliland, Stephen	McDannald, Hugh
Crawford, Mary	Hansbarger, Rebecca	McDannald, John
Crawford, Samuel	Hughart, Ervin	McDannald, Rebecca
Crawford, William	Hughart, James	Moore, Jane
Criser, Mary	Hughart, Martha	Payne, Ann
Dickenson, Adam, Jr.	Hughart, Samuel	Porter, Adam
Dickenson, Charlotte	Hutchinson, Harriet K.	Porter, Martha

Porter, Mary	Sitlington, Thomas	Walters, Benijah
Porter, Rachel	Sloan, Mary	Withrow, Eliza
Porter, Rebecca	Surber, Jane	Woods, Edward
Ryne, Martha	Surber, Levi	Woods, ———, Mrs.
Sitlington, Mary (1)	Surber, Mary	Mingo (negro)
Sitlington, Mary (2)	Surber ———, Mrs.	Bridget (negro)
Sitlington, Nancy	Williams, Elisha, Jr.	

The ruling element in colonial Virginia held that education is a private and not a public interest, and that schooling is to be purchased like clothing or groceries. This is why the subject has only incidental mention in the public records. So far as we know, the first schoolhouse in the Bath area stood on Indian Draft, in or near the basin of Stuart's Creek. It is mentioned in 1779. But ever since the Reformation came to Scotland, the Scotch people have been noted for their zeal in the cause of general education. The ability to read and write was almost universal among the pioneers of Bath. We have found scores of their signatures, often written in a plain, easy hand.

The settlers of Augusta were very much given to litigation. The number of their lawsuits, during the 30 years prior to the Revolution, runs into the thousands. The settlers of Bath seem to have furnished their full proporton. Some persons were exceedingly contentious and were almost constantly in court for years. Most of the suits were for debt. Not a few were for assault and battery. Many others were for slander. If a man gave a note, performed a piece of work, or ran up a bill at a store, the outcome was commonly a lawsuit, and sometimes it dragged through court after court for a number of years. It sometimes looks as though every man was not only all the while in debt, but was holding notes against other persons. It was a common thing for a person to claim damages for being called a thief. It was even more common for both men and women to complain of having immoral behavior alleged against them. Some of these charges are gross in the extreme, and are set forth in the bills of complaint with a frankness that is astonishing. It is evident that the people of old Augusta knew perfectly well how to call a spade a spade.

The pioneers were not meek in submitting to any human authority. The justices of the county court were sometimes "damned" or otherwise insulted while sitting on the bench. In 1754, a woman called William Wilson a rogue, and said that on his "coming off the bench she would give it to him with the devil." At another time, three soldiers came into the court-room and insulted the justices. The court was repeatedly disturbed by rioting in the courtyard or by ball playing. As for the constables they were not to be envied in attempting to discharge their duty. Sometimes they could not serve a writ "by reason of a fresh." One of them says he was "kept off by force of arms." Another says his writ was "not executed case of by a hay fork." A third says, "the fellow gave me neel play." A writ against two settlers near Fort Dickenson was not executed in 1758 "for fear of the Indians."

Micheal Harper complained that three of the Bath settlers burned his house and 500 rails and committed other "enormities." John Bodkin was granted two pounds damages for being accused of stealing a filley. Robert Duffield complained of a certain very contentious and rather pugilistic settler that the said person killed a black mare belonging to him. A woman on Jackson's River was accused by another woman of stealing a cheese, but was granted only one penny damages. A man on the Cowpasture sued Joseph Mayse for speaking of him as a hog thief. In this suit a pioneer of Stuart's Creek deposed that he saw the plaintiff drivng away seven "hoggs" from the plantation of Colonel Lewis and supposed them to belong to Mayse. William Wilson sued two men for using several panels of his fence to catch a horse belonging to one of them; also for burning some of the fencing, whereby eight acres of rye and fifteen of good timothy were ruined. This was in 1757, during the Indian war, and Wilson lost the suit. William Armstrong sued a neighbor for coming at him with "clubs, swords, staves, knives, feet, hands, and sticks," whereby he was knocked senseless and his arm broken. The bill fails to state how many hands and fingers the assailant possessed.

During the Revolution the mines of Wythe county were an important source of bullets and shot. Attempts to manufacture powder were begun at an early day in the Alleghany region, and were continued until until near the middle of the last century. The first powder mill we hear of in Greater Bath was at Fort Mann. Another, on Blue Spring Run in Rich Patch Mountain, is spoken of in 1819.

The first drowning in the Cowpasture that we hear of was that of Garret Phelan, in 1782. The inquest was held at David Frame's.

The coroner's jury consisted of Charles Cameron, James Henry, Patrick Miller, Andrew Sitlington, Robert McCreery, Alexander Black, William Black, David Frame, Jermiah Frame, Matthias Benson, and Sampson Wilson. Wilson was from the Doe Hill neighborhood.

Thomas Feamster "bred a meeting" in 1757 and was its spokesman. He set forth his refusal to muster, saying Captain George Wilson had given to women and children provisions that belonged to the soldiers. He said Wilson's character would become as well known a it was in Pennsylvania. Wilson brought suit for slander and won. One pioneer of the Calfpasture sued another for saying he had stolen two shirts from the neighbor and had been to see a conjuror about it. It was easily within the recollection of the people then living that a woman had been ducked in Princess Anne County for witchcraft.

Previous to the French and Indian war small printed forms were used for writs. From then until the Revolution legal papers were written out by hand, usually in a neat, legible manner. Very small pieces of paper were used, and the lines of writing were near together. This was because of the high cost of paper. The ink was very good and the writing is easily read to-day. None but quill pens were known or used, and unlike steel pens their action is not corrosive.

The large river farms were really plantations, and were spoken of as such. And as these farms took in nearly all the prime tillable land in Bath, the structure of society was rather aristocratic for a mountain region. So often are the planters mentioned as officers of the militia, that one is sometimes inclined to wonder who were the privates.

Money was computed, as in England, in pounds, shillings, and pence. But on this side of the Atlantic, these words applied to values and not to coins. The Virginia pound was worth almost one-third less than the pound sterling, and for this reason English money did not circulate in the colony. In Virginia currency, the pound was worth $3.33, the shilling 16 2-3 cents, and the penny a little more than 1 and 1-3 cents. The hard money in actual use came from the West Indies, and was of Spanish, French, and Portuguese mintage. Thus we read frequently of the pistole, the doubloon, and the "loo-dore," which were gold coins worth, respectively, $3.92, $5.00, and $3.96. It was thus that the Americans became acquainted with the "piece of eight," or Mexican dollar. The former name was because it was divided into eight reals, the real being a silver coin of the value of nine pence, or 12½ cents. The earliest mention of the dollar by name is in 1752, when Adam Dickenson thus acknowledges a payment on a note: "Rec'd of the within 28 dollars."

"Since the gold and silver coins that passed from hand to hand were of so varied a character, it was tedious and inconvenient to turn their values into Virginia money. They were computed by weight, and this is why money scales are often mentioned in inventories of personal property. The silver coins were legal tender at the rate of 3¾ pence per penny-weight, or $1.04 per ounce. Copper pennies were coined for Virginia in 1733. Paper money of colonial issue began to appear in 1755. The ten pound bill was only 2½ by 3 inches in size, was crudely engraved, and was numbered and signed with a common pen. The bill pictured in this book was once held by William Blanton, who asked Charles Lewis to change it for him or get it changed. That planter could not change it himself, and was holding it until an opportunity arrived, when he showed it to Adam Bowyer, the sheriff. Bowyer pronounced it counterfeit, and Lewis gave back the bill to Blanton, who brought suit against the man who had passed it on him.

When a nominal money consideration was written into a legal document, the sum mentioned is usually five shillings. Five per cent was the legal rate of interest. There were no banks, and men who had considerable money on hand were accustomed to hide it. Peter Wright hid some money on Peter's Mountain in so secure a manner that it was not found until a comparatively recent day.

Most of the early settlers of Bath came through Philadelphia, and their merchants often purchased their goods in that city. Thus we can understand the very frequent mention of Pennsylvania money, in which the pound was worth only $2.50. The fact that the Mexican dollar, was worth six shillings in Virginia or New England money, and eight shillings in the money of the Middle Colonies, is the leading reason why the dollar, already a well-known coin, became the unit of the new Federal currency. Under the names of "levy" and "fip," the real and half-real (12½ and 6¼ cents) were legal tender in this country until near the time of the civil war.

LIFE IN THE PIONEER DAYS 73

Certain of the Augusta court records, particularly those relating to suits for debt, throw much light on values in the colonial era. The purchasing power of the dollar was several times greater than it is now. This fact helps to explain why the prices of land and livestock seem so very low. On the other hand, some articles were very expensive; relatively more so than they are now. Whether, on the whole, living was easier than with us can be judged fairly well by studying the values mentioned in the paragraphs below. Most of these have been taken from the law documents which concern the pioneers of Greater Bath.

What land sold for in various years may be found in Chapter III. As to land rent, we find two instances. A farm of 517 acres on Back Creek rented three years for $6.46. James Gay was to pay John Warwick four pounds yearly for three years for 149 acres. A mare could be had for $15, although an extra good horse might come as high as $40. Andrew Lockridge paid $6.17 for a cow, but Valentine Coyle furnished one for $3.58 to Patrick Martin's militia company. Rachel Burnside, perhaps through sheer necessity, sold two cows and a yearling for $10. We find mention of a hog at $2.11, and a sheep at $1.14, although one animal of either sort could ordinarily be had at rather less than one dollar. The one mention of a goose is at 42 cents. Common labor ran from 33 to 50 cents a day, although corn could be gathered and husked for 25 cents, and 33 cents would command the services of a person who could tend store, and post books. James Bourland charged but 50 cents a day for himself, wagon and two horses. But George Lewis, working at a somewhat later date at Warm Springs, charged $1.08 for himself and three horses. Jacob Marlin, a trapper, charged $3.75 for the use of a horse two months. A horse could be kept one week for a shilling, but Michael Harper was charged $5.33 for the wintering of a single horse. Rails could be split for 37½ cents a thousand, although selling as high as $5. A blacksmith would make a mattock for 67 cents. A carpenter charged William Dean 83 cents for making a churn, $2.50 for laying his barn floor, $6.67 for covering his house, and $10 for covering his barn. A bedstead could be made for $1.25, a loom for $5, and a coffin for $2.17. Two pounds—$6.67—would build one of the big stone chimneys of that day, and four pounds would build a log dwelling. David Kincaid's house in 1752 cost him $30. We find $7.50 charged for making a spring house. and only 83 cents for a lime kiln. $10 would pay for a year's schooling. Aminta Usher, servant to Loftus Pullin, worked for $20 a year.

Wheat varied little from 50 cents a bushel and oats 33 cents. Rye was quoted at 25 to 42 cents, corn at 24 to 38 cents, and potatoes 20 cents. Even in the Greenbrier settlement of 1762, corn commanded 33 cents. Flour by the barrel ran all the way from $3.25 to $8.33. Butter was worth five to eight cents a pound. Beef and mutton averaged hardly more than two cents a pound, although there is an instance where we find 400 pounds of bear meat, bacon, and venison billed at $25. In 1749, Joseph Mayse sold a "half buflar" for $1.25. Half a bear carcass is mentioned at 83 cents, and a whole deer at 36 cents. A month's board bill could be satisfied for $3. All condiments were brought from the seaports. It was here that the pioneer "caught it in the neck." Salt was 67 cents a quart in 1745. As late as 1763 coarse salt commanded $2 a bushel, and it cost 83 cents to bring it from Richmond. Tea was $1.56 a pound and coffee $1. Bottled honey was 31 cents. Pepper was 75 cents a pound and alspice 54 cents. Nutmeg was 17 cents an ounce and cinnamon 58 cents. As to sugar, we are sometimes in doubt whether maple or cane sugar is meant. White loaf sugar from the West Indies was sometimes 25 cents a pound. Brown cane sugar was much cheaper.

Clothing was costly. Homemade linen could be woven for six cents a yard, but Irish linen cost $1.08 a yard, ribbon 17 cents, flannel 41 cents, sheeting $1.25, and velvet $3.33. A handkerchief of cotton or linen cost from 25 to 33 cents, while one of silk cost 75 cents. Men's stockings, which came above the knee and were there secured under the ends of the trousers with a buckle, cost 80 to 90 cents. Worsted hose for women was 50 cents and plaid hose 33 cents. Headgear was high or low according to the means of the wearer. A woman's hat is mentioned at $5 and a boy's at 83 cents. But a cheap felt hat could be purchased for 33 cents. Leggins were $1.04, pumps $2, and men's fine shoes $1.41. James Carlile's blue broadcloth coat cost him $5.42. Gloves are listed at 58 cents, a necklace at 33, and a woman's fan at 25. A pair of steel buckles for shoes or knees cost 25 cents, but the man of fashion insisted on silver for both buttons and buckles, and he had his name put on the buttons. Common buttons were 42 cents a dozen, silk garters were 42 cents a pair, and thread was half a shilling to a shilling an ounce. Leather breeches, very generally worn by laboring men, are priced at $3.17 a pair. There were fabrics called osnaburg, callimanco, and none-so-pretty.

The hunter had to be a good marksman, when he paid 56 cents a pound for powder and 21 cents for lead, and turned in beaver skins at 83 cents each. His gunflints and fishhooks cost him about one cent apiece. "Sang digging" was a rather profitable pursuit. In 1755 a Carlile promised 30 pounds of ginseng at Thomas Hicklin's house, and it was valued at $20. Eight years later we find the root quoted at a dollar a pound.

During the Revolution the mines of Wythe county were an important source of bullets and shot. Attempts to manufacture powder were begun at an early day in the Alleghany region, and were continued until near the middle of the last century. The first powder mill we hear of in Greater Bath was at Fort Mann. Another, on Blue Spring Run in Rich Patch Mountain, is spoken of in 1819.

Nails were sometimes sold by count, ten-penny nails coming as high as $1.50 a thousand. A bell and collar cost $1.25 and a horseshoe one shilling. A woman gave 11 cents for a thimble, six cents a dozen for her needles, and 17 cents for a paper of pins. The doctor was charged 33 cents a pound for his casteel soap, 67 cents an ounce for his calomel, and 33 cents for a roll of court plaster.

In their account with John and George Francisco, the Mathews brothers name the following items: Chalk per pound, $1; ten-penny nails per pound, 21 cents; sheeting, 35 cents a yard; one frying pan, $1.25.

Some miscellaneous values are shown in the list below:

Bible	$1.00	Candles, per pound	$ .08
Testament	.33	Knives and forks, per dozen	1.56
Scythe	1.00	Brass knife and fork	.21
Iron pot	1.17	Brimstone, per pound	.17
Iron candlestick	.11	Indigo, per ounce	.17
Handsaw file	.22	Tablecloth	1.33
Steelyards	2.33	Packsaddle	.50
Whip	1.41	Pocketbook	.83
Tallow, per pound	.02	Basin	.37½

Comb	$1.33	Blanket	$2.67
Ivory Comb	.42	Making a jacket	1.00
Horn Comb	.21	Gloves	.58
Rye Brandy, per gallon	.33	Tobacco	.10 to .14
China bowl	.33	Allspice, per pound	1.08

To give some idea of prices at the leading seaport of America, we take the following items from the bills rendered in 1759 and 1760 by two merchants of Philadelphia against two merchants of Staunton:

Tumblers, per dozen	$3.33	Worsted Hose	$ .42
Glasses, per dozen	1.00	Sleeve buttons, per dozen	.09
Flannel	.33	Salt, per bushel	.42
Needles, per thousand	1.12	Bar iron, per pound	.04
China bowl	.33	Bar lead, per pound	.05 3-5
Linen Handkerchief	.14	Brown sugar	.10
Silk Handkerchief	.44	White sugar	.25
Sheeting	.48		

The thinness of population, the fewness of towns, the slowness of travel, and the comparative absence of newspapers and a real postal service, caused the life of the community to move at a slow pace. So late as 1775, there were but two newspapers and 15 postoffices in all Virginia. Postage was so high that many letters were sent by private persons. There were no envelopes, and postmasters read the letters just as gossip now claims that country postmasters are said to read the postal cards. Until 1755, there was no regular service with the British Isles, and if a letter weighed one ounce it cost a dollar to get it delivered there.

The pioneers had little of our modern hurry, but were awake to what was taking place in their own neighborhoods. On matters relating to the colony in general, they were slow to move unless aroused by their better informed leaders. As to anything like a national feeling between the populations of the several colonies, there was nothing worthy of the name.

A journal kept in 1749 by two Moravian missionaries gives us a glimpse into the valleys of Bath after some four years of settlement. These men were traveling afoot from Pennsylvania to the Dunkard settlement on New River, ministering as they went along to the spiritual needs of the pioneers of German birth. They came by way of the South Fork, and at the head of that river they reached on the night of November 13th—November 24th, New Style—an "English Cabin," probably that of Hercules Wilson. Here they warmed themselves by a fire on the hearth and slept on bearskins spread on the floor. Like all the settlers this family had bear meat, and like some of them it had no bread. But on the morning of that day a German woman had given the missionaries some bread and cheese. These eatables they shared with their entertainers.

Next day, after frequent fordings of the Cowpasture, they came either to the Black or the Jackson farm and lodged there for the night. Their host was suspicious and not very willing, but in the morning he was induced to put them over the Bullpasture on his horse, the waters being high. They soon fell in with George Lewis, who was traveling on horseback in the same direction they were going. This man set them across the river at 12 fords. They seem to have parted with him when they left the vicinity of the river and began climbing Warm Springs Mountain. A rain began to fall, and it was dusk when they reached the summit. They were not only wet, but were weary with a hard day's walk. They found an empty hut, which must have stood near the present tollgate. They had nothing for a supper, but made a fire and dried their clothes. In the morning they hurried down the mountain into Warm Springs Valley, and at the first house they had a breakfast of hominy and buttermilk. They speak of the man as a good Presbyterian, but do not give his name. He was probably James Ward. The missionaries do not say a word about the thermal waters. They were in a hurry to get on. They could not speak English fluently, and along this part of the way there were no German settlers. Jackson's River was crossed by swimming and with some difficulty. They speak of "mountains all around." At the close of this day, after crossing Dunlap Creek, they reached a house, perhaps that of Peter Wright. Here they again slept on bearskins, like the rest of the family. While crossing a mountain on their way to Craig's Creek, they heard an "awful howling of wolves."

These Moravians found that the people they met were living like savages, wearing deerskin clothes, and making hunting their chief pursuit. The style of living among the settlers is mentioned as poor in the extreme. But this was in the very infancy of the settlement of Bath, and was during the "wild and wolly" stage of its evolution.

Doctor Thomas Walker, in his diary for July, 1750, says the settlers on Jackson's River "are very hospitable and would be better able to support themselves, were it not for the great number of Indian warriors that frequently take what they want from them, much to their prejudice."

At the date of the Dunmore war, and still more so after the close of the Revolution, there was a comparative degree of prosperity and comfort. Staunton, a village of some 20 houses in 1753, grew into a sizable place and had its third courthouse. To Richmond, which did not become the state capital till 1779, produce was wagoned from the Augusta settlements. After 1783, the Indian peril was a thing of the past. But in the features of local government there was little change, outside of the abolition of the vestry. This came with the disestablishment of the Church of England near the close of the war for Independence.

IX

TEN YEARS OF INDIAN WAR

NTIL 1748, and theoretically until 1763, the Alleghany Front was the western frontier of Virginia. Beyond was the Indian country, claimed by the English and the French, as well as by the natives. The conflict known in American history as the French and Indian war broke out in 1754. It was a final struggle between England and France for control in the Western Continent, and victory declared for the former. Aside from the Iroquois of New York, nearly all the Indian tribes aided the French. They resumed the strife on their own account in the episode known as the war with Pontiac's confederacy. A general peace did not come until 1764.

No Indians were living in Bath when the white settlers appeared, although hunting parties visited these valleys in the fall months. They called at the cabins of the white people and learned to express themselves in the English tongue. By reason of this intercourse they became very familiar with words of insult and profanity.

The points of view of the two races were very divergent. The pioneer despised the native as a heathen, and showed little tact or patience in dealing with him. Because the red man did not cultivate the ground, except to a slight extent, the white man could not see that his claim to the country was worthy of any serious consideration. He did not conceal his desire that the Indian should get entirely out of his way, so that he might have the whole country for himself. On the other hand, the Indian did not like the British-American. His people were very few in number, while the whites were a host. The powerful and ceaseless push of the latter was driving him farther and farther away from the hunting grounds where his own people had followed the chase for generations. There was sentiment in the Indian, and those hunting grounds were sacred in his eyes. He was proud as well as free. He did not give up the hopeless struggle without a long and gallant fight, during which he inflicted far heavier losses than he received. He was cruel in war, after the manner of all barbarians, yet the frontiersman was not far behind him.

There were some curious exceptions to the general rule. "Mad Anthony," for whom Anthony's Creek is named, was an Indian hunter who used to visit Fort Young and tell of the plots of his race. Quite as a matter of course, he was distrusted by both paleface and redskin. White men, taken captive in boyhood, could only with much difficulty he weaned from the life of the forest, and sometimes they fought against their own color.

The shameful defeat of General Braddock in July, 1755, exposed the whole inland frontier to the vengeance of the native. Washington was put in charge of the Valley of Virginia and made every effort to defend it. His position was a very trying one. With only a few hundred militia, untrained, insubordinate, and poorly equipped, he was expected to defend a line 300 miles long. He was under the authority of a royal governor who was stingy, meddlesome, and inefficient, and was also hampered by a legislature that was not only meddlesome but at times incompetent and unfriendly.

Many of the people on the frontier did not think that the colonial government rose to its duty, and they flocked into the upland districts of the Carolinas. There were some others who did not leave the colony, but sought places of greater safety. Those who remained at their homes were in almost constant danger except in the winter season. Rangers, who were known as Indian spies, watched the trails and the mountain passes. They were forbidden to make fires to warm themselves, lest the smoke might give notice to some lurking enemy. A horseman, speeding over the bridlepaths, and shouting "Indian sign" to every person he met, caused the families along his route to make a hurried flight to the nearest stockade or blockhouse. There they "forted" during the times of special danger. Fierce dogs, trained to recognize the odor of the Indian, were an additional means of protection.

And yet the pioneers were wilfully careless. While serving as militia they could not be counted upon to obey their officers or serve out their terms. They disliked to be cooped up in the stockades. At such times they not only took imprudent risks, but they were negligent in sentinel duty. When Washington passed through the Bath area on a tour of inspection, not one of the forts he visited was in a proper condition for defense. There was not one which could not have been surprised with ease. He also writes that the members of his escort conducted themselves in a most foolhardy manner. It is not pleasant to learn of these shortcomings of our ancestors, and to see that their hardships were due in a considerable degree to their own fault. While in service the militiaman received one shilling a day.

The leading stronghold on the Cowpasture was Fort Dickenson. It stood in the midst of the river-bottom, a half mile north of Nimrod Hall and to the west of the stream. There is nothing to mark the exact site. Close to where is now an ancient brick house, a mile north of Fassifern on Jackson's River, was Fort Dinwiddie, the southern limit of Washington's tour of observation in the fall of 1755. Like Fort Dickenson, it stood on the second bottom and near a water supply. Near the Clover Creek mill on the Bullpasture stood Fort George, in the midst of a meadow that has never been plowed, and hence the lines of stockade and covered way may easily be traced. Near the site of the iron furnace at Covington was Fort Young, built in 1756 according to specifications given by Washington. A council of war held in the same year speaks of Fort Breckenridge and Fort Christian, the former 16 miles from Fort Dickenson, and the latter 15 miles from Fort Dinwiddie. They were small stockades and both stood on Jackson's River. It is probable that Fort Christian was but another name for Fort Mann, which stood at the mouth of Falling Springs Run.

There were also fortified houses capable of repelling an ordinary attack. Thomas Feamster, who lived a mile south of Williamsville, hit upon an ingenious device. His house stood near Meadow Lake, a pool more than an acre in extent. In the midst of this water he built a blockhouse supported on piles, some of which remained visible many years. The blockhouse was approached by a foot-bridge, the planks being detachable.

In a letter of September 23, 1755, Robert McClenachan relates that Captain Dickenson had had a "scrimmage" with nine Indians, killing one of them and losing one of his own men. Two Cherokee boys were released and taken to Fort Dinwiddie to remain there until the governor could make known his wish as to what should be done with them. The Cherokees were at this time allies of the English. The writer does not say where the skirmish occurred, and it probably happened on the Greenbrier.

A council of war held at Staunton, July 27, 1756, decided in favor of placing a garrison of 30 men at Miller's Fort, and 60 at Fort Dinwiddie. Miller's Fort stood 15 miles up Jackson's River from Fort Dinwiddie. Forts Breckenridge and Dinwiddie, the former 13 miles from Dinwiddie and 13 from Dickenson, were deemed properly protected by the men already there.

Of the Indian raids into Bath, the earliest we can locate took place near the middle of September, 1756. Within or very near the present county limits, and mainly along Jackson's River, nine men, one woman, and three children were killed, and two men were wounded. Among the slain were Ensign Humphrey Madison, John Byrd, Nicholas Carpenter, James Mayse, and James Montgomery. Joseph Carpenter, David Galloway, and a Mrs. McConnell were captured, but got away. Mrs. Byrd, Mrs. George Kincaid, Mrs. Persinger, and 25 boys and girls were taken to the Indian towns in Ohio. Among the children were six Byrds, five Carpenters, and two Persingers.

During this raid occurred the first attack on Fort Dickenson. Captain Dickenson was absent at a general muster. When Washington came along, about seven weeks later, he remarks that the stockade was in need of improvement. He also remarks that at the time of the attack, the Indians crept close to the enclosure without being discovered and captured several children.

A council of war the same year advised stationing 250 men at Fort Dickenson, 100 at Fort Dinwiddie, and 40 at each of the other forts, Breckenridge and Christian. The only way to have secured garrisons of such strength was to bring soldiers from east of the Blue Ridge.

In the summer of 1757 Fort Dickenson was invested a second time. Again Dickenson was absent, and again there was negligence on the part of the defenders. The approach of the Indians was first known by seeing the cattle of John McClung running toward the fort with arrows sticking in their backs. Several boys had gone outside the stockade to gather wild plums and they were captured. Among them was Arthur Campbell, a militiaman of 15 years who later on became prominent in the annals of southwest Virginia. A girl named Erwin moulded bullets for the men in the fort. Governor Dinwiddie, always swift to find fault, scolded Dickenson for being away and ordered Major Andrew Lewis to garrison the post with 70 men.

TEN YEARS OF INDIAN WAR   83

Between the middle of May and the end of September of this year, we are told of six more men who lost their lives. In this number were Sergeant Henry at Fort Dinwiddie, and John Moore and James Stuart on the Cowpasture. Stuart may have been killed in the second attack on Fort Dinwiddie. James Allen and one Swoope were wounded on Jackson's River. This season, 11 captives were carried away. Among them were James McClung, James Stuart, Jr., Mrs. Moore and her children, and two Cartmill children.

The affair at Fort Dinwiddie was perhaps the same for which John Brown put in a claim. He was helping to convoy some provisions to the fort and the guard was attacked.

In April, 1758, there was still another raid into the valley of the Cowpasture. A man was killed and a boy and a girl were captured. All three of these were servants. During this incursion the Indians are reported as having carried away John and William McCreery. This statement is probably incorrect. One Kephart was a tenant on the McCreery plantation and lost two sons by capture. They made their escape, however.

Fort Duquense fell in 1759. The Indians were now deprived of French support and their raids soon came to a pause. These were not confined to the settlements west of Shenandoah Mountain. The northern and middle portions of the Shenandoah Valley were severely scourged. Staunton and its neighborhood fared better, the natives not coming within five miles of that place. But for some cause the Indians bore a deep grudge against the settlement on Kerr's Creek. Their first foray into that valley seems to have taken place in October, 1759. The assailants came from the direction of Sweet Springs. They are said to have killed 12 persons and carried away 13. With wonderful energy Charles Lewis raised in one night a pursuing party of 150 men, Captain Dickenson heading one of the three companies. The foe was overtaken on Straight Fork, west of the Crabbottom in Highland County. A surprise was intended, but through a mischance it was far from complete, and the Indians escaped wth a loss stated at 20 of their warriors, though it was probably less. The booty they were carrying away was retaken. Thomas Young was killed in this fight and Captain Dickenson was wounded.

The Pontiac war suddenly burst out in June, 1763. It had been planned with great secrecy by the red men and was designed as a simultaneous attack along the whole western frontier. To Cornstalk, a Shawnee chieftain of unusual ability, was assigned the task of dealing a heavy blow on the Greenbrier and the settlements to the southeast. With a strong band he fell upon the unsuspecting Greenbrier settlements, and in a day or two he had blotted them out. One Conrad Yoakum outdistanced the Indians in their progress to Jackson's River, and gave warning to the people around Fort Mann. The settlers could scarcely credit the report, yet they gathered into the blockhouse and sent a courier to Fort Young, 10 miles down the river. Captains Moffett and Phillips set out with 60 men to their relief. The scouts kept cautiously along the river-bank the entire distance. But when the main body reached the horseshoe peninsula immediately below the fort, they thought to gain time by marching arcoss the neck. As a result of their imprudence they fell into an ambuscade and lost 15 of their number, the survivors retreating. This action seems to have taken place July 16th.

The fort was not taken, but the Shawnees followed up their victory over the relief party by going down Jackson's River and then up the Cowpasture. They were seen near Fort Young and an express rode at full speed to William Daugherty's. That pioneer was away from home, but his wife mounted the only horse in the stable and raced up the valley, warning the settlers as she galloped along. Her house was burned but we are told that no scalps were then taken on the Cowpasture. If so, it was during some previous raid that a man was shot while standing on a bluff near the Blowing Cave. His body fell into the river.

The Indian army now divided, one part turning homeward, and the other crossing Mill Mountain to Kerr's Creek, where, only two days after the havoc in Greenbrier, there was more loss by fire and massacre than on the former occasion. This time they had nothing to fear from Charles Lewis, for he was now serving in Pennsylvania under Colonel Bouquet. The other squad seems to have returned by way of Green Valley, near the head of Stuart's Creek. Close to the present home of Jasper C. Lewis, they killed one or more persons, and carried off the wife of Joseph Mayse, her son Joseph, Jr., and another woman, whose name is now unknown. The captors appear to be the same party that attacked the home of William Wilson at the mouth of Bolar Run. They were beaten off, though not until they had wounded the wife of Wilson, and a daughter, and carried away his son Thomas.

Joseph Mayse afterward wrote an account of his experience. His guard camped the first night on the west slope of Warm Springs Mountain, and at a large pine, which continued to stand until a few years since. A lateral root made the spot where the boy was ordered to lie down a most uncomfortable couch. For a while he feared to complain, lest he be quieted with a tomahawk. But his position proving quite unendurable, he nudged the Indian lying by his side and made him understand the situation. The brave made a comrade move over, so as to permit the boy to rest in some comfort. On the Greenbrier the Indians were overtaken by a pursuing force. The pony which young Mayse was riding carried also a coil of rope, and in the confusion caused by the attack, an end of the rope caught on a bush and dragged him off. He was thus restored to his people.

While Cornstalk was falling upon the Greenbrier settlement, a band of Delawares and Mingoes divided on New River, one party going to Catawba Creek and the other to Dunlap. The latter crossed Jackson's River above Fort Young and went on to Carpenter's blockhouse, which stood near the residence of Colonel W. A. Gilliam. Near the house they killed and scalped William Carpenter, after which they plundered the dwelling, took his son Joseph, two Brown children and a woman, and began their return by way of Greenbrier. The shot was heard at Fort Young, but as the garrison was weak, an express was sent to Captain Audley Paul at Fort Dinwiddie. He pursued, and though he did not overtake this party, he came up with and scattered the party returning from the Catawba. The younger Brown became known as Colonel Samuel Brown of Greenbrier. His brother remained with the reds, but visited his mother in her old age. Joseph Carpenter became a doctor in Michigan.

It is probable that the attack on the Carpenters occurred only a day or two after the battle at Fort Mann.

Bouquet's victory at Brushy Run near the site of Pittsburg, brought an early end to the war with Pontiac. The Indians were required to give up the prisoners they had collected during the preceding ten years. In the number were Mrs. Mayse, John Byrd, and doubtless several other persons belonging to the Bath area. One of the restored girls was reared by Captain Dickenson, and she became the wife of James McClung. As in several other similar instances her real name was never learned.

The following letter of the Indian period is the earliest we know of to be written in Bath. It seems to have been addressed to Thomas Lewis.

Jackson's River, May ye 15th, 1755.

Dear Brother,

I have been stopping here several days in purchasing of provisions. I have purchased as much grain as will serve three months, but will have a great deal of deficiency in getting of meat. I propose to march in ye Narrows towards Greenbrier. I think I shall go to Marlings (now Marlinton, W. Va.) in two days, where I purpose to construct a small fort. I hope you will be so kind as to remind Mr. Jones (Gabriel Jones, King's Attorney of Augusta County) to bring pay for my company from Colonel Wood as often as he has an opportunity, which he promised to do. I have nothing that is new to acquaint you of. I am, dear brother, your most affectionate and very humble servant,

ANDREW LEWIS.

A partial list of Captain John Dickenson's Rangers in 1757-59 affords the following names:

Bollar, John (Sergeant)	Hamilton, William	McMullen, John
Carpenter, Solomon	Jameson, Andrew	Persinger, Abraham
Carpenter, Thomas	Johnston, James	Persinger, Jacob
Carrigan, Patrick	Kelly, Thomas (corporal)	Persinger, Philip
Davis, William		Shields, William
Fulton, John	Madison, Humphrey (ensign)	Taylor, John
Galloway, David		Wiley, John
Gillespie, Robert, Sr. (sergeant)	McMullen, Edward	Wiley, Peter

The following is the muster roll of Captain George Wilson's company, August 11, 1756:

Hugh Hicklin—lieutenant	Barton, James	Carlile, Robert (1)
Thomas Hughart—ensign	Bell, Joseph	Carlile, Robert (2)
Charles Gilham—sergeant	Black, William	Davis, Patrick
	Bodkin, James	Deckert, Simon
William Johnson—corporal	Bodkin, John	De La Montony, Samuel
	Bodkin, Richard	Duffield, Robert
PRIVATES	Bright, Samuel	Elliott, Andrew
	Burnett, William	Estill, Benjamin
Adair, Robert	Carlile, John	Estill, Boude

Gilbert, Felix	Knox, James	Miller, Valentine
Hall, Robert	Lewis, George	Miller, William
Harper, Hance	Lewis, John	Phegan, Philip
Harper, Matthew	Long, Stephen	Price, William
Harper, Michael	Mayse, James	Sprowl, William
Hicklin, John	McClenahan, Elijah	Stull, Frederick
Hicklin, Thomas	McClenahan, William	Warwick, William
Jackson, James	Miller, James	Wilfong, Michael
Jordan, Adam	Miller, John	Wilson, Samuel
Jordan, John	Miller, Patrick	

The letter below was written from Sitlington Creek, Pocahontas county, a spot then on the very edge of white settlement, but technically within the Indian domain. The writer subsequently moved to the Cowpasture.

Green Briar September 25th 1766

Dr Brother

This comes to let you know that I am in good health at Present blessed be God for it hoping these will find you and your Family in the same Condition, for tho' we have been long absent from each other, yet neither Time nor distance of Place can remove the Brotherly Affection I have for you. As for my Situation in this Country I live on a Branch of the Mississippi Waters, which is a very fertile Land but it is not yet Purchased from the Indians. I enjoy a reasonable Living; but have been long in a dangerous situation from the incursions of the Savages, yet thro the Protection of God have hitherto Escaped, and had I the comfort of you to Converse with shou'd think myself Happy: But I dare not advise to come to this Country, Yet were I in Ireland and had such a Family as you have and cou'd foresee it no other way, I wou'd bind myself & them before I wou'd stay to be so Oppressed, but you have no Occasion, for if you are unable to pay your Passage, come upon Redemption to Pennsylvania and Brother William will soon relieve you, and as soon as I have an Opportunity I will repay it him.

I had the Comfort of hearing of your welfare by Brother William which gave me great Satisfaction and likewise I heard of Brother Thomas.

I have no Child which makes me the more Desirous to have you hear, my Wife Joins in our Love to you and Family and Sister Elizabeth and her Family and to all old Friends, which is all from your Affectionate & Loving Brother till Death

ANDREW SITLINGTON

X

THE POINT PLEASANT CAMPAIGN

Ten years of nominal peace succeeded ten years of intermittent war. The boundary line between the two races had been pushed westward to the Ohio, and yet England was vainly trying to keep the Americans from settling beyond the Alleghany Front. In the spring of 1774 anoether conflict was in sight. Wanton outrages were being committed by white men as well as red men, and the latter were putting on their war-paint. A campaign aganst the tribesmen was planned at the capital of Virginia. It was arranged that Andrew Lewis, then a member of the House of Burgesses from Botetourt, should lead an expedition to the mouth of the Great Kanawha. He was there to be joined by Governor Dunmore in person with 1200 men from the lower counties of the Valley of Virginia. Thus opened the Dunmore war, waged on the side of the white people by Virginia alone and against the desire of the British government. The white soldiers taking part in it were almost wholly of American birth and nearly all came from west of the Blue Ridge.

The militia were called out in June. During the last week of this month a band of Indians penetrated as far as the Cowpasture, and fired upon Fort Lewis from the steep hill just east of the river. The range was too great for the firearms then in use to do any damage. The redskins shouted to the men within to come out of the "Lewis hogpen" and be accommodated with all the fight they could wish. Charles Lewis was away at the time, and the defenders kept prudently inside. John McClenahan, who had married a Lewis, lay dying in the stockade, and in setting down a mention of his death, his wife said it took place amid the yelling of the savages in the woods.

Charles Lewis was now colonel of the Augusta militia. It was near this time that he wrote the following letter to Colonel William Preston:

Dear Sir—I Received your letter of the 19th of June and will take all oportunity to a Quente you of Every thing that happens here worth your Notice. no Dout but you have herd of ye engagement that Capt Dickenson is had with ye Indians. he had one man killed and his Lieutenant Wounded. a fewe Days ago ye Indians fired at Wm Mcfarlen Neere ye Warm Springs and wounded him slitly. Ye inhabitants of our Frunter is in ye Greates Confuson. they are all gathered in forts. I have ordered out Several Compneys of Militia which I am in hops will put a stope to thir intended Hostilities. I hear that ye Assembly is to Meet ye 11th of Next Month when I hope they will fall on som Method to put an End to ye War. Since I begane to Rite to you I ha'e Re'd by way of Ex(p)ress from fort Pitt that ye Indians is Suing for Pace. as to further perticlers I will Refer you to my Brother (to) home I have sent Capt Connelly letter with ye Indians speech.

I am Dr Sir your Humb Servant

CHAS. LEWIS.

July 9th 1774

The regiment under Charles Lewis formed a part of the column led by his brother Andrew. Among his captains were John Skidmore from the South Branch, Samuel Wilson from the head of the Bullpasture, Andrew Lockridge from the upper Cowpasture, John Lewis from Warm Springs, John Dickenson from the lower Cowpasture, and George Mathews from Cloverdale. At the muster of September 27, their companies numbered, respectively, 32, 25, 28, 21, 56, and 60 men. The total for the regiment was 477. The muster rolls for the above companies do not seem to be in existence, and we are therefore unable to publish the names of the soldiers.

Warm Springs was at this time the western terminus of a wagon road, and several of the Augusta companies were assembled here by the close of August. By September 12, 96 wagon loads of provisions had arrived. Thence to the general rendezvous, where now stands the town of Lewisburg, only a bridlepath was available. For the remaining distance of 160 miles, a trail had to be cut through the woods. It took 19 days to make this part of the march. Colonel Lewis started from the Levels of Greenbrier September 6, his regiment convoying 500 packhorses and 108 beeves. At every camping place a "grass guard" was put out to watch the cattle during the night. Indian spies were all the while lurking in front of the head of the column, and once in a while they fired upon it. Matthew Arbuckle, later a captain in the Revolution, piloted the army to its destination. Ten years earlier, he had gone down the Kanawha with a load of furs. His home was on the James, near Island Ford, and his father, James Arbuckle, was one of the earliest settlers on this part of the river.

At the end of August, Dunmore had not left Fort Pitt, now the city of Pittsburg. His progress down the river was slow to a needless degree. He was to join the other column at Point Pleasant September 20, but 16 days later he was still as far up the river as the mouth of the Hockhocking. General Lewis arrived at the appointed place October 6, and sent William Mann and William Sharp to see where the governor was. They did not return for five days. October 9, Dunmore informed Lews through a messenger that he had changed the plan of campaign. The southern division was now ordered to meet the other some distance west of the Ohio.

Lewis was intending to get ready the next day to move forward from Point Pleasant. Meanwhile a force of Indians, probably rather less than 800, and representing several tribes, had come in between the two armies, paying no attention to that of Dunmore. Their leader was Cornstalk, the Shawnee, one of the most able known in the history of the red race. Before daylight on the 10th, they were across the Ohio, and were stealing down the east bank in the hope of taking the Virginians by surprise. They nearly succeeded in doing so. There was slack discipline in the camp and the men were dissatisfied with the lean beafsteak issued to them. Quite a number were out in the woods hunting game, although the commander-in-chief had given orders that no soldier should go out of the camp or fire a gun. Some of these men, perhaps not always unintentionally, did not get back in time for the battle. Two of the number discovered the approach of the Indians and gave the alarm. Colonels Lewis and Fleming were ordered forward with five companies, including those of Dickenson, Lockridge, and Wilson. They met the enemy half a mile from the camp, but were forced to give ground. Lewis was soon stricken with a mortal hurt and Fleming was severely wounded. A reënforcement was sent to the firing line. Other men were set to work felling trees for a breastwork. Such a protection for the camp should not have been left till the last moment.

Across the tongue of land between the Ohio and the Great Kanawha, the struggle raged until dusk. The opposing forces were only from six to twenty yards apart, every man taking a tree or any other cover that he could find. The forest resounded with the din of rifle and musket and with the yells and curses of paleface and redskin. Above the noise of battle the Virginians could hear the loud voice of the Indian commander, shouting encouragement to his men. Under a better generalship than that of Lewis, the red men fought with a courage and determination that won the respect of their foes. At noon there was a lull. The Indians fell back to rising ground, dealing severe punishment to their pursuers. Not daring to undergo the loss which would come by pressing a direct attack on the new position, yet fearful of the result if the enemy was not dislodged before night, General Lewis sent three companies to go up the Kanawha, and then up a little tributary, so as to assail the left flank of the Indians in the rear. This maneuver decided the long and bitter conflict. Believing this turning movement was by Colonel Christian, whose regment of 300 men from Fincastle county did not arrive until after nightfall, the Indians drew farther back, although their defiant taunts made Lewis suspect that they were reënforced. The white men held the battlefield, although at the time they considered the result scarcely better than a draw. Under cover of the darkness Cornstalk made a skilful retreat across the Ohio, carrying all his wounded with him. It is not believed that the Indian casualties were much more than 100. According to Colonel James Smith, the total number of the dead was 28. Of these, 17 were scalped by the whites. Only one chief was slain. He was the father of the celebrated Tecumseh.

To the Virginians the victory came dear. Their loss is variously stated and no official report is known to be in existence. It is sometimes set as high as 200. Many of the wounded died in the camp owing to the want of competent care. Of the Augusta men 22 were killed and 55 were wounded. Of the company officers under Colonel Lewis, Captain Wilson was killed outright and Captains Dickenson and Skidmore were wounded.

At Point Pleasant, as in most other battles between the whites and the reds, the latter had the fewer men in action and they inflicted the heavier loss. Yet they have not the white man's persistence in battle, and they are not patient under such losses as they received at Point Pleasant. In this instance they were discouraged at their failure to overwhelm their adversaries, and by going back to their villages they gave up the campaign.

After waiting for provisions, General Lewis crossed the Ohio October 17th. Captain Lockridge was left at Point Pleasant with 119 men of the Augusta regiment. When the army had advanced 80 miles, Dunmore sent Lewis an order to return, saying that a peace was being arranged. But the column that had done all the fighting was suspicious of the governor's intention, and the march was continued until the governor put in a personal appearance. Each army returned the way it had come, Lewis leaving 100 men to garrison the fort built on the battleground.

The agreement between the governor and the Indians was a temporary and not a final treaty. The red men were to give up all the prisoners, valuables, and domestic animals that they had taken. They were not to molest any boats on the Ohio, nor were they to hunt east of that river. A more permanent treaty was made the next year. On the side of the whites it was effected by the Americans themselves and not by the tory governor.

The untimely death of Colonel Charles Lewis at the age of 38 was recognized as a public calamity. His personal magnetism and his social qualities made him a leader of men. He was the youngest of the sturdy, forceful sons of the founder of Augusta and the only one that was born in America. No other was so brilliant and promising, or so beloved by the people. He was a captain when 21 and a magistrate when 27. As a fighter of Indians he was one of the most successful. He was fearless, and had he lived through the war of the Revolution, it is safe to affirm that he would have been one of the best known and most efficient of the American generals. Lewis County in West Virginia is named in his honor.

Against the remonstrance of his brother Andrew, Charles Lewis went out on the morning of the battle of Point Pleasant arrayed in a red coat, thus making himself too conspicuous a target. He was stricken by a bullet before he had taken a tree. While walking to the rear, he handed his gun to a soldier, telling the man to "go on and be brave." To those who asked about his hurt, he replied that it was "the fortune of the war."

His untiring energy and the public demands upon his time are attested by the very believable statement that after he came to manhood he was never home more than a month at a time. Like all the Lewis brothers he was practical and thrifty. The tract of 950 acres of fine river bottom that his father selected for him became the plantation of Fort Lewis. He acquired other lands himself, including several surveys on the Greenbrier. His will, dated precisely two months before his death, was proved by John Dickenson and Charles Cameron, the latter being his brother-in-law. The appraisement of his personality, which totaled nearly $4000, was entrusted to John Cowarden, Thomas Feamster, and John and Robert McCreery. Such possessions as 24 horses, 96 cattle, 43 sheep, and 50 hogs made Colonel Lewis a wealthy planter. The will and inventory mention eight slaves and a white man servant, furniture valued at $117.58, a bookcase at $16.67, a looking glass at $10, and a suit of brown clothes at $30. All this indicates a comparative degree of luxury, when we stop to consider that a dollar would go much farther then than now. His watch, scheduled at $30, was probably the one for which his father left hm a special legacy, and provided that his own initials should be engraved thereon as a token of esteem and affection.

Charles Lewis was spare of figure and upward of six feet in height. He was married to Sarah Murray in 1761. Their children were Elizabeth, Margaret, John, Mary, Thomas, Andrew, and Charles. John, who married Rachel Miller, inherited the homestead, where he died in 1843 at the age of 77. Colonel Andrew Lewis wedded Margaret Stuart and died in 1833, aged 61. Charles, Jr. was born a little after his father set out on his last expedition. He was married to Jane Dickenson in 1799 and died only four years later Thomas and Mary lived single. The husband of Margaret was Major Prior.

From miscellaneous courses we gather the following names of men who served in the expedition to Point Pleasant. Nearly or quite all of them must have served under Colonel Charles Lewis:

Carpenter, Jeremiah	Hamilton, John	Reagh, Archibald
Carpenter, John	Hamilton, Thomas	Reagh, John
Carpenter Solomon	Jameson, John	Scott, James
Carpenter, George	McClintic, William	Scott, William
Douglas, George	Knox, James	Shannon, Samuel
Douglas, James	Mann, John	Steward, John
Dunlap, Robert	Mann, William	Steward, William
Gillespie, Thomas	Mayse, Joseph	Ward, James (Capt.)
Hamilton, Isaiah	Milican, John	Ward, Wm. (Sergt.)
Hamilton, Jacob	Persinger, Jacob	Wilson, Wm. (Sergt.)
Hamilton, James		

XI

BATH DURING THE REVOLUTION

ITH respect to Virginia soil there were three stages in the war for American Independence. There was first the campaign against Dunmore, which was confined to the counties on Chesapeake Bay, and it came to an end with the expulsion of the tory governor early in 1776. Next came the invasion by Arnold and Cornwallis, limited to the country east of the Blue Ridge and to the 10 months closing with the surrender of Cornwallis in October, 1781. The last stage was the warfare with the Indians, which was carried on west of the Blue Ridge, and principally west of the Alleghanies. It lasted intermittently from the summer of 1776 until after the treaty with England in 1783. The British never came nearer to Bath than Charlottesville. The only practical danger was from the Indians, and they do not appear to have come inside the present limits of the county.

The soldiers of the Revolution were of three classes: the militia, called out only on special emergency; the provincials, or state troops, enlisted for home defense by the state governments; and the continentals, enlisted for long terms under the direct authority of the Continental Congress. The continentals were trained soldiers and consequently the most efficient and dependable. The militia came direct from their homes on absurdly short "tours of duty." Not only were they untrained, but they were imperfectly under the control of their officers. Hence they were easily demoralized, and at such a time each man took no thought except to look out for himself. They were seldom on the actual firing line, and when they did get into a real engagement, they were very much inclined to take to their heels. Yet on several occasions their behavior was all that could reasonably be asked.

As in the case of other counties, the able-bodied white adults of Bath were with few exceptions enrolled as militia. But the records of the Revolution are so brief and incomplete that we can affirm very little as to the names of its citizens who were enrolled as privates in the militia companies, or in the continental and provincial organizations. With respect to the officers our informaton is more satisfactory.

General Andrew Lewis was placed in charge of the operations against Dunmore, and he soon drove the hated governor to the shelter of the British fleet. His campaign was far from the mountains and on a small scale, and we do not certainly know that any Bath men took part in it. Arnold's marauding career on the lower James, and the approach of Cornwallis in the spring of 1781 were far more serious. Nearly 1700 of the Virginia militia took part in the battle of Guilford, where their conduct was unusually good, owing to a stiffening in their companies of some experienced men who had seen service in Washington's army. Among these troops were militiamen from this county under Robert McCreery, John Bollar, and David Gwin. Gwin's men, and probably the other commands also, rode on horseback until they had crossed the Dan into North Carolina. The horses were then sent home under guard. Robert Sitlington, William Gillespie, and James Sloan were privates under McCreery. Sitlington grieved at the loss of the knife he had used as a gun-rest. "Bullets," he said, "were flying so thick that by God, sir, I had to leave that knife sticking where it was."

At Guilford the Virginia militia gave a good account of themselves. Their deadly rifle-fire repelled several assaults by the redcoats. Cornwallis was virtually defeated and his shattered army was driven to the sea coast. He gave up his attempt to subdue North Carolina and joined Arnold at Petersburg. While the British leader was pursuing the small American army under Lafayette, his cavalry under Tarleton burned the little village of Charlottesville, where the Assembly was in session. The legislature fled to Staunton, and sat there from June 7th to June 23d. But Tarleton remembered his overthrow at Cowpens and did not try to force his way through Rockfish Gap. He seems to have had a wholesome respect for the Scotch-Irish militia of the Valley. The whole British army presently fell back toward the coast.

There were now heavy calls on the militia. Perhaps a larger number of Bath men were at the front than were present at Guilford. On the peninsula between the James and the York they saw fightng under Colonels Robert McCreery and Sampson Mathews,

Mathews had been south of the James the preceding winter, as a part of the force under General Steuben, who was watching Arnold, at Portsmouth. McCreery and Mathews were in the battle of Green Spring, which took place near Jamestown, July 6th. Under McCreery were the horsemen of Captain Peter Hull. Under Mathews were Captains David Gwin, Thomas Hicklin, William Kincaid, and John Brown. Brown was taken prisoner and was succeeded by Charles Cameron, who had served as adjutant. Brown's lieutenant was Robert Thompson. Gwin's subalterns were Lieutenant William McCreery and Ensign Alexander Wright. Hicklin's were Lieutenant Joseph Gwin and Ensign Thomas Wright.

At Yorktown, where the redcoats in Virginia laid down their arms, about 3000 of the state militia were present. There was no further attempt by the British to prosecute the war with their own men. Within and beyond the mountains, the case was different. For nearly three years after their experience at Point Pleasant, the Ohio Indians remained quiet. But being stirred up by British emissaries, whose home government did not scruple to turn loose the savages on women and children as well as men, they once more began to raid the settlements beyond the Alleghanies. Still earlier on the warpath were the Cherokees, who in 1776 became troublesome in the valley of the Holston.

The menace from the Indians was enough to make it necessary to garrison such posts as Fort Dinwiddie. During the two years beginning with the fall of 1776, Captains John Lewis, Robert McCreery, Andrew Lockridge, and Samuel McCutchen were by turns in command at this point. Captain John McKittrick was here in the early summer of 1780. The stockade was burned by a tenant in the spring of the same year, but for what cause we do not know. During the summer of 1777 there was a guard of six men at William Wilson's at the mouth of Bolar Run. Fort Warwick on The Greenbrier was held the same year by Captain John Lewis, and the next year by Captain Samuel Vance, whose lieutenant was John Cartmill. Vance became a lieutenant colonel in 1782.

Augusta companies were also marched into Bath, either to garrison the local posts or to proceed to the Greenbrier and Tygart's Valley rivers, or even to the Ohio and Monongahela. In 1777, John Dickenson, now a colonel, led his regiment to Point Pleasant, whence General Hand was to march against the Indian towns on the Scioto. Through a seeming lack of energy that officer contented himself with announcing the surrender of Burgoyne and then dismissing the troops. A few days before the arrival of General Hand, Cornstalk was treacherously murdered by the militia from Rockbridge. Next May the Shawnees sought to avenge his death by attacking the fort of Andrew Donally in Greenbrier. They were beaten off before the relief column under Captains Tate, Buchanan, and Long could arrive. About this time Captain Lockridge was at Vance's fort, and a year later at Clover Lick, both points being in the Greenbrier valley. So late as 1782 Captain George Poage was stationed at Clover Lick. Even a year later Colonel Sampson Mathews reported an alarm at that place, and the wife of Christopher Graham of the Bullpasture thought it advisable to flee with her child to Deerfield on the east side of Shenandoah Mountain. So far as we know, this was the last Indian alarm in this region, although so late as 1788 Juhn Stuart, of Greenbrier, feared that Indians and foreigners would drive out all the people west of the Blue Ridge. Not until Wayne's treaty with the Indians in 1795 was the peril finally removed.

In 1780, Thomas Hughart, John McCreery, and Andrew Lockridge were respectively colonel, lieutenant colonel, and major of the Second Battalion of the Augusta militia. Other local officers not already named were Captains John Given, James Hicklin, and John Oliver; Lieutenants Samuel Black, James Bratton, Samuel McClintic, and Robert McFarland; and Ensigns Thomas Catrmill, Jonathan Humphrey, and Moses McClintic.

During the war the machinery of local government moved about as usual. Yet there was much hardship. Foreign trade was precarious on account of the British war vessels hovering along the coast. There was no good money except specie. The paper bills issued by the Congress became more and more worthless. In the spring of 1781 it took $140 in paper to go as far as $1 in coin. The previous October, James Bratton, as keeper of an inn, rendered a bill against Anthony Mustoe for $150 for seven meals, four lodgings, and a few glasses of liquor. The taxes were very oppressive, and although they could be paid in produce, some persons refused to pay them at all, and some officers refused to make collections.

To draw the line between patriot and tory, a law of 1777 required that an oath of allegiance be administered to the citizens. Richard Mayse was assigned to this duty in the territory covered by the militia companies of Captains Dean and Robinson.

This district seems to have been nearly free from tory disturbances, such as took place on the South Branch to the northward or in Montgomery County to the southward. In fact, the only exception of which we have any positive knowledge is narrated by Colonel Skillern, of Botetourt, in a letter to Governor Nelson, dated June 26, 1781. He states that about four years earlier, Captain Lapsley had taken as recruits Solomon Carpenter and Samuel Lyons, telling them they were to go into Washington's bodyguard and to have 3½ shillings a day. Finding this representation untrue on their arrival at the army headquarters, the men deserted, came home, and hid in the mountains. At the date of the letter there were supposed to be from 40 to 50 men in their band. Attempts to disperse them and capture their leader had failed. The two men in question came to Skillern's house under a flag, offering to serve subject to call during two years in the county militia or to join George Rogers Clark for two years. Skillern recommends acceptance of the terms. Carpenter, a bold, daring, active man, had been with the Indians some time, and intimated that if his terms were not accepted he would go back to them. His comrades were active woodsmen, well armed with rifles, and might become dangerous. The writer adds that there were parties of tories and deserters in Montgomery and Washington, who were probably in correspondence with one another.

Aside from the officers we have mentioned, the following men of the Dunmore and Revolutionary wars appear to have belonged within the Bath area or nearly so:

Black, Alexander, Jr.	Mayse, Joseph—wounded at Point Pleasant
Black, James	
Black, William	McAvoy, Hugh—killed
Burnside, James	McFarland, Alexander—wounded
Byrd, John	Montgomery, James
Cowarden, John	Sitlington, Robert
Gillespie, William	Sloan, James

Some of the pensioners of the Revolution, whose names appear in

1832, were born elsewhere, or settled in this country after that war. Among them were Richard Cole, an Englishman, who enlisted in Bath in 1780; William Keyser, of Glouchester County; Andrew McCausland and William Bonner, of Pennsylvania; and John Putnam, of Massachusetts.

This chapter would not be complete without some mention of that eccentric and masculine woman, known to American border history as Mad Ann Bailey. She was given this name because of her irascible Welch temper. Her maiden name was Dennis, and she was a native of Liverpool. She came to Staunton at the age of 13, and ten years later wedded James Trotter, who was killed at Point Pleasant. The pair had a son named William, who was born in 1767. Ann Bailey left her child with Mrs. Moses Mann, a near neighbor, put on masculine apparel, and for several years was a hunter and scout. One of her reasons for adopting such an unfeminine career was to avenge the death of her husband. According to tradition she took more than one scalp. Her most famous exploit was her relief of Fort Lee, which stood where the city of Charleston, West Virginia, afterward arose. The stockade was besieged by Indians, the powder gave out, and it was very dangerous for a courier to get past the assailants. But Mad Ann volunteered, rode swiftly on her horse "Liverpool" to Fort Union—now Lewisburg,—and came back with an extra horse with a fresh supply of powder. This was in 1791, when she was 49 years of age. For a year or so, she lived in a hut on Mad Ann's Ridge, on the south side of Falling Spring Run. On one occasion her black horse went on to Mann's without his rider. A party from the stockade went out to follow the trail, and located Mad Ann by airholes in the snow. She had fallen asleep, either from liquor or drowsiness. According to Ann Royall, who knew her in her old age, she could both drink and swear.. In 1785 she married James Trotter. Her last years were spent on the farm of her only son, who settled in Gallia County, Ohio. Eccentric to the last, she refused to live in his comfortable house, and stayed in a cabin near by, which she built herself. Here she died in 1825 at the age of 83. In 1901 her remains were reinterred in the memorial park at Point Pleasant. In personal appearance, Mrs. Bailey was short, stout, coarse, and masculine, yet affable and pleasing. She wore a coat instead of a gown and she could read and write. While ranging the forest she "halways carried a hax and a hauger and could chop as well as any man."

The longest of Colonel Dickenson's letters that we have seen is addressed to General Edward Hand, and is of this tenor:

Point Pleasant Near Fort Randolph
7th Novr 1777

Dear Sr—Colo Skilron from Bottetourt and myself from augusta arived here with our Troops from Each County the 5th Instant whare we flattered our selves of the hapyness of meeting yr Excelency but being Disapointed Do greatly fear that some accident or Disapointment has fell in yr Way Which I should be hearttely sorry for our No. of Troops are Not mentioned here as the strength of the Whol is Inclosed in Capt. Arbuckles Letter agree able to yr Excelencys Instructions to your county Lieutnt. We brought Flour and salt seficiant only to bring us to this place as we ware greatly Detained on our march by Rain and high Waters. We Expected to have met with a seficiant supply of provisions here but to our great mortification found the garison out of salt and very scarce of Flour tho Wile we have Beef are Willing to surmount every Deficasy and hardship until We Either see or hear from yr Excelency. our Troops are extremely good In general and in high spirits Keen for the Expedition under a Commander of so great a Caracter as yrself

I am Dear general tho unacquainted Yr Excelencys most obedient and very Hble Servt

JOHN DICKENSON.

XII

SELIM THE ALGERINE

HE STORY of Selim, a native of Algeria, is perhaps the most picturesque incident in the early annals of Bath. Between 1764 and 1774 Samuel Given was hunting on the Greenbrier. He had at least one extra horse for carrying home the game he hoped to secure. In the top of a fallen tree he espied an object which he at first took to be a wild animal, and he came very near firing into it. A more deliberate glance satisfied him that what he saw was a human being, but not an Indian. Going to the tree he found a man in a most pitiable condition. He was stark naked except for some rags wrapped about his feet. His body was very much emaciated, and his skin was thickly marked by scars and scabs. In a word he was in an advanced stage of starvation.

Neither man could understand the other's language, and they could converse only by signs. The hunter at once made himself a Good Samaritan. He took as good care of the unfortunate stranger as was possible under the circumstances. In giving him something to eat, he prudently allowed very little at first, and increased the amount as the digestive organs of the famished man began to recover their normal tone. After a few days the patient had gained enough strength to be able to ride the led horse. He was now taken to the home of Captain John Dickenson and made welcome after the openhearted manner of the frontier. He remained with Dickenson several months, meanwhile recovering his strength and rapidly acquiring the ability to converse with his new friends. At length it became possible for him to tell who he was, and how he had fallen into the plight from which he was so providentially rescued.

His name was Selim and he was a son of a wealthy Algerine. The father sent him to Constantinople for an advanced education. While the young man was returning home his ship was captured by a Spanish man-of-war. He was transferred to a French vessel bound for New Orleans. The Algerines as well as the other nations of Barbary were at this time great pirates. They made slaves of their captives and were themselves treated with scant consideration whenever they fell into the hands of any of the Europeans. From New Orleans Selim was taken to the Shawnee towns on the Scioto. A white woman, also a prisoner of the Indians, told him by signs that she came from the east. Selim knew there were English colonies on the Atlantic shore and judged correctly that she came from that quarter. He found an opportunity to escape from the Indians, and tried to find the white settlements, so that he might return to his own people.

He had nearly succeeded when stumbled upon by Given. But he had found little to eat except nuts and berries and became too weak for any farther progress. The bushes and briars had torn his clothing into shreds, and these he had wrapped about his feet to give them some protection. His exposed skin had been so often lacerated by thorns and other obstacles as to present the condition observed by the hunter. He had resigned himself to a death by starvation or by wild beasts, and for a last resting place had chosen the top of the tree in which he was found.

Dickenson treated the unfortunate Moor with a noble generosity. He gave him a horse to ride and took him to see the neighbors of the settlement. Selim accompanied his host to Staunton, at a time when the county court was sitting, and there attracted much notice. The attention of the Algerine was particularly fixed upon the Presbyterian minister, John Craig, who lived near the town. Selim asked the privilege of going home with the preacher and the request was granted. He then explained his reason. He told Mr. Craig that during his journey through the forest the pangs of hunger caused vivid dreams. In one of these visions he saw marshaled in military order on an immense plain a vast assemblage of people, all dressed alike. In the distance was a person of distinguished appearance. Every now and then some member of the throng would undertake to go to him, but when half way there would suddenly disappear into a pit. Other persons, who asked directions of an old man standing by himself, passed safely across. Mr. Craig was recognized as the old man seen in the dream, and it was for this reason that Selim asked to go home with him. He wished to be instructed in the principals of Christianity. The French had tried to make him a convert, but his Mohammedan training made him think the use of images by the

Catholics was a form of idolatry. Selim was a quick pupil. He understood the Greek language and probably had a better insight into the meaning of the Greek Testament than the minister himself. Selim embraced Christianity and was baptized at the old Stone Church.

But at length the Moor expressed a longing to go to his old home, and could not be moved from his purpose. Some money was raised through the efforts of Mr. Craig, who also gave him a letter of introduction to Robert Carter, a member of the House of Burgesses from Westmoreland. The legislature was then in session at Williamsburg. Mr. Carter did all that was asked of him, and Selim was thus enabled to recross the Atlantic.

After some years the Algerine reappeared at Dickenson's with a disordered mind. In his lucid moments he said he had been home, but that his father would have nothing to do with him on account of his acceptance of Christianity. At Warm Springs he was much pleased with the gift of a Greek Testament by a young minister named Templeton. He visited Mr. Carter, and wherever he appeared he aroused great sympathy. John Page, when governor of Virginia, took him to Philadelphia and had his portrait painted by Rembrandt Peale, the celebrated artist. From that city he accompanied a man of South Carolina to his home. He returned to Virginia, and in Prince Edward County learned to sing the hymns by Watts. For a while he was an inmate of the hospital for the insane at Williamsburg. At a date unknown, but which must have been some years later than 1805, he died at a private house.

Thus the story of Selim is pathetic as well as unusual. It is gratifying to know that he was treated with great kindness by the strange people he tried so hard to reach.

XIII

EFFORTS TOWARD A NEW COUNTY

E HAVE seen that Botetourt was set off from Augusta in 1769. Eight years later Rockingham and Rockbridge were formed and Augusta was reduced to its present breadth, north and east. But westward it still reached beyond the Alleghanies. The greater portion of it lay to the west of Shenandoah Mountain. This broad and lofty range is indicated by nature as a political boundary. It is even yet very largely a wilderness. Nothing could be more certain than that the people living on the farther side would agitate for a new county just as soon as there might be any possibility of realizing this desire.

Bath was not actually established until the closing month of 1790. And yet it was almost thirteen years earlier that the first petition for this purpose was sent up to the General Assembly. This petition with its signers will be found at the close of the present chapter. Slightly more than a year later there was a second petition, which included the request that the courthouse site be located in the valley of the Cowpasture. A third petition, presented in the very same year—1779—asked that the proposed county include portions of Botetourt and Rockbridge lying in the Cowpasture and Jackson's River valleys. It was represented that in order to attend court some of the petitioners had to travel a hundred miles and cross high mountains and rapid streams. Some of the movers for the new county wanted the valley of the Calfpasture included.

Notwithstanding the energy shown in these efforts, the time was not favorable to immediate action. The people of Virginia had to struggle with high taxation and depreciated paper money. The Revolution had not yet been fought to a finish, and much attention was necessarily bestowed upon the British, the tories, and the Indians. In 1780 and 1781, British armies were ravaging the country east of the Blue Ridge. So we need not feel surprised that no further effort was made until after the return of peace.

In 1785 there was a petition signed by 522 men, John McCreery, Alexander Black, John Kincaid, and John Lewis, of Warm Springs,

EFFORTS TOWARD A NEW COUNTY

being active in the movement. In October, 1788, there was another paper, the petitioners saying that their troubles with the Indians had prevented them from addressing the Assembly at an earlier date. The settlers west of the Alleghany were strenuous in their appeal. They urge as a strong consideration the fact that there was now a wagon road to Kentucky to take the place of the pioneer bridle-path.

The petition below was written by a man of lame scholarship and does not compare favorably with the general run of the formal documents of the colonial era.

13th April 1778

> To the Honble Specker & Gentilmen Deligates setting now
>
> The Petision of the Inhabitance of Cow and Calf pastures Bull pasture Jackson River and Back Creek Humbly Sheweth
>
> That yr petisioners Not only at present but for many years past have Labored under so great and grievous Disadvantages by Reason of the great Distance the most of us yr petisioners Lives from our Courts of Justice from forty and fifty and others Near seventy Miles from our Nearest Court House besides those on our plantation in the upper end of green bryer at thirty and forty miles farther Back Not to Mention Tygers valley which is yet Dependent on Augusta, so it would be Better for the most of us to put up with small Losses and Injuries Don to us than to attend our present courts for common Justice at so great a Distance and specially in theze Extravagant Times therefore we yr petisioners Humbly prays that our great Deficulty and hardships may be Removed by granting us a New county of our Own and as som of us yr petisioners Inhabiters of the Calf pasture are Lately Thrown into Rockbridge County much against our minds and Inclinations as its vastly more Inconvenient than stanton and worse Road, therefore the Whol of us yr petisioners Humbly prays that our County if granted may be struck of from augusta and Rock Bridge Counties by the Dividing Waters on the Top of the North Mountain The Lower End to begin on the Top of sd Mountain square with the Mouth of the Cowpasture River from thence to the Lower End of William Manns plantation at the mouth of the fawling spring on James River then to continue on a south line to the Waters of Green Bryer from the Beginning; the upper End Likewise to begin on the Top of sd North Mountain opposite to the upper Inhabiters of the Calf Pasture and from thence to the hd waters of Cow and Bull pastures then on a South Line to the Waters of Green Bryer from the Beginning; and as our Bounds is very Extensif and Inhabitance plenty in Number and Seficient Curcomstance to make good all Necessary public Buildings Required by Law We Earnestly pray that your goodness may Take our Case into yr consideration and grant our petision alowing our Court House to be Built in the Cowpasture where it may be sentrable and a greed

upon by the Majority of us yr petitioners &c We Rest in suspense in hopes of success in our Request.

And we as in Duty Bound shall pray

Rafe Laforde	John Montgomery	John McCreery
Henry Beard	Joseph Green	Robert McCreery
John Macdonley	David Frame	Mathias Benston
Wm. Rhea	Thomas Feemster	Joseph Green, Jr.
Wm. Jameson	John Feemster	John Kinging
Jas. Crocket	John Wilson, Jenr	James Peebles
Alex. Crocket	Jas. Dunwodie	john hicklin
William Black	Wm. Dunwodie	Thos. hicklin
Alex Black	Wm. Given	Jas hicklin
William Jackson	Wm. Green	William Steuart
John Montgomery	John Carlil	James Stuart
John Montgomery	James Carlil	Edward Stuart
John Montgomery	Robert Carlil	Joseph Beathe
Patrick Miller	John Cartmill	John Miller
John Kinkaid	James Hughart	William McCanles
George Benston	John Cowarding	Thos. Douglas
Jno. Dunlap	Joseph Mayse, Sr.	William Smith
Robt. Loughridge	Joseph Mayse, Jr.	John Beverage
Wm. Loughrilge	george francisco	Robert McMullin
John Loughridge	Chas. Cameron	William Kilpatrick
Andey Loughridge	Robt. peebles	Andr. McCoslin
Joseph Carpenter	Robt. McCree	Thos. Davis
James Botkin	Lofty pullin	George Carlile
James Clements	Loftis pulin, Junr	christopher Graham
Jas. Clements, Senr	Sam Guliam	Ervin benson
John Redman	Wm. Willson	Wm. Jordan
Robt. Duffell	John Smith	John Willson
Stephen Willson	Thomas Cartmill	John Dickenson
Anthony Johnston	Hugh Hicklin	Robert Mcfarland
James Rucker Jenr	Jacob Warwick	Wm. Daugherty, Senr
Samuel McDannell	Robert Hall	John beard
Wm. Daughherty, Jenr	William Griffeth	Richard Maze, Junr
George Daugherty	George Doherty	William Doherty
William Maze, Jenr	Hugh Hicklin	Chas. Donally
Andr. Sitlington	Robert Kinkade	Thos. Fitzpatrick
Saml. Cartmill	abraham hempstall	Robert McCreery Junr
John Redman	Alexr. Crockett, Senr	Elibabb Wilson
Ralph Wilson	Samson Wilson	John Galaspy
Thos. Galaspy, Jenr	Jas. Galaspy	Christian Snider Jr
Christian Snider	Caleb knap	John Brown
Moses Knap	Theophilus Blake	John Blake
John peeble	James Blake	John McCoslin
George Blake		

XIV

ORGANIZATION OF BATH

HE efforts to divide what was left of Augusta County finally bore fruit. The following Act of Assembly was passed December 14, 1790:

SECT. 1. *Be it enacted by the General Assembly,* That from and after the first day of May next, all those parts of the counties of Augusta, Botetourt, and Greenbrier, within the following bounds, to-wit, beginning at the west corner of Pendleton County, thence to he top of the ridge, dividing the head waters of the South branch from those of Jackson's river, thence a straight line to the lower end of John Redman's plantation on the Cowpasture river, thence to the top of the ridge that divides the waters of the Cowpasture from those of the Calfpasure, thence along the same as far as the ridge that divides Hamilton's creek from Mill creek, thence to the Mill mountain, and with the same to the north corner of the line of Rockbridge County, thence along the said mountain crossing the line of Botetourt County, to the ridge that divides the waters of Pad's creek from those of Simpson's creek, thence along the said ridge to the Cowpasture river, thence crossing the said river a direct course and crossing Jackson's river, at the mouth of Dunlap creek, thence up the same as far as the narrows above the plantation of David Tate, so as to leave the inhabitants of the said creek in Botetourt County, thence a direct course to the top of the Alleghany mountain, where the road from the Warm Springs crosses the said mountain, thence along the top of the said mountain opposite the head waters of Anthony's creek, thence a direct course crossing Greenbrier river to the end of the Droop mountain, thence up the same to the great Greenbrier mountain, thence along the said mountain to the line of Randolph County, thence with the same along the said mountain dividing the waters of Monongalia and Cheat from those of Greenbrier river, and thence to the beginning, shall form one distinct county, and be called and known by the name of Bath.

SECT. 2. A court for the said county of Bath shall be held by the justices thereof on the second Tuesday in every month after the same shall take place, in like manner as is provided by law for other counties, and shall be by their commissions directed; and the court of quarterly sessions for the said county of Bath shall be held in the months of March, May, August and November in every year.

SECT. 3. The justices to be named in the commission of the peace for the said county of Bath, shall meet at the house of Margaret Lewis at the

Warm Springs, in the said county, upon the first court day after the said county takes place, and having taken the oaths prescribed by law, and administered the oath of office to, and taken bond of the sheriff according to law, proceed to appoint and qualify a clerk, and fix upon a place for holding courts in the said county, at or as near the center thereof, as the situation and convenience will admit of; and thenceforth the said court shall proceed to erect the necessary public buildings at such place, and until such buildings shall be completed, to appoint any place for holding courts, as they shall think proper. *Provided always,* That the appointment of a place for holding courts, and of a clerk, shall not be made unless a majority of the justices of the said county be present; where such majority shall have been prevented from attending by bad weather, or by their being at the time out of the county, in such cases the appoinment shall be postponed until some court day, when a majority shall be present.

SECT. 4. The governor with advice of the council shall appoint a person to be sheriff of the said county, who shall continue in office during the term, and upon the same conditions as are by law appointed for other sheriffs.

SECT. 5. *Provided always,* That it shall be lawful for the sheriffs of each of the said counties of Augusta, Botetourt and Greenbrier, to collect and make distress for any public dues or officers fees which shall remain unpaid by the inhabitants thertof, at the time the said county shall take place, and shall be accountable for the same in like manner as if this act had not been made. And the courts of the said counties shall have jurisdiction of all actions and suits which shall be depending before them, at the time said county of Bath shall take place; and shall try and determine the same and award execution thereon.

SECT. 6. In all further elections of a senator, the said county of Bath shall be of the same district as the county of Augusta.

SECT. 7. *And be it further enacted,* That all that part of the county of Augusta lying on the headwaters of the Bullpasture and Cowpasture rivers, not included within the limits of the county hereby established, shall be and the same is hereby added to the county of Pendeton.

SECT. 8. The said county of Bath shall be included in the district with the said county of Augusta, for which a court is to be holden in Staunton.

A portion of the original Bath lay in the Greenbrier valley. This was at the request of the people who were living there. About 1796 some of the people on Anthony's Creek several times petitioned to be annexed to Bath.

The first session of the county court of Bath convened May 10, 1791, at the home of the widow of Captain John Lewis. A part of the proceedings took place under a large shade tree, but later in the year the court voted Mrs. Lewis the sum of seven pounds for the use of her two-roomed house.

ORGANIZATION OF BATH

The justices present on the opening day were John Bollar, John Dean, John Poage, William Poage, Samuel Vance, and John Wilson. Sampson Mathews was the first sheriff and Charles Cameron the first clerk, the bond of each being fixed at 1000 pounds ($3,333.33). William Poage became the first surveyor, and Samuel Vance the first coroner. The first attorneys were John Cotton, James Reid, and Archibald Stuart. The members of the first grand jury were Joseph Mayse (foreman), Samuel Black, Thomas Brock, John Dilley, James Hamilton, James Hughart, Owen Kelley, John Lynch, John McClung, Samuel McDonald, John Montgomery, Joseph Rhea, William Rider, Robert Stuart, and Stephen Wilson. There was an appropriation of 25 shillings ($4.17) for blank books for the county officers.

According to the usage of the time, the first court defined the minimum rates for entertainment at taverns. The figures are as below when reduced from shillings and pence to Federal money.

Dinner	.21	Stabling and hay, 1 night	.16 2-3
Breakfast or supper	.16 2-3	Pasturage, one night	.08
Cold supper	.12½	West India rum, per gill	.07
Lodging	.08	Common whiskey, per gill	.04
Corn or oats, per gallon	.10½	Cider, per quart	.08

The first misdemeanor of which the court took notice was the striking in its presence of John McCarty by Abraham Thompson. Thompson was fined $10. Next year both Thompson and Captain Thomas Lewis were summoned to answer the charge of rescuing property from the sheriff. In 1792 it was ordered that 30 lashes on the bare back be administered to a person who had stolen some goods.

The first minister of the Gospel to present the necessary credentials was Charles Clark of the Presbyterian Church. The second—in 1796—was John Pinnell of the Methodist Church.

The portion of the county west of the Alleghany Front was divided into two constable districts.

In April, 1792, Samuel Vance and John O'Hara were elected over John· Brown and George Poage as delegates to the legislature. The largest number of votes polled was 217. The number of men subject to poll tax was 769, and about one-half of them were presented by the grand jury for failing to vote.

After holding office one year, the first sheriff resigned and went to Augusta. He was succeeded by John Bollar, Sampson Mathews, Jr., becoming his deputy.

About this time the first mill license under Bath was granted to Hazael Willams on Lick Run. John Lyle and Michael Bowyer were named as practicing attorneys.

In 1793 a deputy sheriff reported delinquent taxes to the amount of $75.93. The poll tax for that year was $256.33.

And thus the county of Bath was launched upon its independent career.

XV

THE SURNAMES OF BATH

Heads of Families in 1782

HE personal property books of 1872 are the oldest that have been preserved. Tithables, slaves, horses, and cattle are indicated, respectively, by T, S, h, and c. Where a T preceded by a numeral does not occur, there is but one tithable.

List by Captain James Bratton of the Calfpasture:

Adams, Thomas—2T—40S—13h—43c—also 1 chariot
Armstrong, Archibald—11h—16c
Bell, John—4h—12c
Black, Rebeckah—6h—11c
Bratton, James—3S—14h—19c
Bratton, Adam—8h
Bratton, Robert—5S—10h—45c
Carlisle, John—1S—7h—26c
Carson, Thomas—3h
Craig, Alexander—2h—11c
Craig, Samuel—9h—8c
Davis, Charles—4h—7c
Davitt, Tulley—1S—3h—8c
Elliot, John—1S—9h—14c
Fauntleroy, Moore—11S—6h—1c—1 two-wheeled chariot
Fulton, James—1S—6h—15c
Gay, James—10h—3c
Graham, John—7h—30c
Gaham, Elizabeth—2S—7h—25c
Griffith, James—4h—12c
Gween (Gwin), Robert, Sr.—3h—8c
Gwin, Robert, Jr.—7h—12c
Hamilton, Andrew, Sr.—3S—8h—22c
Hamilton, Andrew, Jr.—6h—6c
Henderson, John—2S—1h
Henderson, Joans—2S—12h—52c
Hughart, Thomas—5S—15h—34c
Jones, George—nothing
Kelly, John—4h—9c
Kincaid, John—5h—15c
Kincaid, William—9h—21c

Lockridge, John—3h—10c
Lockridge, William—4h—5c
Lockridge, Samuel—4h—12c
Mateers, William—9h—25c
Mathews, Sampson—14S—26h—45c
McCutchens, Robert—1S—7h—24c
McCutchens, John—1S—7h—19c
Meek, Daniel—6h—19c
Meek, Thomas—3S—4h—23c
Meek, John—6h—16c
Montgomery, Humphrey—1S—7h—15c
Moorehead, Matthew—nothing
Plunkett, John—3h—11c
Poesy (Posey), Thomas—2S
Porter, William—1h—5c
Ramsey, John—4h
Ramsey, ——— — 4c
Salt, Humphrey—2h—13c
Shields, Robert—4h—11c
Stuart, Alexander—8h—23c
Vahubs (Walkup), John—8h—23c
Vahubs, Robert—1S—4h—17c
White, Archibald—4h—5c
Wilson, John—1S—8h—17c
Wright, John—5h—14c
Wright, William—6h—15c

Total: 63 white tithables, 101 slaves, 352 horses, 870 cattle, 2 carriages.

List by Captain John Brown of the Cowpasture:

Beall (Bell), Leonard—4h—10c
Benston (Benson), Mathias—4S—6h—13c
Benston, Ervin—1h—2c
Benston, George—5h—9c
Black, Alexander—2h—4c
Black, William—2S—5h—11c
Bleak (Blake), Theophilus—2h—5c
Bleak, George—4h—6c
Brown, John—6h—2c
Burns, John—2h—2c
Cameron, Charles—8h—2c
Carlock, Hunkrist—5h—15c
Cartmill, John—8h—9c
Cartmill, Samuel—3h—12c
Cochran, Thomas—8S—8h—4c
Cowarden, John—3S—7h—3c
Crawford, Alexander—2S—6h—6c

Crawford, Nathan—6h—8c
Crawford, William—1h
Day, Samuel—2h—3c
Dickey, William—6h—10c
Donally, Charles—2S—17h—13c
Ervin, Charles—5h—18c
Feamster, Thomas—6S—24h—37c
Frame, David—6h—19c
Frame, Jeremiah—3h—10c
Francisco, George—8h—19c
Francisco, Michael—2h—3c
Gillespie, Samuel—3h—3c
Gillespie, Thomas—3h—10c
Gillespie, John—2S—6h—15c
Hicklin, Hugh—9h—13c
Hughart, James—1S—3h—10c
Irvin (Ervin), James—5h
Kenny, James—4h—4c
Kincaid, John—1S—9h—28c
Kirk, Alexander—5h—6c
Knight, James—1h—5c
Laverty, Ralph—8h—10c
Lewis, Sarah—8S—18h—22c
Mais (Mayse), Joseph—10h—25c
Mattinearly, James—1h—1c
Mayhall, Stephen—3h—4c
Mayhall, Samuel—1h—3c
McCaslin (McCausland), John—8h—21c
McCaslin, Andrew—3h
McClung, John—4h—13c
McCreery, Robert—2S—16h—48c
McCreery, John—11h—15c
McDannald, Samuel—9h—7c
McRobert, John—11h—28c
Miller, Patrick—12h—24c
Montgomery, John—5h—22c
Montgomery, James—6h—4c
Moody, Andrew—2h—7c
Moore William—5h—11c
Moses, Samuel—2h—3c
Newton, Joseph—7h—13c
Rhea, William—1S—9h—21c
Rhea, John—1S—6h—14c
Setlington (Sitlington), John—6h—8c
Setlington, Robert—5h—5c
Singlenton, Andrew—12S—8h—44c

Sloan James—6h—14c
Smith, John—5h—4c
Stout Daniel—7h—7c
Stuart, Robert—6h—16c
Swerengen, Van—2h—7c
Thompson, Robert—3h
Thompson, Edward—4h—11c
Thompson, William—2h—9c
Townsend, Taylor—3h—4c
Wildridge, William—2h—6c
Wilson, Samson—3h—2c
Young, William—5h—14c
Young, James—1h,
  Total: 83 white tithables, 61 slaves, 451 horses, 830 horses.

List by Captain David Gwin—Jackson's River and Back Creek.

Bates, Ephraim—5h—9c
Baxter, John—2T—10h—37c
Beans, Jacob—2h—5c
Boreland, John—3T—5S—10h—20c
Bratton, George—3S—9h—12c
Byrd, John—17h—15c
Davis, John—1S—13h—18c
Dennison, John—4h—10c
Dixon, William—1h—4c
Elliott, Richard—4h—18c
Ellis, James—4S—7h—16c
Fitzpatrick, James—3h—5c
Givens, William—1S—14h—15c
Green, John—5h—15c
Gregory, John—2h—4c
Gwin, David—1S—19h—35c
Hamilton, Alexander—1S—6h—18c
Hamilton, Charles—5h—12c
Hamilton, John—10h—12c
Hamilton, Osborn—9h—12c
Hickman, Roger—6h—14c
Hughes, David—3h—4c
Hutchinson, William—1S—8h—20c
Johnson, Samuel—2h—3c
Kelly, Oan (Owen)—2h—6c
Kilpatrick, Andrew—1h—2c
McClain, James—4h—6c
McFarland, Daniel—5h—11c
McLaughlin, James—2h—4c
Nail (Neil), Thomas—2h—5c

THE SURNAMES OF BATH

Rider, William—4h—5c
Robertson, William—4h—7c
Slavin, William—3h—1c
Stout, Hezekiah—1h—4c
Tabley, Jewel—1S—2h—2c
Townsend, Ezekiel—2h—5c
Townsend, James—2h—7c
Vance, Samuel—2S—10h—28c
Vance, Martha—1S—8h—14c
Waid (Wade), John—4h—10c
Warren, Obijah—1h—1c
Willson, William—4S—26h—35c
Willson, Stephen—11h—30c
Willson, John—13h—24c
Wright, Elizabeth—4h—9c
Wiley, Alexander—4h—3c
Wiley, Robert—4h—16c
Total: 46 white tithables, 28 slaves, 293 horses, 568 cattle.

List by George Poage—Greenbrier River:

Anderson, Thomas	Guy, John	Rucker, James (1)
Barker, James	Hencher, John	Rucker, James (2)
Blaik, Thomas	Hutchinson, Robert	Sharpe, William
Blakeman, Adam	Jarvis, Thomas	Stuart, Ralph
Blakeman, Moses	Lowry, Alexander	Sutton, Joseph
Carson, James	McCarty, James	Tackett, Christian
Cartmill, Thomas	McCollum, John	Tackett, Lewis
Docherty, Michael	Moore, David	Tackett, Francis
Drenon, Lawrence	Moore, Levi	Tanner, James
Drenon, Thomas	Moore, Moses	Taylor, William
Dunlap, Alexander	Offill John	Tracewell, Edward
Galford, Thomas	Poage, George	Warwick, Jacob
Gillespie, Jacob	Reaugh, James	Warwick, William
Guy, (Gay), James	Rogers, John	Wiatt, Leonard

The total was 43 tithables, 460 horses, 543 cattle. Jacob Warwick had 80 horses, 88 cattle. William Warwick had 22 horses, 34 cattle. Dunlap had 44 horses and 24 cattle.

List by Captain George Frazier—Cowpasture, below Botetourt Line—(1783):

Beard, James—1S—4h—10c
Beard, Samuel—1S—4h—11c
Beaty, Robert—2T—4h—10c
Cairns, Michael—2h—15c
Carrigan, Patrick—3h—9c

Cashady, Thomas—1h
Clendening, John—1S—8h—17c
Cooper, James—4h—11c
Daugherty, William—3S—4h—5c
Davidson, William—2T—3S—5h—16c
Fleming, James—2S—6h—6c
Fogle, Philip—2h—4c
Fogle, John—3h—3c
Frazier, George—1S—5h—13c
Galloway, William—8h—26c
Galloway, William—1S—4h—7c
Galloway, Robert—9h—13c
Gilliland, James—2h—11c
Gillispie, Simon—2S—5h—13c
Gore, Michael—3h—4c
Griffith, William—7h—10c
Haines, Joseph—2h—7c
Haines, Benjamin—4h—5c
Haines, Betty—1S—2c
Hanley, Mary—2S—2h—3c
Hill, Robert—3S—11h—20c
Hughes, Aaron—5h—9c
Insminger, John—2h—5c
Insminger, John Jr.—1h,
Lingnecker, Mary—2h—4c
Maze, William—5h—15c
Maze, Richard—2S—6h—13c
McColgan, Edward—2T—1S—6h—11c
McKay, Archibald—1c
McMurray, William—1S—8h—22c
Miller, Henry—2h—3c
Muldrough, Jean—2h—2c
Muldrough, Hugh—7h—21c
Muldrough, William—4h—3c
Musson, Jean—2h—2c
Nighswinger, John—5h—11c
Roberts, Abel—2h—6c
Roop, Nicholas—2h—4c
Scott, James, Sr.—2T—1S—9h—9c
Scott, James, Jr.—5h—7c
Shanklin, Richard—8h—7c
Shaver, Sebastian—2T—2S—11h—21c
Simpson, James—3S—5h—17c
Stewart, James—2h—9c
Thompson, Joseph—2h—2c
Vaught, Casper—2h—12c

Walker, James—2h—7c
Wooley, William—2T—9h—12c
Total: 23 tithables, 10 slaves, 102 horses, 212 cattle.

List by Captain John Bollar—Jackson's River, below Botetourt Line—(1783):

Armstrong, James—6h
Armstrong, Robert—11h—11c
Barbery, Thomas—3h—3c
Barratt, William—nothing
Boller, John
Bullitt, Cuthbert—3S—8h—24c
Carpenter, Jeremiah—5h—6c
Clark, Joseph—2h—6c
Corder, William—1c
Cottle, Benjamin—1h—2c
Craig, James—3h—9c
Davis, William—1h—3c
Davis, James—3c
Dean, John—8S—11h—28c
Doylton, William—nothing
Edwards, Jeremiah—5h—4c
Elliott, James—7h—20c
Fitzpatrick, John—nothing
Fitzpatrick, Thomas—nothing
Harvie, Thomas—1h
Jones, Henry—2h—3c
Jones, John—1h—3c
Jones, John—3h
Kender, Peter—nothing
Kimberlane, Adam—7h—5c
Kincade, Andrew—7h—17c
Kincade, William—3h—9c
Lilley, William—3h—4c
Mann, Jean—1S—8h—10c
Mann, Moses—2h—9c
Mann, Moses—7h—2c
Mann, Esau—3h—3c
Massie, Thomas—7S—41h—30c
McCalister, Thomas—1S—8h—11c
McCalister, James—2T—7h—5c
McCalister, Garrett—1h
McClintoch, William—6h—21c
McClintock, William—5h—5c
McClintock, Robert—4h—7c

McDuff, John—3h—5c
McGart, John—3h—11c
Milholland, Thomas—nothing
Morren (Morris?), Bernard—3h—4c
Morris, Richard—22h—18c
Price, Evan—3h
Price, Zachariah—1h—1c
Robinson, James—3S—5h—17c
Robinson, James—5h—5c
Robinson, William—3h—7c
Scott, John—5h—6c
Scott, James—1h—3c
Slath, John—1h
Smith, William—4h—11c
Sprowl, William—4h—7c
Thompson, Martha—1h—3c
Trotter, Ezekiel—3h—3c
Wall, Thomas—1h—5c
Wall, Thomas—1h—5c
Ward, William—1h—2c
Wright, Peter—2S—10h—38c

Total: 29 tithables, 7 slaves, 130 horses, 209 cattle.

Heads of Families in 1791

First District—Samuel Vance, Assessor.

Alexander, John
Anderson, John
Anderson, Thomas
Arskin (Erskine), John
Barnet, Thomas
Baxter, John
Beathe, Joseph
Benson, Mathias, Sr.
Benson, Mathias, Jr.
Benson, George
Benson, Erwin
Berry, John (Captain)
Bevins, Thomas
Black, William
Blacke, Samuel
Blaik, James
Botkin, James
Botkin, Thomas
Bourland, Andrew
Boyles, David
Bradshaw, John
Brinkley, John
Brock, Thomas
Brown, Joseph
Brown, John (Captain)
Buck, Charles
Burne (Burns), Petter
Burner, Abraham
Burns, John
Byrd, John (Back Creek)
Byrd, John (Jackson's River)
Byrd, Thomas
Byrd, Jacob
Cailer, Mathias
Cameron, Charles (Colonel)
Campble, William
Carlile, John
Carlile, Robert of John
Carlile, Robert of Robert
Carlile, James
Carlile, Rachel
Carpenter, Joseph
Cartright, Jesse
Chapman, George
Chesnut, Sophia (widow)
Cleek, Jacob
Coberly, Thomas
Cochran, David
Collins, John
Conell, William
Cook, Stephen
Court (McCourt), James
Cowardin, John
Crane, John
Crawford, Nathan
Crawford, William
Crump, John

THE SURNAMES OF BATH 119

Cutlip, George
Davis, William
Davis, James
Deever, John
Denison, Mary (widow)
Dickey, William
Dickenson, John (Colonel)
Dilly, John
Dinwoody, William (Captain)
Diverix, John
Dixon, William
Dizard, William
Donoly, Charles
Donoly, Mary, (widow)
Donovan, Peter
Donovan, Charles
Dougherty, Michael
Drinen, Thomas
Duffill (Duffield), John
Edde, John (constable)
Elliott, John
Erwin, Gerard (Jared)
Erwin, John of Jared
Erwin, John
Erwin, Charles
Erwin, James
Evins, Ebram
Femster, Thomas
Fisher, William
Fletcher, Robert
Fletcher, William
Forbes, Alexander
Fox, Jane (?)
Frame, David
Fuller, William
Fulks, (Fultz) Nicholas
Gabbart, John
Galford, John
Garnett, Absalom
Gates, David
Gillespie, Jacob
Gillespie, Samuel
Gillespie, William
Gillespie, John
Givens, Robert (constable)
Givens, William
Godard, John
Graham, Christopher
Graham, Felix
Graham, William
Graves, Richard
Green, William
Gregory, Isaac
Gregory, Joseph
Gregory, Mary (widow)
Griffen, Abner
Gum, Ebram
Gum, John
Gwin, David
Gwin, Joseph
Hamilton, James
Hamilton, Alexander, Jr.
Hamilton, Osborn
Handly, James
Harris, Ebram
Hicklin, Thomas
Hicklin, James (Capt.)
Hicklin, John
Hickman, Roger
Hinkle, Isaac
Hively, Jacob
Houchon, Moses
Houchon, William
Hubbard, Petter
Hughart, James, Sr.
Hughart, James, Jr.
Hughart, John
Hutcheson, James
Hutcheson, Jacob
Ingram, Ebram
Ingram, Job
Irick, Coonrod
Johns, Isaac (1)
Johns, Isaac (2)
Johns, William
Johnson, Bartholemew
Kelly, Hugh
Kelly, Owen
Kelly, Thomas
Kelso, James
Kime, Henry
Kinkaide, John
Kinkaide, James
Kinkaide, Joseph
Knight, James (constable)
Knox, Jeremiah
Lafferty, Ralph
Layton, Thomas
Lewis, John, Esq.
Lewis, Andrew
Lewis, Margaret (widow)
Leytch (Leach), John
Lockridge, James
Lockridge, William
Lockridge, Jean (widow)
Lowney, Alexander
Lunsford, Reuben
Matheny, Archibald
Matheny, Luke
Mathews, Sampson (Colonel)
May (Mayse) William
Mayze, Joseph
Mayze, Isaac
Mayze, Rebecca
McCab (?), John
McCallister, John
McCartney, Andrew
McCarty, Elijah
McCarty, John
McCashlin (McCausland), John
McCashlin, John (2)
McCashlin, Andrew
McClung, John
McCollom, Daniel
McCollom, John
McDonald, John
McDonald, Samuel
McGlaughlin, Hugh
McGalughlin, Hugh (taylor)
McGlaughlin, John

ANNALS OF BATH COUNTY

McGlaughlin, John (Cowpasture)
McGlaughlin, James
McGlaughlin, Daniel
McGoverny, James
McLey, John
Miles, George
Miller, Charles
Miller, James
Miller, Patrick
Miller, John
Montgomery, John
Moor, William
Moor, John
Moor, Levi, Sr. (constable)
Moore, John, (Pennsylvania)
Moore, Mary (widow)
Moore, Moses, Sr.
Moore, Moses, Jr.
Moore, Robert
Moore, George
Moore, Levi, Jr.
Morison, Hugh
Mullinix, John
Munroe, Daniel
Neel, John
Neel, William
Nicholas, Lewis
Nicholas, William
Nicholas, Zephiniah
Notingham, William
Odle, Sylvanus
Ofriel, Jeremiah
Peebles, John
Phelps, Isaac
Poage, George
Poage, James
Pullins, Loufty (Loftus)
Pullins, John
Pullins, Jonathan
Pullins, Samuel
Ray, Joseph
Reah, John
Reah, William
Redman, Samuel
Rian, George
Richardson, Robert
Rider, William
Roberts, John W.
Robinson, John (Captain)
Robinson, Thomas (constable)
Robinson, John
Robinson, Petter
Robey, Patrick
Rodgers, John
Rose, Jesse
Ruckman, David
Ruckman, Thomas
Russell, John
Scott, Henry
Sharp, William
Shaw, George
Shrewsbury, Samuel, Esq.
Sigafoos, Petter
Sitlintown, John
Slavin, Isaiah
Slavin, William
Slavin, John, Sr.
Slavin, John, Jr.
Slone, Jenny (widow)
Smith, Joseph
Stephenson, James
Stiff, John
Stuart, Robert
Stuart, James of Robert
Stuart, William
Stuart, Edward
Stuart, John
Stuart, James (constable)
Sybert, Nicholas
Swearingham, Van
Tait, David
Taylor, William
Townsend, Ezekiel
Townsend, Robert
Townsend, Solomon
Turner, Edward
Tygart, Joshuah
Tygart, Samuel
Vance, Samuel, Esq.
Viers, Gideon
Waide, Leonard
Walgrave, Francis
Wall, Charles
Wallace, Thomas
Walsh, Edward
Wanless, Stephen
Warick, Jacob, Esq.
Warick, John
Warick, William
Waring, Abijah
Watson, Samuel
Webb, John
White, Valentine
Whitman, George
Wiley, Alexander
Wiley, Robert, Sr.
Wiley, Robert, Jr.
Willoughby, Benjamin
Wilson, John Esq.
Wilson, Stephen
Wilson, William
Winder, James
Winder, John
Wooden, Bill

There was a total of 476 tithables, 132 slaves, 1376 horses, 6 studs, and 4 "carriage wheels."

Second District—John Oliver, Assessor

Alderman, Ezekl Alford, Talithain Armstrong, Robert

THE SURNAMES OF BATH 121

Armstrong, Robert, Jr.
Armstrong, Isaac
Armstrong, James
Barker, Thomas
Barkly, James
Barkly, Joshua
Barnett, Robert
Barnett, William
Baty, Andrew
Bently, Rosanna
Boller, John
Brindly, James, Sr.
Brindly, James, Jr.
Brindly, William
Buckly, James
Buckly, Joshua
Bumgardner, Jacob
Byrnsides, John
Calaghan, Dennis
Casebolt, John
Casebolt, Henry
Clarke, Christopher
Cochran, Thomas
Cole, Richard
Cotton Benjamin
Crawford, William
David, Thomas
Davis, James
Davis, Daniel
Davis, John
Davis, Richard
Day, Joseph
Dean, John, Esq.
Deene, John
Dodridge, William
Douglas, John
Edmanson, James
Edwards, Jeremiah
Erwin, James
Erwin, John (river)
Ewin, James
Ewin, Joshua
Ewin, William
Evans, Griffith
Evins, Aaron
Fisher, Philip
Fitzpatrick, Daniel
Fitzpatrick, John
Foster, Luke
Fry, Jacob
Gibson, John
Gilliland, Samuel
Gilliand, Catherine
Grattan, David
Greenlee, James
Griffith, William
Hanceford, William
Hannah, David
Javins, Daniel
Johnson, John
Johnson, Samuel
Jones, John
Jones, John W.
Keckley, Valentine
Kenison, Charles
Kenison, David
Kenison, Nathaniel
Kimberland, Adam
Kinkead, John
Kinkead, Robert
Kinkead, William
Knox, William
Kuykendall, Simon
Lewis, James
Linager, Isaac
Linch, John
Lonsdale, William
Mann, James
Mann, Jane
Massingbird, George
Maze, Richard
Maze, William
McClintick, Alexander
McClintick, Robert
McClintick William
McClintick, Alice (widow)
McCollister, James
McCollister, Moses
McCollister, Richard
McDonald, Hugh
McDuff, John
McKenny, Samuel
McNeil, Abraham
McNeil, John
McNeil, Thomas
Milholland, Thomas
Mitchel, Robert
Morris, John
Morrison, James
Mourning, Bernett
Nales, Stephen
Nants, (Nance), James
Nants, Lydia
Oldram, William
Oliver, Daniel
Oliver, Thomas
Peacock, David
Paine William
Parker, Thomas
Poage, William
Powel, Caleb
Power, Elizabeth
Prince, Evan
Reah, Robert
Reid, James
Richards, John
Robinson, William, Sr.
Robinson, William
Robinson, James, Esq.
Robinson, James
Robuck, James
Rupe, Bernett
Rupe, Mary
Salisburg, William
Salmon, Jacob
Saxton, William
Scott, James
Scott, John
Scott, Robert
Sitlington, Robert
Smith, William
Smith, John
Smith, Lily
Smith, Sarah
Stinson, (Stevenson), Jas.
Stinson, James, Jr.
Stinson, David

Sprowl, Alexander
Sprowl, John
Stuart, Henry
Surber, Henry
Swearingen, Samuel
Switcher, John

Syms, James
Thompson, Abrm
Thompson, Joseph
Thompson, John
Thompson, William

Trotter, Ezekl
Waddle, Alexr
Walker, Charles
Wilson, Robert
Wyatt, Reuben

There was a total of 224 tithables, 44 slaves, 664 horses, and 5 studs.

Grand total for Greater Bath: Tithables, 790; slaves, 176; horses, 2040; studs, 11; carriage wheels, 4.

PRESENT SURNAMES

The surnames below are grouped according to color, and are taken from the books of the county treasurer, as the list stood, June 1, 1913. The abbreviations are these: W for Williamsville District, M for Millboro, WS for Warm Springs, and C for Cedar Creek. Where a figure follows such abbreviation, it indicates the number of taxable individuals bearing the same surname. Where no figure is given, there was only one such person.

WHITE

Adams—M
Agnew—WS, 2
Ailstock—M, 6
Alphin—C
Anderson—WS, 2
Ayers—C
Baldwin—WS
Bartley—M
Barksdale—M
Beard—WS
Beckner—C
Bell—C
Bird—W—WS
Black—M—C
Blakey—C
Blankenship—C
Bogan—WS, 4
Boleyn—C
Bonner—WS, 10
Botkin—W—C
Bowers—C, 2
Bowman—M, 2

Bradley—M—C
Bradshaw—W
Bragg—C
Branscome—C
Bratton—M, 3—WS, 4
Bright—WS, 3—M
Brill—W
Brinkley—W, 4—C
Brockway—M
Brooks—M, 2
Brown—M
Bulger—M
Burger—C
Burns—W, 10—WS, 3—C, 2
Bussard—WS—C
Butler—W, 3
Byrd—WS
Callahan—C
Cameron—W—C
Campbell—W, 3—WS—C, 2
Canthorn—M
Carpenter—W, 6—C, 4

Carroll—WS
Cash—WS
Cauley—WS, 6—M—C, 4
Challender—C, 2
Chaplin—C, 3
Chapman—C
Chestnut—WS, 2
Clark—W, 3
Clarkson—M, 2—C
Cleek—M—WS, 6—C, 3
Cobb—WS
Connor—C, 3
Corbett—WS, 2
Cosby—C
Coursey—W, 2
Crawford—W
Criser—M—WS, 5—C
Crummett—WS
Curry—W, 3—WS, 4
Curtis—M—C
Daggy—M, 2
Daniel—M
Darnell—M
Davenny—M
Davenport—M
Davidson—M
Deaner—C
Deeds—M, 6
Dempsey—M
Dickenson—M, 2
Dineen—C
Douglass—M, 3
Doyle—WS
Driscoll—C, 2
Dudley—C, 3
Dunn—C
Durham—M, 2
Eagle—W
Eakle—WS, 2
Ebert—C
Edenton—C
Edmondson—M, 2
Elliot—WS
Ervine—W, 2
Erwin—WS
Eskins—WS

Estes—M
Faircloth—W
Fertig—M—C
Fisher—C
Fitzgerald—C
Fleishman—C
Ford—C
Foster—WS
Fountaine—C
Foutz—WS
Fox—WS, 2
Fuller—C
Gardner—W
Garing—WS
Garland—M
George—WS
Getty—C
Gillespie—C, 2
Gillett—WS, 5
Gillock—M
Ginger—WS, 3
Goode—M
Grady—M
Graham—W
Graybeal—WS
Greaver—C
Green—M—C—WS
Grinsted—C
Grose—C, 6
Grose—C, 6
Gum—WS, 3—C
Gunton—C
Guy—C
Gwin—WS, 4—C, 2
Hahn—C
Hall—W—C
Halterman—W
Hamilton—WS, 2—C
Hammack—C
Harruff—W—M, 2
Harper—C, 2
Harris—M
Harrison—C
Hawkins—M
Hayslett—M
Hefner—WS, 2

Helminstoller—C
Helms—WS
Hepler—M, 3
Herman—C
Hevener—W—C
Hicklin—W, 2
Hickman—M, 2—WS
Hicks—WS, 2
Hillman—C
Hiner—WS
Hite—W
Hively—WS
Hodge—W, 7—M—WS, 6—C, 2
Holland—M
Holmes—W
Hoover—WS—C, 10
Hopkins—C, 2
Hornberger—C
Jack—W—M
Jackson—W, 6—C, 2
Jeffrey—C
Johnson—M—C, 7
Jones—WS
Jordan—W
Karr—M
Kay—WS
Kayton—C
Keller—M
Kelley—W—WS—C
Kellison—WS, 2
Kelso—W
Kenney—W, 2
Keyser—WS—C, 10
Kimberlin—C
Kincaid—W, 2—M—C
King—M—C
Kirby—M
Knittel—C
Kuhn—M
Lair—M
Lamb—C
Landes—M—WS—C, 2
LaRue—W, 2—WS—C
Law—W—WS, 2—C, 2
Lawrence—M, 2
Layman—C, 2

Leach—C
Lemon—M
Lewis—W
Lightner—WS, 3
Lindsay—WS, 2
Lininger—C
Linkswiler—M
Liptrap—W
Little—C
Loan—W, 5—M, 5
Lockridge—W, 2—WS, 4
Loving—C, 3
Lowe—WS
Lowman—M, 3—C
Lyle—M, 8
Mackey—W, 3
Madison—M
Manasse—C
Mann—WS, 2
Marshall—W, 7—C
Matheny—M, 4
Mathews—C
May—M, 2—C
Mayse—W, 3
McAllister—WS, 4—C, 3
McClintic—W—WS—C, 3
McClung—W, 3
McCormick—W—M, 2
McCoy—M, 2
McCray—C, 2
McCune—W
McDannald—WS
McDonald—WS
McElyee—C, 4
McFadden—WS—C, 2
McGowan—C
McGuffin—WS, 2
McLaughlin—M, 2—C, 4
McMansmay—WS, 2
McMullen—C
McNeil—W
Mede—C
Miller—W, 2—M, 3—WS
Mines—WS, 3
Mustoe—C

Neff—W—M, 3
Newcomer—C
Newman—C
Noffsinger—M
Northern—C
Nutty—C
Oden—C
O'Farrell—WS, 2—C
O'Mara—C
Page—W
Pateson—W
Payne—WS, 2—C, 2
Peery—C
Pelter—M
Peters—M, 2
Phillips—MC
Plecker—W
Pole—C, 4
Porter—M—C
Powers—C
Preston—W
Pritt—W—WS, 4—C
Puffenberger—W—WS, 2
Putnam—M, 3
Rader—W
Ramsey—M
Ratliff—W
Reed—WS
Revercomb—W, 4—C
Reynolds—M
Rhea—M, 5
Rice—C
Richards—C
Richardson—C, 3
Richie—C
Rider—WS, 3—C
Riley—M—WS
Roberts—W, 5
Robertson—W—M
Robinson—W—M—WS, 2—C, 2
Rodgers—W, 3—WS, 3
Rorke—WS
Rose—WS
Ross—W, 2—M
Rosser—W
Rowe—W—M—WS

Rucker—M
Rule—W
Rush—WS
Rusmisell—W, 2
Rutherford—C
Ryder—W
Schosleo—W
Scott—C
Shaffer—WS, 2
Shanks—W, 3—M
Sharp—WS, 2—C
Shaw—C
Sheesley—WS
Sheffer—M
Shelton—WS
Showalter—WS
Simmons—W—M, 2
Simpson—M, 3
Sively—WS
Slosser—M
Smith—W, 2—M—WS—C, 8
Snead—C, 2
Snider—WS
Snyder—C, 2
Snodgrass—WS, 2
Sprouse—C, 2
Stephenson—W—M—WS, 2
Sterrett—C
Sterry—C
Stimson—C
Stinespring—C
Stombeck—M
Swadley—W, 2
Swartz—WS—C, 2
Swearingen—W, 3—M
Sweet—C, 2
Taliaferro—C
Tankersley—W
Taylor—W, 2
Terrell—W, 2—C, 2
Thacker—C
Thomas—M—WS, 2—C, 6
Thompson—M, 3—C, 3
Tidd—C
Todd—C
Tomblin—C

Townson—C
Trainor—W
Trostle—WS
Tucker—C
Tuller—C
Vance—C
Van Derveer—M, 2
Van Lear—M
Venable—WS
Vees—M, 4
Vines—WS
Wade—W, 2—M
Wallace—W, 2
Wallin—C
Walton—C, 2
Wanless—W, 3
Warren—M—C, 2
Warwick—W—WS, 3
Watson—M—C
Weaver—C
Webb—WS
White—M, 2
Wilfong—WS
Wiley—WS
Wilkenson—WS, 2
Williams—W—M, 2—C, 4
Wilson—M
Wine—WS
Wiseman—W, 2
Withrow—M, 3
Wood—M, 3
Woodzell—W—M—WS, 2—C
Wright—M—C
Zimmerman—WS, 3—M

XVI

A LIST OF EARLY MARRIAGES

HIS list of marriages that are more or less associated with Bath history is compiled chiefly from the marriage bonds on record at Warm Springs. Names in parentheses are those of consorts. The dates are those of the bonds. Where a parent is mentioned it is nearly always because the son or the daughter was under age at the time. It is to be remembered that a bond, like a license at the present time, was not invariably followed by a marriage.

Previous to 1852, the applicant for a marriage permit in Virginia had to execute a bond in the office of the county clerk. The purpose of the bond was to make the person answerable for any infraction of the law that might occur. The bond was likewise a license. It was signed by the groom and by one other person, usually the prospective father-in-law. When an applicant for matrimony was under age the consent of the parent was filed with the bond. But occasionally the bride wrote the consent herself. Sometimes the security on a bond was tendered in a quite informal manner, as will appear in the letter below. A consent as well as a bond had to be witnessed by two persons.

Below are given a letter, which speaks for itself, and a specimen consent:

Hot Springs May the 14th 1793

Sr this is to Certify that I have no objecksons agenst Mr. Jas Henry and my Daughter Nancy a getting Married therefore if youl Be pleased to Grant Mr. Henry License for the Purpose youl oblige yours Sir Martha Jevons

Friend White,

Mr. George Norton Came to me this day and told me he was so farr on the Road to you for License to get Married, and he Complains that he hase no Money to pay you with, if it is no disadvantage for you to lay out of the Money, I will see you paid in a short time, and likewise I will be answerable for all damages in giving him the License   I am Sir yr Humble Servant

James Kelso

June 26, 1793

1. Armstrong, John (Polly Crawford)—1790
2. Armstrong, John (Jane Kincaid of Robert)—1797
3. Armstrong, Archibald (Nancy Scott)—1797
4. Baxter, William (Margaret Toms)—1788
5. Beard, Robert (Sarah Mitchell of James)—1785
6. Berry, John (Janet Given)—1790
7. Betty (Beaty), Andrew (Agnes Sitlington of John)—1786
8. Black, William (—— ——)—1764
9. Black, Alexander (Mary Ann Ham)—1793
10. Black, George (Elizabeth Miller of Patrick)—1796
11. Bourland, William (Sarah Dean—or Mary?)—1786
12. Bratton, James (—— ——)—1774
13. Bratton, Adam (Elizabeth Feamster of Thomas)—1788
14. Bratton David (Agnes Kirk of John)—1799
15. Brown, Josiah (Jane Waddell)—1801
16. Burns, Peter (Jane Miller)—1789
17. Burns, John (Margaret Monroe)—1801
18. Burns, Polly (James McCourt)—1792
19. Burns, Eva (John Miller)—1791
20. Burnside, Alexander (Elizabeth Gilliland of John)—1800
21. Carlile, John (—— ——)—1762
22. Callison, Mary of Daniel (Benjamin Delany)—1801
23. Clark, Samuel (Jane Mathews of Sampson)—1790
24. Cleek, Elizabeth (Daniel McGlaughlin of John)—1795
25. Cleek, Sophia (William Hartman)—1801
26. Cleek, Margaret, (Benjamin Potts)—1792
27. Coffey, Margaret of James (John McWilliams)—1781
28. Corbett, Mary of Samuel (Joseph Chestnut)—1794
29. Crawford, William (Martha Cooper)—1786
30. Crawford, James (Mary ——)—1786
31. Crow, Thomas (Nancy Donally of Charles)—1789
32. Davis, James (Ann Estill)—1786
33. Dean, John (—— ——)—1758
34. Dean, Sarah (James Venable)—1797
35. Dean, Mary (Samuel Depew)—1787
36. Dickenson, Martha (John Shrewsbury)—1793
37. Dickenson, Nancy (Joseph Kincaid)—1795
38. Donally, Andrew (—— ——)—1766
39. Donally, Catharine (James Ward)—1800
40. Daugherty, William (Mary Bridge)—1786

A LIST OF EARLY MARRIAGES

41. Daugherty, Isabella (William Nicholas)—1796
42. Elliot, Archibald (Sarah Clark)—1748
43. Elliott, Abraham (Nancy) Campbell)—1786
44. Elliott, Wiliam (Agnes McCampbell)—1788
45. Estill, Solomon (—— ——)—1773
46. Ewing, John S. (Rebecca Cackley)—1801
47. Ewing, William (Mary Taylor)—1791
48. Ewing, Jean (Moses Moore)—1786
49. Feamster, William (—— ——)—1763
50. Fitzpatrick, Mary (John Jones)—1792
51. Frame, Elizabeth (John Duffield)—1790
52. Frame, Mary (George Roebuck)—1795
53. Frame, John (Martha Daugherty of Michael)—1798
54. Francisco, John (Eizabeth S. Lewis)—1798
55. Gay, Thomas (Mary Swearingen)—1791
56. Gay, Samuel (Margaret Mustoe)—1799
57. Gillespie, Mary (Samuel Blake)—1792
58. Gillespie, Rachel of Jacob (John Sutton)—1795
59. Gillespie, John (Comfort Griffith)—1798
60. Gillespie, James (Elizabeth Gillespie of Simon and Rebecca)—1779
61. Gillespie, Robert (Mary Galloway)—1791
62. Gillespie, William (Margaret Eddy)—1792
63. Given, William (Agnes Bratton)—1764
64. Given, Samuel (Elizabeth Robertson)—1785
65. Given, William (Rebecca Kenny of Matthew)—1789
66. Given, Adam (Nancy McGuffin)—1797
67. Given, Isabella of Agnes (Isaac Duffield)—1795
68. Graham, Sarah (James Waddell)—1798
69. Graham, James (—— ——)—1763
70. Graham, Lancelot (—— ——)—1763
71. Gregory, David of Mary (Margaret Warrick)—1786
72. Gregory, Elizabeth (John Robinson)—1800
73. Gregory, Isaac (Hannah Given)—1790
74. Griffith, Mary (Peter Flack)—1793
75. Gwin, David (Violet Crawford of William)—1790
76. Gwin, James (Jane Hicklin of John)—1792
77. Gwin, Robert (Ursula Robinson of Peter)—1793
78. Gwin, (—— ——)—1765
79. Gwin, Robert (Margaret Elliott of William)—1785
80. Hall, James (Nancy Hicklin of Thomas)—1785
81. Hall, Jane (Robert Hutchinson)—1788
82. Hamilton, James (Rachel Vance of Samuel)—1786
83. Hodge, William (Martha Benson of George)—1800
84. Hughart, Thomas (—— ——)—1761
85. Hughart, Mary Elstock of Joseph of Louisa County)—1799
86. Hughart, James (Nancy Thomas)—1792

87. Hughart, Jane of James (Edward McGlaughlin)—1796
88. Jackson, Rhoda (Edward Morris)—1795
89. Jackson, H——. (John Townsend)—1786
90. Jackson, Elizabeth (David Caruthers)—1786
91. Kelly, Mary (Patrick McGraw)—1798
92. Kelly, James (Margaret Sloan)—1796
93. Kelso, James (Elizabeth Sitlington)—1789
94. Kincaid, Andrew (Ann Poage)—1785
95. Kincaid, David (Jennie Lockridge of Robert)—1800
96. Kincaid, Ferdinand (Margaret Fulton of James)—1799
97. Kincaid, James (Jane Curry)—1791
98. Kincaid, James (Margaret Wiatt)—1793
99. Kincaid, John (Mary Dinwiddie)—1786
100. Kirk, Robert (Martha Moffett)—1785
101. Knox, Alice (Francis A. Dubois)—1801
102. Knox, Elisha (Nancy Parker)—1801
103. Knox, John (Sarah Robinson of Joseph)—1793
104. Knox, William (Sarah Acklin of Green-Craig County)—1792
105. La Rue, Abraham (Sarah Lower)—1792
106. Laverty, Ralph (—— ——)—1764
107. Lewis, Charles (Sarah Murray)—1762
108. Lewis, Charles (Ann Honce)—1792
109. Lewis, John (—— ——)—1793
110. Lewis, John (Rachel Miller)—1789
111. Liptrap, Isaac (Mary Bright)—1785
112. Mann, Thomas (Elizabeth Armstrong of Robert)—1792
113. Marshall, Robert (Jean Vance)—1792
114. Mayse, Isaac (Ruth Hicklin of Thomas)—1788
115. Mayse, Joseph (Agnes Hicklin of Hugh)—1787
116. Mayse, Nancy (George Shaw)—1787
117. Mayse, Richard (—— ——)—1760
118. Mayse, Robert (Margaret McClenahan)—1790
119. McAvoy, Robert (Sarah Burns)—1798
120. McCallister, Garnett (Ann Sprowl)—1792
121. McCallister, John (Mary Kincaid)—1800
122. McCartney, Lucy (Zachariah Barnett)—1792
123. McCarty, Timothy (Jane Waugh)—1800
124. McCausland, Mary (Samson Sawyer)—1790
125. McClintic, Jane of Robert (James Brown)—1800
126. McClintic, Samuel (Susanna King of Adam)—1793
127. McClung, John (Mary Stuart of Benjamin)—1788
128. McClung, John, Jr., (Jane McClung)—1793
129. McClung, Elizabeth of Joseph (John Moore)—1793
130. McClung, Margaret (James Musson)—1797
131. McCreery, John (Martha ——)—1762
132. McCreery, Robert (Mary ——)—1764

A LIST OF EARLY MARRIAGES 131

133. McCreery, John (—— ——)—1771
134. McCreery, John of Robert (Margaret Black of William)—1787
135. McMullen, Edward (—— ——)—1759
136. WcWhorter, David (Barzillai McCorkle of Robert)—1800
137. Means, High (Nancy Armstrong of Robert)—1785
138. Milhollen, Sarah (Jeremiah Simms)—1800
139. Miller, Patrick (—— ——)—1785
140. Milligan, John (Isabella Doak)—1786
141. Montgomery, James (—— ——)—1765
142. Montgomery, John (—— ——)—1753
143. Montgomery, John (Sarah Hicklin)—1785
144. Morris, Richard (—— ——)—1761
145. Morris, Frances (Abraham Garnett)—1794
146. Payne, Lewis (Nancy Davis)—1794
147. Porter, Amelia (Nimrod Bogges—Boggs?)—1801
148. Porter, James (Catharine Hughes)—1795
149. Porter, Nancy (Robert Nutt)—1800
150. Ramsey, Charles (Polly Mounts)—1801
151. Ramsey, William (Sarah Fulton)—1794
152. Rhea, Elizabeth (Tolliver Wright)—1797
153. Rhea, James (Margaret Still)—1800
154. Rhea, Robert (Catherine Bailor)—1798
155. Ross, John (Mary Harvey Davis)—1795
156. Ross, James (Elizabeth Griffin of William)—1795
157. Scott, Hugh (Betsy Bell)—1800
158. Smith, Barbara of William (Joseph Warman)—1794
159. Smith, James (Elizabeth Wilson of Robert)—1794
160. Smith, John (Sarah Moore of Levi and Susanna)—1794
161. Sprowl, William (—— ——)—1757
162. Stephenson, David (Mary Davis)—1783
163. Stephenson, James (Margaret Smith)—1796
164. Stephenson, Robert (Jane Smith of John)—1798
165. Stephenson, Susanna (William Hughes)—1801
166. Stewart, Isaiah (Martha Stewart)—1786
167. Stuart, Henry (Sarah Moore)—1791
168. Stuart, James (Nancy Moore)—1794
169. Swearingen, Alexander (Sarah Layne)—1800
170. Swearingen, Samuel (Hannah Scott)—1798
171. Tharp, Daniel (Margaret Barkley)—1795
172. Thompson, Hannah (Peyton Walker)—1794
173. Thompson, Thomas (Jean McClung)—1795
174. Trotter, Christopher (Prepare McClintic of William)—1786
175. Usher, Ann of Robert (Hugh Donaho)—1795
176. Usher, Jean of Robert (Clements Graham)—1791
177. Usher, James (Catherine Whitesides)—1788
178. Vance, Samuel (—— ——)—1763

179. Vance, Mary of James (William Bridger)—1795
180. Waddell, Isabella of Alexander (James Boggs)—1797
181. Wallace, Matthew (Sarah Brown)—1801
182. Ward, James (Catharine Donally)—1800
183. Warwick, John (—— ——)—1771
184. Warwick, John (Mary Poage)—1794
185. Warwick, Margaret (Adam See)—1794
186. Wilson, John (—— ——)—1769
187. Wilson, George (Elizabeth McCreery)—1750
188. Wilson, Jane (Cornelius Vanosdale)—1785
189. Wooton, William (Jane Gilliland)—1793

CROSS-INDEX TO ABOVE LIST

Acklin—104
Armstrong—112, 137
Bailor—154
Barkley—171
Barnett—122
Bell—157
Benson—83
Black—134
Blake—57
Boggess—147
Boggs—180
Bratton—63
Bridge—40
Bridger—179
Bright—111
Brown—125, 181
Burns—119
Cackley—46
Campbell—43
Caruthers—90
Chestnut—28
Clark—42
Cooper—29
Crawford—1, 75
Curry—97
Daugherty—53
Davis—146, 155, 162
Dean—11
Delany—22
Depew—35
Dinwiddie—99
Doak—140
Donaho—175

Donally—31, 182
Dubois—101
Duffield—51, 67
Eddy—62
Elliott—79
Elstock—85
Estell—32
Feamster—13
Flack—74
Fulton—96, 151
Galloway—61
Garnett—145
Gillespie—60
Gilliland—20, 189
Given—6, 73
Graham—176
Griffin—156
Griffith—59
Ham—9
Hance—108
Hartman—25
Hicklin—76, 80, 114, 115, 143
Hughes—148, 165
Hutchinson—81
Jones—50
Kenny—65
Kincaid—2, 37, 121
King—126
Kirk—14
Layne—169
Lewis—54
Lockridge—95
Lower—105

Mathews—20
McCampbell—44
McClenahan—118
McClintic—174
McClung—128, 173
McCorkle—136
McCourt—18
McGlaughlin—24, 87
McGraw—91
McCreery—187
McGuffin—66
McWilliams—27
Miller—10, 16, 19, 110
Mitchell—5
Moffett—100
Monroe—17
Moore—48, 129, 160, 167, 168
Morris—88
Mounts—150
Murray—107
Musson—130
Mustoe—56
Nicholas—41
Nutt—149
Parker—102
Poage—94, 184
Potts—26
Robertson—64
Robinson—72, 77, 103
Roebuck—52
Sawyer—124

Scott—3, 170
See—185
Shaw—116
Shrewsbury—36
Simms—138
Sitlington—7, 93
Sloan—92
Smith—163, 164
Sprowl—116, 120
Still—153
Stewart—166
Stuart—127
Sutton—58
Swearingen—55
Taylor—47
Thomas—86
Toms—4
Townsend—89
Vance—82, 113
Vanosdale—188
Venable—34
Waddell—15, 68
Walker—172
Ward—39
Warman—158
Warrick—71
Waugh—123
Whitesides—177
Wiatt—98
Wilson—159
Wright—152

XVII

SEVENTY YEARS OF BATH HISTORY

IN THIS chapter we can give only some of the leading facts in our local history for the period of just seventy years between the organization of Bath and the war of 1861.

The original Bath lay astride the Alleghany Front and was at least three times as large as the present county. The reduction to the present boundaries has been by four steps.

The line between Bath and Pendleton was 20¼ miles long as reported in the survey of 1793. It is described as leaving North (Shenandoah) Mountain opposite the lower end of John Redmond's plantation, and by a course running N 63½ degrees W, crossing Shaw's Fork below the dwelling of Thomas Deverick's, the Cowpasture below the land of John Redmond, the Bullpasture below the house of Joseph Malcom, and Crab Run below the house of Joseph Bell, about 2½ miles above the Blue Hole. Thence to the top of the Alleghany, no houses are named.

The first curtailment took place in 1796, when a strip averaging three miles in breadth was annexed to Pendleton, the new line running through the Dinwiddie Gap and crossing the Cowpasture at the mouth of Shaw's Fork. The second and largest reduction came in the winter of 1822-23, when the counties of Alleghany and Pocahontas were established. The third was when Pendleton and Bath were shortened to make room for Highland. The last was in 1847 and was very small. It consisted of a slight change put into the Bath-Alleghany line where it crosses the Cowpasture, so that Sheppard Gilliland and Orlando Griffith might be citizens of Alleghany.

The original line between Bath and Alleghany is thus described:

> (From the) top of Alleghany mountain where the public road crosses to Anthony's Creek; thence to the mouth of the draft at Benjamin Thompson's (deceased) on Jackson's rivr so as to leave the said public road in Bath, and with the road as the dividing line between Alexander McClintic and Benjamin Thompson; thence, with the dividing line, crossing the river, to top of mountain; thence with top of mountain to intersect

line run by William Herbert, and with said line to top of mountain at Henry Massie's; thence direct to Cowpasture just below William Griffith, leaving him in Bath; thence on direct line to top of Mill Mountain in Bath line; thence with top of same to corner of Rockbridge on mountain top; thence with Rockbridge line between the heads of Simpson's Creek and Bratton's Run to top of North Mountain, passing Collier's Gap, and thence with boundaries of Alleghany as per Act.

The section of Bath west of the Alleghany Front went to form the greater part of Pocahontas County. A petition of 1812 had stated that a third of the people of Bath were living between 25 and 50 miles from the courthouse.

The progressive shrinking in the county limits will largely account of the fluctations in the census returns, the figures for six decades being as follows:

1800—5508	1830—4002
1810—4838	1840—4300
1820—5231	1850—3426

The falling off between 1800 and 1810 was not because of a diminished area. It was due to the heavy emigration then moving into the seemingly boundless West. But since Bath shrank into its present dimensions in 1847, the population has doubled, and there has been no falling off in any ten-year period.

It is well known that a domestic animal will sometimes return to the former home, regardless of the wishes of the owner. This is usually soon after the migration. But in 1810 a horse returned from Kentucky after a residence there of 15 years. It was summer time, and instead of going at once to the Mayse place, where he had belonged, the animal thought it the proper thing to resume business on his old grazing range on the mountain.

In 1853 there were seven election precincts: Courthouse, Cedar Creek, Hamilton's, Cleek's Mill, Williamsville, Milton, and Green Valley.

Because of its summer resorts and its fertile river bottoms, Bath has always had a large proportion of negroes as compared with other mountain counties. Between 1810 and 1860 the percentage of blacks increased from 19 to 27. In the latter year this county had 946 slaves and 78 free colored persons, as against 402 slaves and 27 free colored in the adjacent county of Highland with its then larger total population.

A sidelight on material conditions appears in the circumstance that while 2117 horses were reported in 1833, there were only six coaches, five carryals, and two gigs. The total tax in that year was $837.24.

With respect to its county seat and its courthouse, Bath has had a somewhat checkered career. For the county buildings, Mrs. Margaret Lewis offered to donate two acres adjacent to Warm Springs Run, and to give free access to a cold spring. But she was in straitened circumstances, and payment was made for the land. In 1795, her son, Thomas L. Lewis, conveyed one acre to Bath County for $100. For the May term of 1792 the court sat in the clerk's office, and in the next month it met in the upper, or debtor's, room of the new jail. It would not seem that the county was then entertaining any boarders in its jail.

In April, 1795, a committee was appointed to prepare plans for a courthouse of stone, the building to be 20 by 30 feet in the clear, two stories high, and not to cost more than 500 pounds ($1666.67). The members of the committee were John Bollar, John Dean, John Lewis, John White, and Andrew Moore. For drawing the plans, William Mathews was to be allowed $3. But no courthouse appears to have been ready for more than twelve years after the county was organized. The first one was finally built opposite the grounds of the Warm Springs hotel. The brick structure is yet standing, and though vacant is a serviceable building.

After 1822 there were petitions for and against the removal of the county seat to the twin hamlet of Germantown. Until Highland County was created, there was violent opposition to such removal. It is only within quite recent years that the change has been effected.

The justices appointed at the time of the organization of Bath were these:

John Bollar	John Lewis	James Poage
Charles Cameron	Sampson Mathews	Samuel Shrewsbury
Alexander Crawford	John Oliver	Samuel Vance
John Dean	John Peebles	Jacob Warrick
John Dickenson	George Poage	John White
John Kincaid	William Poage	John Wilson

Warrick and the Poages were from beyond the Alleghany. Peebles and Wilson lived in what is now Highland County. Crawford and White seem to have represented the Alleghany area. Crawford and Dickenson refused to serve. Bollar, Mathews, and White comprised the committee to build a jail, which was the first county building to come into existence. Cameron, who lived at Fassifern, used a little stone building on his farm as the first county clerk's office.

The later justices, for the 32 years during which Bath was "Greater Bath," were the following, so far as we can ascertain their names. The dates are for the earliest year in whch we find mention of the persons:

Berry, John—1812
Brown, John—1794
Crawford, William—1793
Davis, Jesse—1813
Dean, William—1801
Dean, William M.—1812
Dinwiddie, William—1796
Erwin, John—1794
Gatewood, Thomas—1801
Gay, Robert—1812
Hamilton, James—1801
Hicklin, James—1801
Hill, Richard—1815
Hite, Keeland—1813
Holcomb, Timothy—1795
Johnson, Bartholemew—1795
Jordan, John—1814
Jordan, Solon—1813
Kinkead, Joseph—1801
Kinkead, Thomas—1801

Lewis, Andrew—1801
Lewis, Charles A.—1812
Lockridge, William—1797
Mason, Moses—1812
Massie, Henry—1814
McClintic, Alexander—1812
Milhollen, Thomas—1796
Moore, Levi—1796
Robnson, James—1792
Shrewsbury, John—1797
Sitlington, Robert—1797
Sitington, William—1812
Sitlington, George—1814
Slaven, Stewart—1815
Tallman, James—1812
Walker, Joe—1796
Warwick, John—1794
Warwick, Andrew J.—1814
White, Valentine—1796

After the reduction of the county in 1823, and previous to the war of 1861, we find the following sheriffs:

Robert Sitlington—1823
Alexander McClintic—1828
James Hamilton—1834
William McClintic—1837
John Sloan—1838

Archer P. Strother—1848
Andrew H. Byrd—1849
Samuel Lewis—1851
Andrew H. Byrd—1857
Adam G. Cleek—1858

Until 1852 the justices of the county courts of Virginia were appointed and served without pay. They now became elective and received a per diem allowance. About this time the county was divided into four districts, each of which was entitled to four justices. For a while the districts were designated as First, Second, Third, and Fourth. Later, they were given the names of Cedar Creek, Warm Springs, Williamsville, and Millboro. In 1860 the valuation of real and personal property was $3,156,238. There were 16 churches: 6 Baptist, 4 Presbyterian, 4 Union, 1 Methodist, and 1 Episcopalian.

In 1794 Virginia was called upon for a quota of 4800 men to be used in putting down the Whiskey Insurrection in the southwest of Pennsylvania. The commander of the national troops was Governor Henry Lee, the father of General Robert E. Lee. As "Light Horse Harry," he had made a brilliant record in the Revolution. Some Bath men served in this army, but we have not list of their names. The following letter by one of them was written to a friend at home:

> Camp at Simpson's, the Center of Aligany 32 miles short of Beason Town[1] & 8 from the Big Crossings[2], Sunday Morning, Oct. 26, '94.

Dear Mustoe

Wee are hear Lying on our ores waiting for Better weather. It has been Verry wet Since Friday Evening Last and appears to Continue this Evening. Wee would Reached Beasontown had the weather been Feavorable. Wee will march to Pit[3] at all events & there Remain Some time. There will be about 2000 Men Kept there this winter to be Composed of Volenteers from the whole army when Collected on Imediate Drafts from the home Militia if the Volenteers Cannot be Procured. there will be Nothing to be Don but to Reduce them to Proper Subordination, which will be Easily Effected as they are Almost frighted to Death. the Great Breadford made his Escape Eight Days ago Doan the River and Left Some fine farms. it is Supposed one of them will be head Quarters this winter. Brackenridge, Gattes, Cook, & some others As yet Says they will Stand their Tryal in hopes for Mercy. a Captain Higgens—Express from that Country Came to Genl Morgan a Thursday Last who Informs there Never was so affrighted a People, when they find the Army so near them. Genl Morgans Division to which I Belong are the advanced part. My Compny Drew Riffles. there is one Regiment of Riffle men in the Division Commanded by Colo. Crisup from Maryland. wee are about 500 strong.

A Military Life is a fine one. Waron[4] Says if Ever he Volenteers it

---

[1]Now Uniontown, Pennsylvania.
[2]A ferry on the Youghiogheny.
[3]Pittsburg.
[4]Probably Abijah Warren.

again the Devil May be his Captain. for my own Part I am as happy as the Nature of my Situation will admit of—a fine apatite & Plenty to Eat and Drink, wet Cold Ground to Ly on. wee Ly Down & get up Contented. I Procured the Quarter Masters Appointment for Fliegan, which is a handsome one. he Lives in My family. So of Course when Joined with the Stof wee shal Not Want. So hears to You & the two Whites, Cochran, & Oliver, & the rest of the Boys about the Springs. Just Merridian, the Publick pays for all. Fliegan Joins the Lott. My Love to Dolly & the Childer. I shall Soon see them when I Return.

As Yours
W. CHAMBERS

In 1822 many Bath citizens signed a petition for the removal of the state capital from Richmond. The reasons given were that Richmond would be too much exposed in case of war; that its warm climate makes it uncomfortable for mountain legislators to attend summer sessions; and that the luxurious habits of its people were distasteful to the petitioners.

As already observed, there was a comparatively full population in 1790 and a considerable degree of prosperity and comfort. The further progress of this county, before the upheaval of 1861, was at a steady and substantial pace, so far as agricultural interests were concerned. With respect to highways and the summer resorts, the advance was more marked. Geography has been kind to Bath. The several openings among the mountain ridges between the Iron Gate and the Sister Knobs are doorways to through lines of travel between East and West. Even before 1800, what was then considered a good road led over the Alleghany divide and down the Great Kanawha to Ohio and Kentucky. The Harrisonburg and Warm Springs Turnpike, built some years later, was a still better road. It was lined with taverns and was traversed by the stages that conveyed visitors to and from the summer hotels. It was thronged with numerous freight wagons and with droves of cattle and other domestic animals. In 1857 the pike was partially superseded by the Virginia Central Railroad, which in that year had extended its line to Jackson's River station, a few miles west of Clifton Forge. War checked the advance of the iron path, but in 1867 work was resumed, and under the name of the Chesapeake and Ohio, it has grown into a very important thoroughfare.

With respect to slavery, a few clauses in the will of Andrew

Sitlington are of interest. One of them leaves several slaves to his wife and concludes with this wish: "And though I give them entirely into her disposal to do unto them as she pleases, yet I cannot help expressing confidence in her humanity and tenderness that she will grant them their freedom in some reasonable time after her death." He desired such emancipation as to slaves over the age of 25. Males under 25 were to be "bound out to honest, industrious persons to become industrious and moral, and taught to read and write, so as to understand Scripture and keep their accounts." Females were to be bound until 21, and taught "to read, at least, and to habits of industry and morality, so that they may be good and useful members of society." But Sitlington did not deem it prudent or expedient to free the male negroes under the age of 25. The freed negroes were to contribute to the support of any of their number who might become infirm.

The interest in popular education appears in a petition by Patrick Maloy and fifty-seven other persons, the names having been procured about 1842. We quote some extracts from this paper.

(There is) no legal provision for the proper location and construction of schoolhouses, for supplying well-qualified teachers, or for testing the quality of such as profess to teach; no superintendent of schools, nor general regulations for the proper management of them, or the proper selection and supply of textbooks. The fund appropriated for the education of poor children is not only deficient in amount, but often negligently and injudiciously administered. Much of this precious fund has been wasted in paying for abortive scraps of tuition. We hold it to be manifestly just and proper, that the people should all contribute according to their ability,, to the great object of diffusing the blessings of education through all classes of our citizens.

It was not until 1846 that Virginia adopted any plan for free public tuition, and even this was not comprehensive.

An advanced stand against intoxicants is disclosed in a vigorous petition, probably written by John H. Ruckman. It was presented to the General Assembly, January 15, 1840, by William Lockridge. We give below its opening and closing sentences.

Those laws by which the sale of intoxicating drinks are legalized and licensed were originally dictated by a benevolent wish to restrict the sale and use of such drinks. They were intended to keep the means of intoxication away from the drunkard, but leaving them entirely open to sober men. Were the system perfectly successful we should deem it highly objectionable, as tending to debase respectable citizens into drunkards. But it is a matter of perfect notoriety that it imposes no practical restraints whatever upon any person.

If the laws will continue to permit sinks of vice, poverty, and crime to stand open night and day, the same laws must continue to provide poor-houses, prisons, gallowses, and graves to receive the victims. Can it be necessary to keep up this state of things forever? Does the public good require that in these United States 50,000 men shall spend their whole time in manufacturing and selling a deadly poison, both to body and soul, and that these men shall destroy 25,000,000 bushels of grain yearly, while the people are suffering for bread? And is it necessary that 30,000 of our fellow citizens shall annually go down to the drunkard's grave, leaving their wives widows and their children orphans? Does the public good require such a sacrifice? Is there no remedy? Has law nothing to do with humanity? There is a remedy. Repeal the liquor laws, and in their stead provide suitable penal enactments against the further sale and distribution of the poison.

A century after the first appearance of Selim the Algerine there was another incident of a quite unusual character. A stranger appeared in this county one summer, who never revealed his name and went to much trouble to avoid meeting people. He would hide if a person were coming in his direction and likely to encounter him. He occupied a vacant mountain cabin near Bath Alum. An old colored woman came once a week to keep the habitation in order. When he needed provisions, he would place the order and the necessary money on a stump, and then go off with his gun until the woman came back with the supplies.

One day the negress found him in a delirious condition and called a doctor, under whose ministration the man recovered. There was a long talk with the mysterious patient, who was found to be a cultured gentleman of pleasing personality. One day the caretaker brought him a letter and photograph which pleased him greatly. In taking leave of his physician, he told the latter he was going home and that they would never see one another again. The stranger had money and paid all his bills. Who or what he was, or where he came from, were things that never became known in Bath. The conjecture esteemed most plausible was that the eccentric behavior was due to a love affair.

The letter with which we close this chapter was written from Indiana. Captain James Bratton, the father, was living near Millboro. The original letter is in the possession of W. A. Bratton.

"Montgomery County October th. 20. 1812.

Honoured father and mother I embrace this opportunity of informing you of our welfare. At present that we are well thanks be to the giver of all mercies hopeing that these few lines will find al in the same state of health. We have had a young daughter born April th eight the name is Betsy Dunlap We are highly pleased with our moving to this county as yet I have not purchased land as yet but I expect in few days to get place where we shall settle upon As to going to the Wabash I have defered as the indians appears to be very troublesome there yet we have had a very late account from the frontiers and the killing the people on the frontiers every Chance they get the mounted volunteers that went from this state against the indians are now all Coming home the have cut all the corn burnt there towns in all this work there never an indian appared against them the footmen are to stay during the winter nothing more but remain your loving son and daughter till death

"ROBERT AND ANNE BRATTON"

"Remember us to William Crawford and the family likewise to John Poter and his family Brother David and his family are well."

XVIII

BATH IN THE WAR OF 1861

URING the war of 1861 this county adhered to the Confederate government. A large share of the able-bodied men were absent in the Southern army, and the hotels in Warm Springs valley were converted into military hospitals. Bath did not itself come within the sphere of important military operations. There were slight skirmishes at Williamsville and Millboro, but no engagement of importance. Yet the Federal cavalry several times raided through the valleys and thus brought the people face to face with some of the aspects of actual warfare.

The men serving on the county court for the term 1860-64 may well be termed the "war justices." Their names are as follows:

First District: Alexander H. McClintic (president), Anthony Mustoe, William W. Shields, George Mayse.

Second District: Aaron G. McGuffin, Osborne Hamilton, Roger Hickman, ———.

Third District: Moses McClintic, William C. Burger, Stephen Wanless, John Carpenter.

Fourth District: Thomas Sitlington, John U. Dickenson, Addison McClung, Robert P. Williams.

It is a very exceptional fact that Bath supplied from one of ts households a general of brigade rank to each of the contending armies. They were sons of William H. Terrell, an eminent lawyer who filled the position of commonwealth's attorney in 1860-64. Brigadier-General William R. Terrell, a graduate of West Point, took his stand with the Union, and his artillery was very instrumental in saving the day for the Federals at Shiloh. He was killed in the battle at Perryville, Kentucky, October 8, 1862, and was buried at West Point. Brigadier-General James B. Terrell, a graduate of the Virginia Military Institute, went with the South, and was killed in the battle of the Wilderness in 1864. He was serving as colonel at the time, but his commission as brigadier-general had already been signed. The Terrill brothers were descendants of the McCausland family, now extinct in Bath.

To deal as directly as possible with the way in which this county experienced the vicissitudes of the struggle, we present some data taken in chronological order from the pages of the county records.

1861

Jim, a slave of Mary C. Frazier, was acquitted, April 21st, of the charge of feloniously conspiring to plot, rebel, and make insurrection. But as he was of bad reputation, a bond of $150 was demanded from his owner.

The county court ordered, May 14th, that $1500 be appropriated out of the forthcoming levy to arm and otherwise equip a troop of cavalry. Charles R. McDannald was appointed its agent for this purpose. A patrol of 16 men was appointed July 9th, according to an act of Assembly. The poll tax voted was $4.25.

1862

Martial law was proclaimed by the Confederate president, March 29th. An order from General Heth requiring a provost marshal in Bath, Robert B. Matheny was recommended for the position. Salt being scarce, John P. McDannald was authorized, April 8th, to borrow money for the purchase of 100 sacks, the fund so used to be repaid out of the next levy. At the same time, and in pursuance of a military order, all free able-bodied negroes between the ages of 18 and 45 were ordered to report. Of these, 12 were required to work the road between Milboro and Warm Springs. There being no election at the usual time, of sheriff and commissioner of the revenue, a special election was ordered for November 27th. December 9th, 12 patrols were ordered, three for each district.

1863

A smallpox hospital was ordered, January 13th. On the same day it was decreed that $3500 be applied to the relief of destitute families, the justices acting as distributors. Notes to this amount, in denominations of one dollar, fifty cents, and twenty-five cents, were ordered to be printed and then signed by the presiding justice By order of the Secretary of War, five free negroes were drafted to chop wood on the Virginia Central Railroad.

There was a requisition on the county, February 13th, for 40 slaves between the ages of 18 and 45, the purpose of the call being to employ them in building fortifications around Richmond. The answer was that of the 781 slaves in 1862, there should have been available 104; but that some had been removed from the county by their owners, others had been sold because of the nearness of the enemy, while from 14 to 16 had escaped, and from 12 to 15 were physically unfit for service. As the draft was therefore deemed much too heavy, the War Department reduced the requisition to 30, a third of whom were to go to Richmond. Wiliam Shumate was detailed to have charge of the party.

In March, John Cleek was appointed an agent to procure cotton and yarn from the South. It was announced that goods thus purchased were for use and not for speculation. A special election was ordered for May, but none took place. A claim of $584 against the county was allowed, December 8th. It was for flour to the amount of 14 barrels and 61 pounds. On the same day the sheriff was ordered to make a list of all indigent soldiers honorably discharged, and also a list of the widows and minor children of deceased soldiers.

In September, there was a call for 20 slaves between the ages of 18 and 55. The answer was returned that the number of such was still further reduced, from 15 to 20 having lately been abducted by the Federals.

1864

Bonds to the amount of $15,000 for the relief of destitute soldiers were ordered, January 12th. Ten slaves were requisitioned. in February, but only about 30 of the class asked for were reported as now in the county. At the May election, Charles R. McDannald was chosen clerk, Adam G. Cleek sheriff, and William McClintic surveyor. The poll tax for the 350 tithables was fixed at $10, and to pay the allowances for the destitute. a levy of 2½ per cent. was ordered on the assessment of $2,266.125. The Federal inroads causing the production of foodstuffs to be less than the needs of the population, it was asked that the head tax might be paid in money. In December there was a requisition for five slaves beween the ages of 17 and 50, the draft to be supplied by individuals individualy owning a number equal to the call. It was replied that there were but two such persons. One of these had lost seven by capture within 18 months. Some negroes had been secreted, and others had been stolen away. There was a request that six millers, five blacksmiths, two shoemakers. and one tanner be exempted from detail service.

In October, Smith Darnell was allowed $13,743.10 of the depreciated currency for the relief of the destitute in the First District.

1865

It was announced in January that a third of the slaves had been abducted. In April the county court ordered that any surplus of provisions which might exist should be distributed at prices not to exceed the following figures: Wheat, per bushel, $50; corn, $30; rye, $30; buckwheat, $30; potatoes, $15; bacon, per pound, $11.

The last session of the court under the Confederate government was held April 14th. The clerk was ordered to remove the records to a place of safety.

The next session was held August 21st, the members being James L. Bratton, John Carpenter, John Cleek, Sr., Smith Darnell, Osborne Hamilton, Charles H. Hughart, Alexander H. McClung. and Addison McClung.

XIX

THE BATH SQUADRON

N MAY, 1861*, a company of the young men of Bath, eager for the fray, responded promptly to the call of the governor of Virginia The patriotic daughters of the county soon raised the funds to purchase a beautiful silk flag. This was presented on the Saturday preceeding the departure of the company from Staunton on its way toward the northwest. The speech of presentation was by Nicholas K. Trout, Mayor of Staunton. The flag was received by Captain A. T. Richards, of the company with these words: "We will cherish it as we will our wives and sweethearts."

The Bath company was a cavalry command. It marched under sealed orders to Philippi, W. Va., where it reported to Colonel Porterfield, commanding the Confederate forces there. It rendered good service in picketing and scouting, during the interval up to the surprise by the Federals under General Kelley. In this engagement, L. P. Dangerfield of the company, lost a leg by a minie ball, he and a member of another command being the first Virginia soldiers to be wounded in the war. On the other hand, A. M. McClintic[2] wounded General Kelley by a ball from his flintlock pistol.

Because of the hasty retreat from Philippi, the company was so unfortunate as to lose its beautiful flag. It was in its case in the company's wagon, and in the suddenness of the early morning attack was overlooked. The retreat continued to Beverly, where General Garnett took command. With other troops the Bath Cavalry were advanced to Laurel Hill, northwest of Beverly. While here being drilled in the duties of the soldier, they continued to do good work in picketing the roads leading toward the Federal position. Early in July General McClellan advanced from Buckhannon by the Staunton and Parkersburg pike, and overpowered after a gallant resistance the

---

[1]This account is condensed from articles written for the Bath News by Lieutenant A. C. L. Gatewood. His letters relating to events after the battle of Gettysburg were not available to us.

[2]John W. Sheffer, according to another account.

Confederates on Rich Mountain. Pegram and his men were captured but were released on parole to return to their homes and there remain until regularly exchanged. Among the prisoners were the Bath Greys under command of Captain S. A. Bonner. Pegram's men reported kind treatment by McClellan and his army. After their exchange the Greys were transferred to the cavalry service and were now commanded by Captain W. D. Ervin. Their assignment was to the 18th Virginia Cavalry of Imboden's Brigade.

General Garnett began his retreat the evening of July 9th, intending to make a stand in the mountain passes near Huntersville. But learning that the road to Beverly was in the hands of the Federals, his only way to escape was northeastward through Tucker County. At Corrick's Ford—now Parsons—he gave battle and was killed. McClellan, an old friend and classmate at West Point, had his body embalmed and sent to his family. From the Cheat River to Petersburg, Garnett's men had nothing to eat except fresh beef killed on the road and eaten without salt or bread. At Petersburg there were supplies for the famished soldiers. After a rest the march was continued to Monterey, where within a few weeks General R. E. Lee took command and advanced into Pocahontas County. The Bath Cavalry were assigned to his army, being put into a battalion commanded by his son, Major W. H. F. Lee.

The summer was unusually wet and there was much sickness from measles and typhoid fever. The country from Valley Mountain, where General Lee made his headquarters, down to Huntersville is dotted with the neglected graves of soldiers, especially the Georgia troops. The Bath Cavalry were at Huntersville till late in the fall. when from the great difficulty of provisioning the army, the command was odered into winter quarters at Bath Alum, and afterward at Rockbridge Alum.[1]

Early in May it was known that a foraging party from Milroy's army was in the neighborhood of Williamsville. With a view of bagging the detachment, the Bath Cavalry set out at 2 P. M., and at

---

[1]Because of the recruits who came in at these places, the Bath Squadron was divided into two companies, F and G, commanded, respectively, by Captains A. G. McChesney and F. A. Dangerfield.

night were near the foraging party. At daylight they took position on the Burnsville road a little way out from Williamsville. It was by this road that the foragers were to return to McDowell. A picket on an opposite hill within observation of the foragers was to fire his gun as a signal for the attack. The train was captured, only a few shots being fired. A Federal refusing to surrender was wounded in the shoulder by J. W. Warwick, Jr. The booty amounted to 15 prisoners, 25 wagons, and 105 horses. Because of high water in the Cowpasture, and the danger of being intercepted if the return were by the Burnsville road, the wagons were set on fire. The wounded Federal recovered. He was a cousin to Mrs. Felix Hull, of McDowell.

Just after the battle of McDowell, which took place May 8th, the two companies, a fine looking and well mounted body of troops, were ordered to report at Staunton. Company G was put on detached service, to scout down the South Branch toward Franklin. Company F was sent to Richmond, and thence on picket duty toward Fredericksburg. Early in July, Company G was sent to Gordonsville to picket the Rapid Anna near that place. July 4, a scouting party from Company F, under command of Lieutenant Henry McClintic, was surprised in Caroline County. Six men escaped, but four—E. B. Williams, M. P. Surber, W. H. Tinsley, and C. Cochran—were captured. After this occurrence, there was some skirmishing with Kilpatrick's men. July 25th, Company F was put into the 17th Battalion, Virginia Cavalry. In a skirmish early in August, Company G lost three men. The captain and A. M. McClintic were wounded and captured and William Thompson was killed. The company, now under Lieutenant Joseph Mayse, was ordered to McDowell on detached service. Shortly afterward the 17th Battalion was detailed to convoy to Richmond the 600 prisoners taken in the battle of Cedar Run. It then rejoined Stonewall Jackson's army, and accompanied it on the flanking movement which brough on the second battle of Manassas. Its position was on Jackson's extreme left. This force reached Middleburg August 28th, where an unusual hospitality was shown to the men, the chronicler being careful to mention that never before had he seen so many pretty young ladies in a small town. But the sound of cannon toward the southeast made it necessary to resume the march, and that night the cavalry were deployed as videttes in front of the infantry. Next day the 17th supported Chew's Battery.

After the Federal lines were broken on the 30th, the cavalry were sent in pursuit.

While General Lee was moving across the Potomac into Maryland, the 17th Batallion and the 12th Virginia Cavalry were ordered to make a demonstration on Martinsburg to keep the Federals there from reënforcing Harper's Ferry. This brought on an engagement at Darkesville, Sept. 6th. The loss of Company E, which was armed with double-barelled shotguns, was four killed and six wounded. Early in November, General W. E. Jones took command of Ashby's old brigade of which the 17th was now a part, and was left in charge of the lower Shenandoah Valley. The 17th was stationed seven miles north of Winchester in order to scout the roads toward Romney. Company G joined the battalion here, and during the remainder of the war the two Bath companies were never separated. In December, Jones made a reconnoissance toward Moorefield. About the middle of February companies I and K were added to the 17th Battalion, which became known as the 11th Virginia Cavalry. Lieutenant A. J. Ware became captain of Company F, and Henry McClintic the first lieutenant. Between Edinburg and Woodstock the 11th encountered the 13th Pennslyvania Cavalry, February 26th, and captured over 200 men.

In April, Colonel L. L. Lomax, a graduate of West Point, took command of the regiment, which on the 21st of the same month, as a part of the brigade under General Jones, began a raid into West Virginia. The whole command was in fine order, the men having fresh mounts. Starting from near Harrisonburg, and moving through Brock's Gap to Moorefield, the South Branch was found so high that it was necessary to go 10 miles up the river to find a ford at all practicable. The crossing was with much difficulty and danger, one member of the 6th Regiment being drowned. At Greenland Gap a Federal force of 150 men was captured, though after considerable delay. At daylight on the 26th, "Red House" was reached. This was a point on the line of Garnett's retreat, nearly two years earlier. The command passed through Preston County, greatly harrassed by bushwhackers. At Evansville the soldiers were permitted to help themselves to the goods of the merchants. One fellow, not knowing what he wanted, tied about a dozen pairs of hoop skirts to his saddle. But General Jones made him get off his horse, put on a pair, and then prominade up and down the street in the presence of the other troops, at the same time giving him a verbal reprimand for burdening his horse with such baggage. The 12th Regiment gained the name of "Calico 12th," from its taking back to Dixie more of that brand of cloth than any other command.

Jones advanced to Morgantown, some of his command pushing onward nearly to Uniontown. He next seized Fairmont, where he captured without any fight the 105th New York Infantry, and some Home Guards, a total of about 800 prisoners. They were released on parole, the Home Guards with the promise that they would behave better in the future. At this town the fine railroad bridge was destroyed. This act was a severe blow to the Federal cause. A pontoon bridge had to be used for the next six months, and a permanent one was not constructed until after the war. Near Bridgeport there was a hot skirmish, in which Company G lost two men. Upon reaching the town some damage was done to the railroad and rolling stock. It was here at Bridgeport that Imboden was to meet Jones, after which the united force was to capture Clarksburg and then wreck the railroad bridges and tunnels in the direction of Parkersburg. But the other command not appearing, Jones moved to Philippi, and learning that Imboden was at Buckhannon, he joined him there, and the united forces advanced to Weston, where they rested a few days. Imboden then went to Sutton, while Jones struck the railroad again, this time at Pennsboro, tearing up the track from that point to Cairo. He then moved to Burning Springs on the little Kanawha, where a vast quantity of oil was set on fire, turning the river into a flaming lake for 12 miles, and killing the timber within a hundred yards of either bank. The next objective was Sutton, where the 11th was detached from the bribade, rejoining it at Warm Springs. After this the old camp near Harrisonburg was reoccupied. The raid had lasted 30 days and was very fatiguing, but resulted in the infliction of much damage and the capture of much livestock.

After a short rest, Jones was ordered to join General J. E. B. Stuart at Culpeper, where in June there was a review of the whole cavalry corps. The spectacle was very imposing. Next day the great cavalry battle of Brandy Station took place, in which the 11th captured a battery and routed a large force of cavalry. For this achievement, Colonel Lomax became a brigadier general. The next fight was at Upperville, where both the Bath companies sustained some loss. In the advance of Lee's army into Pennsylvania, the 11th was on the extreme right, and at Fairfield repulsed the 2d U. U. Cavalry (regulars), this being the regiment of their commander-in-chief before the war.

At the close of this year, General Rosser became the brigade commander. The campaigning of 1864 took place in the valleys of the Shenandoah and the South Branch.

XX

ROSTER OF CONFEDERATE SOLDIERS

EARLY all of the soldiers from Bath in the Confederate army served in the 11th Cavalry and the 52d Infantry of the Virginia Line. The services of the cavalry command are related in a special chapter. The 52d Infantry served first in the brigade of General Edward Johnson, and took part in the battle of McDowell. Then and afterward it was under Stonewall Jackson in the Valley of Virginia and East of the Blue Ridge.

The following roster is a consolidated list, gathered from the rolls collected some years since by the veterans of the county. It is not intended to include men who were not residents of Bath between 1860 and 1865, nor who were not honorably discharged from the Confederate service. The list does not assume to be complete or perfect. It has had the best revision we could command, but the War of 1861 now lies more than 50 years in the past and hence it is all but impossible to attain absolute accuracy.*

So far as our information will permit, each name is followed by these particulars:

1. The company (indicated by letter) and the regiment (by number) in which the soldier served, the regiment being understood to be infantry unless otherwise mentioned.

2. The soldier's rank. Where no rank is mentioned it is to be understood that he was a private.

3. Facts as to being killed, wounded, or taken prisoner, and where and when.

4. If still living, his postoffice address in August, 1917. Where no state name follows the name of the state, an address in Virginia is to be understood.

Names of military prisons are sometimes mentioned in the case of prisoners of war.

Names followed by a star indicate the soldiers who went out on service May 13, 1861, these being the first ones to go from Bath.

The following abbreviations are used in the list:

Capt—captain	wd—wounded in action
Lt—lieutenant	m wd—mortally wounded
Sergt—sergeant	cp—taken prisoner
Corp—corporal	d—died of sickness during the war
Qmr—quartermaster	D—died since the war
k—killed in action	ukn—whereabouts unknown

ROSTER

Acord, George—F—11 Cav—k Wilderness, '64
Adams, William—K—52
Ailstock, Simon—Grays
Ailstock, C. F.—F—11 Cav
Ailstock, Jordan—G—11 Cav—cp—d, prison
Ailstock, Zerubabel*—G—11 Cav—3d Corp.—D
Anderson, William H.*—G—11 Cav—4th Corp.—cp—ukn
Anderson, Samuel—F—11 Cav—4th Corp —D
Archie, Robert—G—11 Cav—D
Archie, Stephen P.—K—52—D
Armstrong, Dr. J. M.—G—11 Cav—Ass't Surgeon—Ardmore, Okla.
Ayers, Stephen P.—K—52
Baldwin, Peter—?—52—D
Beaty, George—Grays—D
Bennett, ——— —Grays—unkn
Bess, Andrew J.—unkn
Bethel, James S.—K—52
Bogan, S. W. B.—?—18 Cav
Bolton, John—Grays
Bonner, S. A.—F—11 Cav —Lt—k Wilderness '64
Bonner, Andrew G.*—Bath Cav
Boone, Walter—K—52—4th Sergt
Booth, ——— —F—11 Cav—West Virginia
Bratton, Andrew S.—F—11 Cav—2d Sergt—D
Bratton, William A.*—F—11 Cav—k—Blackwater '64
Bratton, John F.—F—11 Cav—Bolar
Bratton, James—F—11 Cav—D
Bratton, J. M.—G—11 Cav—Millboro
Bright, Thomas—Grays
Bright, John—Grays—D
Bright, David—Grays—D
Bryan, Dr. C. P.

---

[1]We are indebted to Mr. George W. Wallace for a revision of the roster.

Burger, David—F—11 Cav—D
Burger, Samuel C.—G—11 Cav—D
Burger, William C.—K—52—1st Lt—D
Burns, M. C.—K—52
Burns, Aaron W.—K—52
Burns, Lewis F.—K—52—D
Burns, Hughart M.—?—18 Cav—D
Burns, Pressley—G—11 Cav—D
Burns, John —G—11 Cav—Tex.
Burns, Michael N.—K—52—1st Corp—m wd '62
Burns, Joseph
Carpenter, William R. N.—K—52—d '62
Carpenter, J. W.—?—18 Cav—Burnsville
Carter, Thomas—Grays—D
Cauley, Lee—G—11 Cav—McClung
Cauley, Brown—?—11 Cav—McClung
Chandler, Samuel—F—11 Cav—West Virginia
Chandler, David—?—11 Cav
Chandler, Stround—Grays
Clark, James M.—K—52
Cleek, Eli*—G—11 Cav—D
Cleek, James*—G—11 Cav—D
Cleek, George W.—F—11—Cav—2d Corp.—cp—Darkesville '62—Bolar
Cleek, D. G.—F—11 Cav—wd, Wilderness—'64—D
Cleek, Thomas*
Cleek, Adam G.*—K—52—D
Cleek, Jacob—K—52—D
Cosby, Benjamin—G—11 Cav—D
Cosby, John—G—11 Cav—d, home
Cosby, David—G—11 Cav—D
Coyner, Robert—Grays—D
Coyner, William—Clifton Forge
Criser, William H.*—G—11 Cav—D
Criser, T. J.—G—11 Cav.—D, 1898
Criser, J. Lewis*—F—11 Cav—D
Criser, John S.*—F—11 Cav—Warm Springs
Criser, Robert J.*—F—11 Cav—D
Curry, Alexander—K—52
Curry, Martin V.—K—52—D
Curry, Samuel M.—K—52—D
Curry, Peter S.—K—52—3d Corp—D
Curry, Andrew*—G—11 Cav—D
Curtis, Joseph—Grays
Daggy, John H.—K—52—D
Danellor, William—G—11 Cav—2d Corp—k Blackwater '64
Danellor, F. G.*—unkn

Dangerfield, F. A.*—G—11 Cav—Capt—w and cp, '62—D
Dangerfield, Leroy P.*—wd, Philippi '61—D
Dean, William*—F—11 Cav
Deeds, John L.—D
Dickenson, John S.—F—11 Cav—1st Corp—D
Donovan, Stephen—G—11 Cav
Douglas, B. R.—F—11 Cav —Sitlington
Douglas, Calvin—Grays—k Fisher's Hill '64
Dunlap, Joseph M.—F—11 Cav —1st Sergt
Erwin, William D.—Grays
Erwin, Dr. James R.—G—11 Cav —k Wilderness '64
Foster, David C.—K—52
Fry, James—G—11 Cav
Fry, William—F—11 Cav —D
Garrison, John W.—K—52
Gatewood, A. C. L.—F—11 Cav —2d Lt —wd Darkesville '62
Gay, David*—ukn
Gay, Henry—ukn
George, Samuel F.—ukn
Gibson, Lewis—F—11 Cav
Gibson, Stephen—Grays—D
Gillespie, Joseph G.*—F—11 Cav—m wd '64
Gillespie, John W.—K—52
Gillett, James—K—52—Warm Springs
Gillett, Andrew W.—K—52—Flood
Gillett, John W.—K—52—D
Gillett, William R.—K—52—Color Sergt —D
Gillett, Daniel—Grays—Tex.
Ginger, James*—G—11 Cav —D
Ginger, George—F—11 Cav —k Orange '62
Ginger, Frank—Grays—D
Ginger, Samuel—Grays—Warm Springs
Gladwell, John—G—11 Cav —D
Glendy, R. G.*—G—11 Cav —4th Sergt —D
Glendy, Thomas—G—11 Cav —D
Glendy, John—G—11 Cav —D
Glendy, Benjamin—G—11 Cav
Gordon, James W.—ukn
Green, B. W.—Grays—ukn
Green, William—G—11 Cav —k Upperville '63
Gross, Henry—F—11 Cav k Wilderness '64
Gross, William A.—D
Groves, John, Jr.—K—52
Gwin, J. S.—F—11 Cav
Gwin, James K. P.—F—11 Cav —D
Gwin, William—F—11 Cav—d. diphtheria

Hamilton, Charles*—F—11 Cav —k Edinburg '62
Hamilton, Joseph E.*—F—11 Cav —D
Hamilton, John A.—F—11 Cal—Rockbridge Co.
Hamilton, Charles B.—K—52
Hamilton, C. A.—K—52
Harouff, James—Grays—D
Harris, William—Grays
Haynes, —— —Grays
Heffner, Zebulon—K—52
Hickman, L.—F—11 Cav —D
Hicks, William E.—D
Hite, Allen—D
Hively, Thomas—G—11 Cav —d, home
Hively, George W.—K—52—D
Hodge, James, W. D.—F—11 Cav —D
Hodge, Joseph—Grays—D
Hodge, Reuben—D
Hodge, William—Deerfield
Hoover, John A.—K—52—D
Hoover, Jacob A.—K—52—D
Hoover, William A.—K—52—3d. Sergt —D
Hoover, Samuel—K—52—2d. Corp —D
Hoover, David—G—11 Cav —D
Hopkins, W. H.—G—11 Cav —1st. Sergt —wd Upperville, '63—D
Hughart, Charles A.—K—52—D
Hughart, Robert—Grays—D
Husk, Thomas R.—C—11 Cav —ukn
Huzer, William J.—K—52—ukn
Jack, David—Grays—D
Jack, William, Z. B.—K—52—D
Jack, John H.—K—52—D
Jackson, George—ukn
Jackson, Peyton—G—11 Cav —Richmond
Johnson, —— —G—11 Cav
Jordan, James—F—11 Cav
Jordan, John—F—11 Cav —D
Jordan, William—F—11 Cav —D
Jordan, William D.—Grays
Jordan, William C. S.—Grays—D
Karnes, William H.—G—11 Cav —wd. Brandy, '63—D
Keatz, John—ukn.
Keizer, Marshall D.—K—52
Keizer, H. G.—K—52
Kenny, James—Grays—D
Keyser, James—F—11 Cav —D
Keyser, D. W. C.—F—11 Cav —D

Keyser, Hezekiah*—F—11 Cav
Kincaid, Thomas M.—K—52—D
Kincaid, Floyd—D
Kincaid, James N.—D
Kincaid, Joseph B.*—G—11 Cav —D
Kirpatrick, William, R.—K—52
Kirkpatrick, C. T.—Bolar
Lair, John—D
Landes, Joseph—F—11 Cav
Landes, James
Lange, Henry—G—11 Cav—k Edinburg, '62
Lange, William—unk
Lange, John—G—11 Cav
Law, Aaron—F—11 Cav—k Wilderness, '64
Law, James—G—11 Cav—D
Law Benjamin H.—G—11 Cav—McClung
Law, Stephen—G—11 Cav—D
Lawrence, William—Grays
Lewis, Jasper C.*—G—11 Cav—2d Sergt—Green Valley
Lindsay, John A.—K—52—2d Lt
Lindsay, William
Lindsay, R. D.—?—18 Cav—McClung
Lindsay, Paul—D
Linkswiler, Joseph—K—52—D
Linkswiler, James—K—52—D
Liptrap, David—K—52
Loan, Samuel—K—52—D
Lockridge, Cooper*—G—11 Cav—D
Lockridge, Jacob
Lockridge, David—F—11 Cav—2d Sergt—wd—d, home
Lockridge, L.—Churchville—F—11 Cav—D
Lockridge, John W.—G—11 Cav—D
Lockridge, Andrew J.—?—31—D
Lockridge, Lewis C.—Grays—D
Lockridge, William—D
Lowman, James D.—G—11 Cav—D
Lyle, William A.—K—52—D
Lyle, John—Grays—D
Lyle, Samuel—Grays
Lyle, Benjamin F.—?—18 Cav
Marshall, J. M.—D
Marshall, William—Grays
Martin, W. A.—F—11 Cav
Matheny, Oliver T.—Grays—D
Mayse, Allen—G—11 Cav—D
Mayse, Thomas—G—11 Cav—D

Mayse, Joseph*—G—11 Cav—1st Lt—D
Mayse, Charles F.—G—11 Cav—Fort Lewis
Mayse, Dr. George—G—11 Cav
Mayse, Anderson—F—11 Cav—D
McAllister, John W.—McClung
McChesney, A. G.—F—11 Cav—Capt—resigned, '63—D
McClintic, W. S.—G—11 Cav—D
McClintic, Adam A.*—G—11 Cav—k, Cedar Creek, '64
McClintic, Robert S.—G—11 Cav—k, Patterson's Creek
McClintic, A. B.—G—11 Cav—D
McClintic, John—F—11 Cav—D
McClintic, James—K—52—D
McClintic, Henry—F—11 Cav—1st Lt—D
McClintic, A. M.—G—11 Cav—2d Lt—wd and cp, '62—D
McClintic, G. T.—G—11 Cav—3d Sergt—Tex.
McClung, W. T.—K—52—McClung
McClung, John—Grays—D
McCray, William—Grays—Hot Springs
McDannald, William C.*—F—11 Cav—D
McDannald, George W.—F—11 Cav
McDannald, J. P.—F—11 Cav—Qmr Sergt—D
McDannald, S. Crockett*—G—11 Cav—d, disease, '62
McDannald, W. K.—G—11 Cav—D
McElwee, John—F—11 Cav—d, '64
McElwee, Francis—F—11 Cav
McElwee, William D.—Grays (?)
McElwee, "Bud"—F—11 Cav
McElwee, Divis—F—11 Cav
McElwee, Bernard F.—F—11 Cav
McGuffin, James—F—11 Cav—2d Lt—resigned, '62—D
McMath, Samuel—G—11 Cav—D
McMullen, John—K—52
Miller, John M.—K—52
Miller, Andrew*
Moffett, W. B.—F—11 Cav
Moore, W. H.—F—11 Cav
Moore, —— —Grays
Morris, Joseph
Mustoe, M—F—11 Cav—3d Corp—D
Mustoe, George—F—11 Cav—D
Neff, Allen—?—18 Cav—D
Oliver, C. H.—G—11 Cav
Oliver, Charles—Grays
Oliver, Joseph—G—11 Cav—k (?)
O'Mara, James—F—11 Cav—D
Painter, Alexander—Grays

Painter, James—Grays—D
Painturff, J. H.—F—11 Cav
Palmer, George—Grays
Payne, Charles—G—11 Cav
Payne, George—D
Payne, Lewis—F—11 Cav—4th Corp—cp, Darkesville, '62
Payne, W. G.—F—11 Cav—2d Corp—Charlottesville
Payne, William H.*—F—11 Cav—Alderson, W. Va.
Payne, J. E.—F—11 Cav—Warm Springs
Phillips, Wiliam*—G—11 Cav
Phillips, Thomas*—G—11 Cav
Porter, Andrew S.—F—11 Cav—wd—D
Price, Henry—F—11 Cav—D
Pritt, James—K—52
Propst, James—D
Putnam, Albert—D
Putnam, Samuel—Grays—D
Ratcliff, Warwick C.—K—52—D
Ratcliff, James P.—K—52—D
Ratcliff, William—Grays—D
Ratcliff, —— —Grays—D
Ray, J. Shaw—D
Ray, Thomas T.—Grays—D
Rider, Jacob M.—K—52—D
Ritchie, William*—G—11 Cav—D
Ritchie, Joseph—G—11 Cav
Rithway, William—D
Rogers, Stephen—G—11 Cav
Rogers, J. H.
Rosser, John—F—11 Cav—k, Wilderness, '64
Rourke, Charles K. S.—K—52—D
Rowe, John A.—D
Rucker, —— —Grays—D
Shelton, Thomas A.—K—52—D
Shultz, John—F—11 Cav—D
Shumate, John R.—G—11 Cav
Shumate, William H.*—D
Silver, Joseph—F—11 Cav—Color Sergt—k, Cedar Creek, '64
Simpson, George—G—11 Cav—D
Simpson, John F.—G—11 Cav—D
Simpson, William—G—11 Cav—Millboro Springs
Simpson, Michael—K—52
Sittlington, Alexander H.—F—11 Cav—D
Sively, George L.—F—11 Cav—D
Smith, John—K—52
Smith, James M.—K—52—d, '62

Smith, James—G—11 Cav—D
Smith, Charles—G—11 Cav—D
Smith, Stewart—G—11 Cav—wd—Millboro
Smith, James—F—11 Cav—d, '63
Snead, Anthony—K—52—4th Corp—D
Snead, William—F—11 Cav
Snead, Robert V.—F—11 Cav—D
Snead, Samuel—K—52—D
Snead, John—K—52—D
Sprouse, William—Grays—D
Sprouse, Walker—K—52—D
Stewart, James H.—F—11 Cav—D, 1894
Stinespring, James—Grays—D
Stinespring, Jonathan—D
Surber, M. P.—F—11 Cav—cp, '62
Swartz, John—G—11 Cav
Swartz, Samuel R.—F—11 Cav—cp, Darkesville, '62—D
Swartz, Lewis R.—F—11 Cav—cp, Darkesville, '62—D
Swearingen, James N.—K—52—D
Swearingen, William—Grays—D
Taylor, Almond S.*—G—11 Cav—D
Thomas, Charles—F—11 Cav—Augusta Co.
Thomas, Charles A.*—G—11 Cav—Hot Springs
Thomas, David—F—11 Cav
Thomas, George—F—11 Cav—D
Thomas, Jacob—G—11 Cav—k, Wilderness, '64
Thomas, John J.—K—52
Thomas, John M.—Grays
Thomas, Samuel B.*—F—11 Cav—D
Thompson, Benjamin—G—11 Cav—k, Wilderness, '64
Thompson, Charles*—G—11 Cav—D
Thompson, George—G—11 Cav—D
Thompson, Henry—F—11 Cav
Thompson, Mason—G—11 Cav—d, home
Thompson, William*—G—11 Cav—1st Corp—k, Orange, '62
Tinsley, James—F—11 Cav
Tinsley, William H.—F—11 Cav—cp, '62
True, Thomas—G—11 Cav—D
Tuning, Benjamin—Grays
Tyree, Larkin B.—K—52
Tyree, W. W.
Vance, Charles—Grays—D
Venable, William G.—k Cedar Run '62
Vess, George W.—K—52—k Cedar Run '62
Vess, Jacob—Grays—D
Wallace, Andrew—G—11 Cav—mt Wd—Patterson's Creek

ROSTER OF CONFEDERATE SOLDIERS 161

Wallace, Christopher R.*—F—11 Cav —D
Wallace, John S.—Sunrise
Wallace, M. W.—11 Cav—3d Corp—cp, Darkesville—d, Camp Chase '62
Wallace, William H.—Lewiston, Wash.
Walton, Benjamin F.—K—52—Capt—mstwd Port Republic '62
Walton, John A.—K—52—k, Port Republic, '62
Walton, Thomas—F—11 Cav —K
Ware, A. J.—F—11 Cav—Capt—D—1898
Warwick, John A.*—G—11 Cav—3d Lt—D, 1900
Warwick, J. W., Jr.—G—11 Cav —Hot Springs
Wilfong, Jacob—F—11 Cav —Hot Springs
Wilkenson, James—F—11 Cav —D
Wilkenson, Robert—G—11 Cav —Warm Springs
Williams, Anthony M.*—G—11 Cav
Williams, Charles—Grays—D
Williams, E. B.—F—11 Cav—1st Corp—cp '62
Williams, Erasmus F.*—G—11 Cav —Hot Springs
Williams, Harry—G—11 Cav
Williams, James*—G—11 Cav
Williams, Lewis H.*—G—11 Cav
Williams, Thomas—K—52
Williams, T. J.—F—11 Cav —Healing Springs
Wilson, William—K—52
Windom, John—F—11 Cav
Windom, Charles W.—K—52
Wine, Robert E.
Withrow, Jacob E.—G—11 Cav
Witt, J. J.
Wood, P. A.—F—11 Cav—d, prison
Wood, Frank—Grays—d, prison
Woodzell, William—G—11 Cav —Warm Springs
Woodzell, George—K—52
Woodzell, Benjamin—Grays—D
Wright, John—Grays

XXI

CLOVERDALE

N THE northeast of Bath is the elevated, fertile valley lying between Walker's and Shenandoah mountains. The summers are cool, the scenery is attractive, the grazing is superior. The position is on the natural route used by the Harrisonburg and Warm Springs Turnpike. The timbered mountains, containing deposits of iron ore, give the locality a prospective industrial importance. Last, but not least, this belt of upland, known as Cloverdale, or the Wilderness, is associated with some interesting events in American history.

John Mathews, an immigrant from Ulster, settled about 1742 in Rockbridge County a little above Balcony Falls. Of his ten children Sampson and George acquired fame and fortune. When only about twenty-one years old, Sampson was a reader in the "chapel of care" near his father's home. His services were discontinued in 1759 owing to the partial depopulation of the neighborhood as a result of the Indian war. In 1762, or perhaps earlier, these brothers went into the mercantile business at Staunton. Their store, which was at the northeast corner of Beverly and Augusta streets, seems to have been on the lot which they purchased in 1760 for $100. Their business prospered and they opened stores at other points. With Jacob Lockhart as a partner they conducted one at Lexngton. They also acquired considerable land. In 1765 they bought a large tract near Staunton between the famous hills known as Betsy Bell and Mary Gray. In the same year they purchased 1200 acres on Elk Run, this being the starting-point of their Cloverdale estate. The price was 61 cents an acre. Five years later they patented 2080 acres adjacent. They also owned several small tracts on the Cowpasture.

Like most Virginians of the time previous to the war of 1861, Sampson and George Mathews preferred the country to the town. They at length made their home on the Cloverdale purchase, George styling his residence "Market Hill." He lived here until 1785. Sampson removed to Augusta in 1791. A little before the outbreak of the Revolution in 1775 the brothers built a store at Cloverdale.

Their success in business demonstrated their executive ability. Being also of great energy and influence, they were drawn irresistibly into public and military life. Sampson was nominated for a seat on the county court in 1765, when he could not have been more than twenty-eight years old. He was by this time the proprietor of the most fashionable of the hostelries at Staunton. George was likewise a member of the court and in 1770 was sheriff of Augusta. In 1776 he represented the county in the House of Burgesses.

In the Point Pleasant campaign, Sampson Mathews had charge of the commissary department of the army under Lewis. As a colonel of militia he saw active service in the war for American Independence. In July, 1781, he was quelling the tory organization of William Ward in Pendleton. A little later he was leading his regiment in the Yorktown campaign. In the preceding year he was a member of the State Senate. He favored the formation of Bath and took an active part in its organization. He died in Augusta in 1807 at the age of about seventy. His first wife, to whom he was married in 1759, was Mary, a sister to his partner, Jacob Lockhart. Other sisters were the wives of Matthew Arbuckle and William Ward of Greenbrier. The last wife was Mary, a daughter of Jacob Warwick. His sons identified themselves with Greenbrier County. It is curious to note that in spite of the services of Colonel Mathews he was so lax in the matter of intoxicants as to expose himself to the action of the grand jury by selling them contrary to the regulations of law.

The following is one of his official letters during the Revolution:

Cloverdale 26th Sep 1781

Sir

  I Recd your Excellencys favor (of the 14th Instant) on the 24th I have ordered 200 beef Cattle & 30 Waggons Loaded with stores & Spirits to be at Colo Esoms ordinary on Saturday the 6th nex month & So proceed with all Expedition To the army & Expect at Least 150 or 160 head of Cattle & 20 or 25 Waggons will at that Time make their appearance

  I also will forward in about 5 Days after 80 or 100 cattle & 5 or 6 waggons, which will be the whole that Posibly can be furnished from ye County. I have the honor to be with Much Esteem & Respect

Your Excellencys
obt humbl Servt
SAMP MATHEWS

It was the younger brother, George, who became the more prominent man. When only twenty-two years old he led a band against the Indians and was victor in a sharp skirmish, the foe losing nine of their number, against three on his own side. In the Point Pleasant campaign he commanded a company under Colonel Charles Lewis. Not one of his 60 men was under six feet in height, and many stood six feet two inches. It was these husky fellows who helped to decide the day at Point Pleasant. His company was one of the three that turned the flank of Cornstalk's line and caused the Indians to think the Fincastle regiment had come to the rescue.

Soon after the Revolution broke out, George Mathews was made lieutenant colonel of the Ninth Virginia Regment of the Continental Line. For a while he was stationed east of the Chesapeake. He then joined the army under Washington and in February, 1777, was promoted to the rank of colonel. At Germantown, his regiment, 400 strong, was a part of the left wing under General Greene. This able leader had turned the British right, and the Americans were on the point of gaining a complete victory, when a thick fog settled over the field. In the confusion that followed, the "tall Virginians" of Mathews were outflanked, but did not surrender until reduced to the equivalent of a single company. Colonel Mathews received several wounds in this battle and was not exchanged until December, 1781. His health being somewhat impaired by his long captivity, he retired to Market Hill to provide for the needs of his large family. General Greene, who put a high estimate on his ability, importuned him to join the army in the South. Mathews at first demurred. He wrote Greene that he had been in easy circumstances when the war began, but was now "with care & rigid economy endavoring to presarve from rail want a wife and eight helpless children." But he yielded to Greene's wishes and took command of the Third Virginia Regiment. When the British evacuated Charleston in 1782, he had the satisfaction of turning the tables on his late captors by riding into the city by the side of his commander-in-chief.

The visit to the South led to his removal to Georgia in 1785. As a representative from his adopted state he sat in the First Congress, 1789-91. He was governor of Georgia in 1787-8 and again in 1793-6. He was also a member of its first constitutional convention. During hs second term as governor, Mathews signed very reluctantly and under pressure the charter of the Yazoo company to lands in what is now Alabama and Mississippi. But the concern was fraudulent and shares of its stock were distributed among members of the legislature to influence their votes. After a hot fight the graft was exposed and came to grief. The governor was not designedly a party to what went into history as the "Yazoo land steal," and did not line his own pockets through its corruption. But his popularity was temporarily eclipsed. John Adams nominated him for the governorship of Mississippi Territory, but withdrew his name owing to the reluctance of the senate. Mathews was so angry that he rode horseback to Philadelphia, strode into the president's room wearing his old sword and his three-cocked hat, and gave the first magistrate of the land a a "tongue lashing." But as he was a Federalist, like Adams himself, he was soon pacified.

At the outset of the war of 1812, Mathews was a brigadier general of militia and was stationed on the frontier of Florida, then under the ownership of Spain. He was also appointed one of two commissioners to receive Florida, if offered to the United States, or to seize it if any third power attempted to do so. Mathews was an expansionist and believed in taking over the peninsula. He abetted the insurgents in Florida, occupied the fort on Amelia Island, put out the Spanish officials, and raised the American flag. Spain remonstrated at what was technically a breach of international law, and as the administration did not choose to incur the risk of fighting two enemies at the same time, Mathews was removed. He was on his way to Washington to talk to Madison as he had talked to Adams, but was taken ill at Savannah and died there in 1812 at the age of 73.

General Mathews was a short, heavily built man, with a florid face and light red hair. He walked very erect with his head thrown back. He was of eccentric manner and very positive convictions, not conceding that any man was his superior except Washington himself. He was married in 1762 to Ann Paul. Two of his sons were given land in Ohio and two daughters had lands in Kentucky.

According to some authorities, Mathews County, Virginia, was named for George Mathews.

In the year of his return to Augusta, Sampson Mathews mortgaged the Cloverdale tract of 2080 acres to Gabriel Jones, a once famous lawyer who lived near Port Republic. Shortly afterward a portion was conveyed to Samuel Blackburn and the remainder to other persons.

General Blackburn, who married Anne, a daughter of George Mathews, in 1785, was born about 1758 and was admitted to the bar in 1796. He was a graduate of Liberty Hall Academy—now Washington and Lee University—and a soldier of the Revolution. He went first to Kentucky and then to Georgia, to practice law, but the clamor against his father-in-law caused him to leave the latter state in disgust. He returned to Virginia and built the old brick mansion on what is now called the "Wilderness" property. In 1824 he had 1000 acres under cultivation. Blackburn was an orator and a criminal lawyer of repute. While sitting in the General Assembly he secured the passage of an anti-duelling law. In politics he was a Federalist. He died in 1835, freeing his 40 slaves by will and giving $500 to the Staunton Bible Society. There were no children and the estate fell into neglect.

John Kephart had been a lessee of Cloverdale in 1789. The property at length passed into the hands of Louis C. Barley, of Alexandria, who has acquired mountain lands adjacent until his holdings aggregate 47,000 acres.

Judge Barley is a great friend to industrial development and has put himself to much effort in the way of developing the natural resources of Bath. It is through his exertions that a railroad spur has been built up Mill Creek to afford an outlet for the millions of feet of merchantable lumber on the mountain sides. There is a reasonable hope that this beginning will lead to a permanent railroad. This would prove of much moment in the future development of this and nearby counties.

XXII

THE CALFPASTURE VALLEY

THOUGH not a portion of Bath, the main valley of the Calfpasture is closely associated with this county. At the time of early settlement it was undoubtedly open ground, and was shut off from the country around Staunton by timbered mountains. Access to the Cowpasture was rendered easy by Panther Gap and by the great depression at the south end of Shenandoah Mountain. Some of the pioneers, or members of their households, speedily began to move in this direction, thus establishing ties of relationship and interest with the people of Bath.

The valley of the Little Calfpasture is more distinctly a part of the great Valley of Virginia, and is not considered in the present chapter. On the other hand, Mill Creek, though coursing mainly in Bath, is a tributary of the Great Calfpasture. Locally, the two Calfpasture streams are known as Great River and Little River.

Actual settlement on Great River can scarcely have begun much earlier than 1743. The author of *Annals of Augusta* claims that this valley was settled quite as early as the district around Staunton, yet offers no evidence in proof. The records of Augusta, especially the muster rolls of 1742, do not support the statement.

The first constables were Robert Graham and William Hodge, appointed February 28, 1745. William Jameson was made a captain the same year to succeed Alexander Dunlap, appointed in August, 1743. In 1744 Henry Gay was made a lieutenant.

Acting under an order of council, John Lewis and James Patton surveyed in 1744 a tract nearly fifteen miles long, but nowhere more than about one and one-eighth miles broad. Their map shows it cross-sectioned into twenty-three lots, the first lying where Goshen now stands and the last rather to the north of Deerfield. With a single exception, every lot had already been taken by some settler. The following tabular statement shows consecutively the number of the lot, the name of the settler, the acreage, the purchase price, when stated in the deed, and the early transfers of title. In those instances where the deed was issued to some other individual than the original settler, the name is given in brackets. The name of a wife is also thus given.

1. Alexander Dunlap (John Dunlap)—625—$68.69—295 acres sold to Robert Dunlap, 1761, for $333.33.
2. William Jameson—170—$20.87.
3. Thomas Gilham—168—$18.86—sold, 1752, by Thomas (Margaret) Gilham to James Lockridge for same price—resold, 1767, by John Dickenson to William Thompson for $200.
4. Robert Crockett—370—$41.15—sold, 1760, by pioneer's sons:—James (Martha) and Robert, Jr. (Janet), both of Mecklenburg County, N. C., to William Thompson for $200—295 acres sold by Thompson, 1767, for $166.67.
5. David Davis—290—$29—sold, 1749, by Lewis and Patton to John Poage.
6. Thomas Weems—525—$31.10—sold, 1768, by Thomas (Eleanor) Weems to William Given for $723.33.
7. Henry Gay—694—$33.39—100 acres sold, 1769, to James Frasier for $33.33.
8. Francis Donally—266—$30.02.
9. Robert Gay—519—$57.89.
10. Samuel Hodge—449—$47.97.
11. John Miller—316—$70.08—sold by John (Ann) Miller to John Ramsay, 1757.
12. Loftus Pullin—252 (240?)—$26.92—sold to James Shaw, 1760, for $30—sold by Shaw to John Ramsay, 1768, for $150.
13. Robert Bratton—834—$96.67—400 acres sold to James Bratton, 1771, for $133.33.
14. James Lockridge—280—?—sold by James (Isabella) Lockridge to Andrew Lockridge, 1764, for $66.67.
15. John Graham—696—$79.58—150 acres sold to James Graham (son), 1763, for $16.67.
16. Robert Gwin—544—?—sold by William (Agnes) Gwin to Robert Lockridge, 1766, for $575.
17. John Preston—1054—$31.15—520 acres sold by William (Susanna) Preston to Mary Preston, 1762, for $333.33. The same sold by Mary Preston to Robert Lockridge, 1763, for $366.67.
18. William Warrick—1060—$118.67—sold, 1745, to John Kincaid.
19. James Carlile—600—$65.39—250 sold, 1753, to John Carlile, and sold by him, 1762, to Thomas Hughart for $166.67—200 acres sold by John (Mary) Carlile to Thomas Adams, 1796, for $391.67.
20. Jacob Clements—457—$51.67—202 acres sold, 1751, by Jacob (Mary) Clements to John Campbell for $66.67, and sold by John (Ann) Campbell, 1768, to James Carlile for $250.
21. John Campbell—308—$34.17—208 acres sold by Samuel Campbell to William Lockridge, 1769, for $713.33.
22. James Carter—300—$33.38—sold to Robert Gay, 1746.
23. John Wilson—600—$66.

Not all the original claimants were actual settlers on the survey, but lived on the Beverly or Borden grants and took lands here for speculation or for their sons. This seems to be the case with Crockett, Davis, Donally, Miller, and Preston. Miller is named as a resident of Albemarle.

The first deeds were issued mainly in April and July, 1745, and in Orange County. Carlile, Graham, and Weems did not take deeds until 1748.

Mention of the Calfpasture families in general is given in a later chapter. Thomas Adams came from New Kent County and was a local magnate. He was one of the exceedingly few men of his time to own a "chariot." By his will he freed a slave, "as there is no man to whom I consider myself under greater obligations than to my slave, Joe."

James Carter was a millwright, and his mill is named in early road orders. He was in the Carolinas in 1748, but must have returned. He died in 1768.

The Calfpasture families not only took a very prominent part in settling the valleys of Bath and Highland, and afterward those of Greenbrier and Pocahontas, but they helped to people the uplands of the Carolinas. They were also prompt in taking a share in the settling of Kentucky. In 1779, Captain James Gay and Alexander Dunlap, Jr., headed a party which settled in the blue-grass region of that state and founded Pisgah church, said to be the first Presbyterian organization in Kentucky. The school which grew up by the side of the church developed into Transylvania University.

Gay, who was but twenty-one years old when he turned westward, had served under Andrew Lockridge. His second wife was Elizabeth, a daughter of John Dunlap. He was himself a son of James Gay, who married Jean Warwick. Alexander Dunlap, Jr., married his sister, Agnes. Major Samuel Stevenson, whose mother was a daughter of John Warwick, was a third member of the emigrating party, and he also wedded a Gay. Thus the Gays, Dunlaps, and Stevensons, as well as the Hamiltons, Kinkeads, Warwicks, and other Calfpasture families, have gained both affluence and prominence in the Bluegrass State and other commonwealths of the Great West. A Warwick gave his name in a changed spelling to Warrick County, Indiana. Lieutenant-Governor Walkup, of California, was a descendant of Captain John Walkup, who came to the Calfpasture about 1760.

So great was this exodus that in time it nearly extinguished the Calfpasture surnames of the Revolutionary period.

Because of the homogeneity between the early populations of Bath and the Calfpasture, there were many persons who thought the latter region should be included in the new county. Geographic considerations appeared to link it with Bath rather than Augusta. But there was a difference of opinion on this matter among the inhabitants of the Calfpasture itself, and the stronger voice prevailed.

Rocky Spring church was built on an acre deeded in 1773 by Andrew Kincaid, Jr., to the "trustees of a congregation of dissenters." These trustees were James Bratton, Lancelot Graham, Andrew Hamilton, Thomas Hughart, William Kincaid, and Andrew Lockridge.

It seems to have been on the Calfpasture that Charles Knight was to have $60 for teaching one year, every half Saturday or every other Saturday to be free time. In case of an Indian alarm Knight was to have the privilege of being lodged in the neighborhood.

The names below are appended to a petition of May 27, 1779. The signers are not in favor of being included in a new county lying mainly to the west of Shenandoah Mountain:

Armstrong, Archible	Gay, William	McCutchen, Joseph
Armstrong, John	Griffith, James	McCutchen, Robert
Armstrong, Thomas	Graham, John	McCutchen, William
Armstrong, William	Graham, John	Meek, Daniel
Bell, John	Graham, William	Meek, John
Black, John (1)	Gwin, Robert (1)	Meek, Samuel
Black, John (2)	Gwin, Robert (2)	Meek, Thomas
Bratton, Adam	Hamilton, Alexander	Moorhead, Matthew
Bratton, Robert	Hamilton, Andrew	Plunkett, John
Byrnes, John	Henderson, James	Ramsay, John
Carlisle, James	Henry, James	Reagh, James
Carlisle, John	Hoge, John	Right, William
Cashader, Micol	Kinkead, David	Stewart, Alexander
Clark, James	Kinkead, John	Vacob, Joseph
Davis, Charles	Kinkead, Thomas (1)	Vachub, Matthew
Divet, Tolly	Kinkead, Thomas (2)	Vachube, John
Elliot, John	Kinkead, William	Vachube, Robert
Fortner, William	Martin, Samuel	Walker, John
Fulton, James	Martin, William	White, Archible
Fulton, John	Marton, John	Wright, John
Fulton, Thomas	McCutchen, John	

Additional Names on an Undated Petition.

Aikman, William	Craig, William	Montgomery, John
Armstrong, W. M.	Hodge, Andrew	Mongomery, John
Barker, Edward	Jones, William	Meteer, William
Berry, James	Lockridge, John	Moor, William
Butler, Patrick	Lockridge, Samuel	Page, James
Carson, Thomas	McConnell, Alexr	Peery, James
Craig, Alexander	McNight, Tadey	Thompson, Alexander
Craig, James	McCutchen, James	Youll, William

XXIII

THE BATH OF TODAY

THERE are really two Bath Counties in Virginia. They occupy the same geographic area, but are very unlike one another.

There is first the old Bath, given to agriculture and stockraising, and peopled by the descendants of the pioneers and the later comers. Since the war of 1861 its advance has been at a leisurely pace, such innovations as modern farm machinery, the silo, the telephone, and the automobile being primarily due to influences from without. Toward the other Bath, its attitude is very much that of a spectator. In some measure the old Bath is directly or indirectly supported by the other, but between them there is in the nature of the case but little community of feeling.

There is second the tourist Bath, created by the mineral springs, the mountain climate, and the shortness of time in which it may be reached from the great centers of American population. This Bath is largely though not wholly localized in Warm Springs valley. The characteristic human element in the tourist Bath is the throng of visitors, most numerous in spring and fall. To these must be added the families who have built mansions or cottages, so as to make this valley an adjunct home. And as a great share of the inflow is from the city of New York, distant only a night's journey by the express train, it is hardly an exaggeration to call Hot Springs a detached suburb of the great American metropolis. The people who frequent the hostelries of Warm Springs valley are mainly of the wealthy and exclusive classes. It is thus that between them and the native element, save in exceptional instances, there can be little in common. Each Bath lives to itself.

Dependent on and called into being by the tourist Bath is a third population which is characteristically a labor class. This element is quite considerable in number and quite varied in composition. It is largely derived from without the county, and in a great degree it is concentrated in Warm Springs valley. This class has had much to do with the steady increase of the total population. To the north is

Highland with an almost exclusive agricultural interest and a slowly declining population. To the south is Alleghany, where a diversified industrial interest heavily dominates, and because of which the aggregate population tends to increase.

The visitor who makes a comprehensive tour of Bath is struck by the seeming smallness of the number of people on the farms, and by the large areas of hill and mountain which remain very nearly as much a wilderness as they were when the first pathfinders arrived. The river-bottom lands have been continuously occupied since the dawn of settlement. Not a few of the holdings are owned by progressive farmers and are valuable properties. But the natural increase in population has ever been much more inclined to migrate to newer regions than to reduce to tillage the much inferior uplands. No large inroad has been made into these, and on some roads one may travel several miles without passing a house. The imperfect railroad facilities are somewhat adverse to intensive farming, which has the effect of arresting the decline in population of strictly rural communities. Yet there is an increased demand for the minor products of the farm, and a beginnig has been made in commercial orcharding.

Turning to Warm Springs valley, whose limestone soils point to grazing farms, one is impressed by the extent to which this exceptional basin has been turned into a recreation ground. The present considerable population is dependent on the soil only in a slight degree.

The main line of the Chesapeake and Ohio railroad touches just one limited stretch of good agricultural land; that which is immediately tributary to Millboro Station, where quite a village has grown up. After coursing through it two miles, the steel track plunges into a tunnel, beyond which it follows the exceedingly rough and almost unpeopled valley of Padd's Creek. The branch line from Covington merely traverses a few miles of the indifferent Cedar Creek valley and reaches only to the upper end of Hot Springs Gap.

A complete railroad development of the Virginias would include a through line from the Potomac to the upper James by way of the South Branch and Jackson's River valleys. At all events, an electric line through this long district could be of great service to it, and the necessary motive power could be secured by harnessing the rapidly flowing rivers.

The metallic resources of this county are not inconsiderable, but must await the hour when the ores that are more readily reduced have diminished greatly in amount.

The future of Bath is to be read in its past and present. It will remain to a somewhat increasing extent a recreation field for the tourist element. Agriculture will slowly become intensive and its output more valuable. Relatively, the rural population will hold its own, and is not likely to be supplanted in any marked degree by a tide of new immigration. The highways will very noticeably improve, both with respect to roadbed and bridges. The present degree of inconvenience in reaching the outside towns and markets will diminish. In a word, we may confidently expect that the county will develop into a still better place in which to live.

Since 1860, the increase in population is shown in these census returns:

1870—3795   1900—5595
1880—4482   1910—6538
1890—4587

Considered by districts, there are these contrasts between 1890 and 1910:

	1890	1910
Cedar Creek	867	2472
Millboro	1542	1418
Warm Springs	1058	1360
Williamsville	1120	1258

In 1910, the whites numbered 5362 and the negroes 1176. Of the whites, 115 were of foreign birth, and 134 were of foreign or mixed parentage. Of the foreign born, 28 were from Italy, 20 from Greece, 17 from Germany, 15 from Sweden, 14 from Ireland, and 12 from England. Only 12 of the 115 had taken the trouble to make themselves fully naturalized ctizens. Of the negroes 276 were classed as mulattoes. The white males were 2821 and the white females 2541. The males of voting age were 1818, although but 527 of the number cast ballots for the three leading presidential candidates of 1912. Of these 1818, there were 111 illiterate whites and 83 illiterate negroes. The persons between the ages of 6 and 14 were

1332, of whom 842 were in school. The dwellings numbered 1195 and the families 1225. The average of persons to the family was 5.3, against 4.9 for the state at large.

The 563 farms of the county had a valuation per acre of $6.05. They covered 41,323 acres of improved land, which is one-ninth of the entire surface. Of the farms 13.2 per cent. were operated by tenants. There were 1475 horses, 80 mules, 5980 cattle, 3711 hogs, and 16608 sheep and goats. The value of all farm property, including improvements and domestic animals, was $2,958,186. The acreage and yield of the leading farm crops present this exhibit:

Corn	4,405 acres	112,895 bushels
Wheat	2,567 acres	36,816 bushels
Oats	459 acres	6,912 bushels
Potatoes	198 acres	18,345 bushels
Hay	8,027 acres	8,645 tons

XXIV

ALLEGHANY COUNTY

ALLEGHANY was carved out of Bath, Botetourt, and Monroe, Bath contributing the most important portion. The Act of Assembly creating the county was passed January 5, 1822. A portion of Monroe was annexed in 1843, and a very small portion of Bath in 1847. On the other hand a part of Alleghany was annexed to Craig in 1856.

Nearly all the preceding chapters of this book deal very much in matters which concern the Alleghany area as well as the Bath. Also, what has been said of the general characteristics of the mountains, streams, soils, climate, plants, and animals of Bath applies nearly as well to Alleghany. The climate of the valleys is a little warmer because the altitudes are less.

A striking difference in the physical geography lies in the circumstance that in this locality every mountain ridge east of the Alleghany Front opens to give passage to the James, just as the corresponding ridges 200 miles northward open to give passage to the Potomac. In each instance nature has indicated a route for an important line of railway between the Atlantic seaboard and the Great West. As a consequence of this continuous cleft in the ridges of Alleghany, Jackson's and Cowpasture rivers, and Dunlap and Potts creeks are converging streams, and each is followed by a railroad line. And since the mountains of this county are stored with mineral wealth, the transportation and industrial interests very much outweigh the agricultural.

The counties of Pocahontas and Alleghany were created during the same session of the legislature. It is said that the intention was to call the western county Alleghany and the eastern Pocahontas, but that the heedlessness of the engrossing clerk caused the names to be transposed. The first should have had the name Alleghany, since it lies in the midst of what are in this latitude the loftiest heights of the Appalachian system.

Alleghany has a length of 40 miles, a breadth of 26, and an area of 462 square miles. The census figures by decades are these:

1830—2816	1880—5586
1840—2749	1890—9283
1850—3515	1900—16330
1860—6765	1910—19921
1870—3674	

By districts the population in 1910 was as follows:

Boiling Spring	2794
Clifton	4415
Covington	6974
Clifton Forge (city)	5748

By the last Federal census Alleghany had 574 farms, of which one-sixth were operated by tenants. The valuation per acre was $7.43. There were 32,699 acres of improved land, covering about one-ninth of the county. The value of all farm property, inclusive of improvements and domestic animals, was $2,092,552. There were 1267 horses, 68 mules, 4563 cattle, 2487 hogs, and 5558 sheep and goats. The leading crops were as follows with respect to acreage and yield:

Corn	5,023 acres	121,048 bushels
Wheat	2,535 acres	28,456 bushels
Oats	659 acres	8,389 bushels
Potatoes	434 acres	43,159 bushels
Hay	4,210 acres	4,376 tons

Alleghany has three times as many people as Bath, yet its total farm valuation is 3 per cent. less. The leading farm crops rank about the same, but Alleghany stands much lower in its number of farm animals. It outclasses the older county in such minor crops as potatoes and cabbages, and in orchard and small fruits. The explanation of the above facts is quite plain. Outside of the limited bottom lands, neither county is well enough suited to general farming. The uplands are too rough and stony. But in grazing and fruit culture, and in some other specialized lines, these counties can hold their own against many others. The future of agriculture in this mountain region lies not in the time-honored field tillage, which is adapted only to level or nearly level lands, but in those special products which are indicated by soil, climate, and contour, and by the nearness to large markets. Mountain counties are constrained to give much attention to general field crops so long as they are remote from market. But as soon as this remoteness is removed and they are brought into competition with prime agricultural districts, general tillage is forced into the background, no matter how ample the marketing facilities may be.

The highways of Alleghany are in better order than those of Bath, and a considerable mileage is macadamized.

As early as 1800 there were several furnaces and forges with a capacity of one to three tons a day. They used charcoal and water-driven triphammers. Stoves, pots, skillets, and pipe were manufactured before the war of 1861.

The mountains of this county contain immense deposits of iron ore. There are now six large furnaces, but it is useless to expect that iron mining will assume very great dimensions, so long as there are large beds of loose ore in the Lake Superior region that can be scooped up with a steam shovel.

The other mineral resources are of much importance. They include very large deposits of limestone, in addition to cement rock, marl, magnesia, brick, clay, and slate.

Among the scenic features and natural curiosities is the cascade where Falling Spring Run, itself the outlet of a mammoth spring, passes through Little Mountain by a watergap. Toward the lower end of the gap the waters plunge 70 feet over a precipice of marl and enter the deep lower valley leading to Jackson's River. One is now almost compelled to speak of the fall in the past tense. The waters have been turned aside in order to give better excess to the immense cliff of marl which the stream has built up from the leachings of the limestone strata in the upper valley. The manufacturing plant is located at the railroad station of Barber on Jackson's River. From the standpoint of the picturesque, it is to be regretted that the cascade has been done away with, at least for a time.

A waterfall of far greater volume occurs in Jackson's River, where that stream passes through White Mountain between Covington and Clifton Forge. It was described by Jefferson. A little below Clifton Forge the same river passes through the Iron Gate, a short, sharp-sided gorge that has much the same form as the notch which is cut into a tree in the process of felling. A railroad track follows one side of the defile and a wagon road the other. Midway between Covington and Hot Springs is the Natural Well. The opening is only about three feet in diameter, but not far below the surface the well widens very greatly, forming a considerable cavern.

The James River and Kanawha Canal was projected to Covington, but never built above Buchanan. A convention was held at Covington, October 19, 1846, to discuss the improvement of the James and the Great Kanawha. Delegates came from the county itself, and from Bath, Botetourt, Greenbrier, Kanawha, Mercer, Pocahontas, Roanoke, and Rockbridge. The meeting was in favor of bringing the canal to Covington and then securing a railroad. If this were denied it was claimed that the region would be almost depopulated by emigration to the West. It was shown that most of the counties represented were virtually without a market, owing to the prohibitive cost of transportation. Coal, wheat, and fruit could not be sent abroad, and the attention of the farmers had to be centered on stock growing. With the canal at Covington, it was asserted that there would be a probable increase yearly of 15,000 tons of traffic in farm produce and 8,000 tons of merchandise. The cost per ton in moving freight could thus be reduced from $5 to $1.50.

In 1857 the rails were laid to Jackson's River. Ten years later, construction was resumed, and by the end of 1872 there was a through line to the Ohio. The influence on the later history of Alleghany has been very marked.

Covington was designated as a town in 1833 and incorporated in 1873. In 1840 it contained about 50 houses. In 1867 it was still an inland village looking much like those county seats that still lie remote from the railroad. Even in 1890 the population was only 704. Since then Covington has steadily grown into a little city that was credited with 4234 people in 1910, and is larger today. Its industrial interests are very important. Far in the lead is the extensive plant of the West Virginia Pulp and Paper Company, opened in 1900. Others are an extract plant—the only one of its kind in the United States—an iron furnace, a tannery, machine shops, brick works, an ice factory, and two large flouring mills. The pulp and paper works are the second largest in the country. Most of the growth of Covington having taken place within the last twenty years, the town has a quite modern appearance. In fact, the size of the place is not in proportion to its industrial and commercial importance.

Twelve miles down Jackson's River is Clifton Forge, an incorporated city and politically independent of Alleghany County. It is situated among very bold river-hills, and unlike what is true of Covington, there is a very inconsiderable amount of arable land in the near vicinity. Clifton Forge is the metropolis of the county, having a population in 1910 of 5748. Originally the site of an iron furnace, Clifton Forge is now almost exclusively a railroad town ,and is a division point in the Chesapeake and Ohio system. What there is of river-bottom is covered by the railway yard with its extensive sidings. It is here that the James River division leaves the main line and runs with a constant down grade to Richmond, 231 miles distant. This was at first an independent road, and was built as the Richmond and Alleghany. The easy down grade is why this line is used mainly for freight, all express trains using the main line.

The minor towns of the county, such as Lowmoor, Iron Gate, and Longdale, are exclusively industrial, and are mainly devoted to the smelting of iron. The population of Iron Gate by the last census was 600.

The first meeting of the county court was held at Covington, March 18, 1822. William Herbert was the first surveyor and sheriff, Oliver Callaghan the first county clerk, Thoms Crutchfield the first commonwealth's attorney, and William S. Holloway the first commissioner of the revenue.

The number of men liable to poll tax was 534. The first levy was $1361.70, out of which there was an appropriation of $1068 for the first county buildings.

The following is a list of the justices previous to the time when they became elective instead of appointive. The names with a star are those who were present on the opening day of the first court. The names with a date are those whose commissions were subsequent to July, 1823:

ALLEGHANY COUNTY 181

Allen, John—1831	Keyser, Joseph D.*
Aritt, Michael*	Kincaid, Robert
Aritt, John	King, Charles—1839
Bishop, Jacob—1846	Knox, Rev. Elisha
Boswell, John L.	Pitzer, John L.—1846
Callaghan, John*	Mann, Moses H.
Callaghan, Charles	Mann, Lewis T.—1846
Carpenter, Samuel—1838	Morton, William F.—1846
Crow, John	Persinger, John
Davis, Jesse*	Persinger, Peter
Harry, John—1831	Persinger, Lee—1839
Harnsbarger, Sebas	Sancy, Sampson
Haynes, William H.	Smith, Henry—1831
Holloway, John*	Steele, Isaac
Holloway, William G.	Warren, James—1839
Hook, Stephen	

Of the original board, Massie and Keyser were empowered by the legislature to administer the oath of office to the other members. The justices elected in 1852 were as follows:

First District: Peter Helminstoller, William Herbert, John C. Taylor, James Warren.

Second District: Jacob Bishop, Samuel Brown, Jr., Lewis F. Mann, Thomas Richardson.

Third District: John A. Black, James Harnsbarger, John J. Paxton, James Shanklin.

Fourth District: Samuel Carpenter, Charles King, Madison Hook, William F. Morton.

The recommendations by the first court for officers of the militia were these: Colonel, John Crow; Lieutenant-Colonel, John Persinger; Major, William H. Haynes; Captains, Moses H. Mann, Anthony Brennemer, George Arritt; Lieutenants, Jacob Fudge, Moses Smith.

Further recommendations for the First Battalion, 128th Regiment, were as follows: Captain, John Callaghan; Lieutenant, Cornelius Vanstavern; Ensigns, David Johnson, William Mann, Joseph Pitzer. For the Second Battalion, they were Robert Griffith as captain; William G. Holloway and Barton Shawver as lieutenants, and George Pitzer and Alexander Johnston as ensigns.

The first tavern license was granted to Fleming Keyser.

The town of Covington, as orignally laid out, comprised 120 lots, each a quarter acre in size.

The first board of school commissioners—for 1843—were Joseph Damron, Andrew Damron, Charles King, John McD. Mann, Alexander Rayhill, Sampson Sawyers, Henry Smith, Isaac Stull, James Warren.

In 1860 there were several naturalizations, especially of Irish. There were hundreds of that nationality in the county during the construction of the Virginia Central Railroad.

We now pass to the leading documentary features of the War of 1861, as given in the county order book.

1861

The grand jury for the March term was thus constituted: William F. Morton (foreman), John H. Stone, Jordan Helminstoller, Asbury Matheny, Samuel Boyer, Peter Boyer, Dennis Callaghan, William Scott, Joel Kindell, Elias Hook, George Carson, Michael Karnes, Peter Dressler.

The entire county court was present at what may be termed the first war session held April 27th. The members were Andrew Fudge, G. McDonald, George Stull, Lee Persinger, Madison Hook, Thomas T. Shumaker, Charlton Shirkey, Beale V. Keyser, John I. Haynes, and Davis Williamson. At this session it was announced that two volunteer companies were organized and on duty in a tented field, and that other companies would soon be organized.

For the equipment and support of these volunteer companies, there was an appropriation of $6000, raised by a loan. The board to adjust and settle all claims arising out of this fund were C. Bias, James Burk, William F. Clark, Thomas J. Daggs, Colonel Charles Dressler, William G. Holloway, Madison Hook, Edwin Jordan, John Mallow, James M. Montague, Lee Persinger, John L. Pitzer, William M. Scott.

The "war sheriff" was John J. Stack.

The poll tax was $3.50 per tithable, and there was a levy of two per cent. on official salaries.

1862

In March Andrew Damron was authorized in case of need to remove the public records to a place of greater safety.

The levy was $6375.53.

William C. Clark was directed in August to buy 2500 bushels of salt in Washington County.

A great scarcity of wagons was reported.

In November, William P. Rucker was arraigned under a charge of treason for acting as provost marshall under the Wheeling government, for compelling citizens to take an oath to uphold the Federal government, for burning the railroad bridge over the Cowpasture, for appropriating horses and wagons, ofr carrying off slaves, and for mortally stabbing Michael Soice in April, 1861.

1863

In January, William C. Clark was employed to buy 800 bales of cotton yarn, 1000 yards of osnaburgs, and 3000 yards of brown domestic. The actual purchases were 225 bales of cotton and 800 yards of cotton cloth.

Out of 595 slaves the county was required to furnish 27 between the ages of 18 and 45 to work in the Confederate service.

In August there was appointed a committee of safety,, consisting of Thompson McAllister, Peter Byers, William F. Clark, Joseph Irvin, Charlton Shirkey, and William Damron.

It was ordered that C. F. Johnson be paid $25 for removing the county records.

Colonel Samuel Carpenter was made salt agent.

The court states that early in the war ten per cent. of the population had volunteered for the Confederate service; that 200 families of soldiers were now in need of support; that there had been two invasions by Averill's cavalry; that many slaves had absconded, and that if the quota of forty slaves asked by the War Department were insisted upon, desertions from the army would follow.

1864

W. F. Clark was authorized to borrow $10,000 to buy 2000 bushels of corn for destitute soldier families.

It was announced that the Federals under Averill, Duffie, and Crook in their advance, and Hunter in his retreat, had taken everything they could lay their hands on; that there had been unprecedented drouth; and that it was impossible to supply the people and the soldiers unless the Confederate government should release the payment of tax in kind and permit payment in money.

In September wheat was worth $8.11.

The tax on real and personal property was 1½ per cent.

1865

W. F. Clark was an impressing agent.

There was a good deal of felony.

At the special term held April 24th, a resolution was passed, stating that the surrender of Lee had greatly demoralized the citizens, and that both soldiers and citizens were taking government property by force. Captain John Carpenter, of Carpenter's Battery, was ordered to take possession of all government property now in private hands, and turn it over to the state.

At the session of May 5th, it was represented that there was not enough grain on hand to support the soldier families till harvest. Twelve days later, the grain distributors were ordered to receive no more Confederate money in payment of grain, but only specie or its equivalent.

The county court did not meet again until August 21st.

Alleghany had only five soldiers in the Mexican War, but their names are not at our command. In 1843 there were only thirteen schoolhouses.

The real and personal property valuation in 1860 was $3,156,238. The churches were fifteen—nine Methodist, four Presbyterian, and one Union.

We close this chapter with three legends. The first claims that some peaceable Indians lived in White Rock Gap near Lowmoor, and frequented the distillery of Michael Karnes; and that by appointment the nearby farmers met at the distillery, looked up the Indians, and exterminated them.

Another states that Katherine Vanstavern taught the children of the four families once living on the site of Clifton Forge. An admirer was Harry Gorman, a graduate of William and Mary College. Two Indians came one day to the door of the schoolroom. Gorman fired upon them from the woods, killing one and causing the others to run. Very naturally, this led to the lovers becoming engaged. But before they were married, Katherine was seized by five Indians and taken bound in a canoe to the camp of the red men lower down Jackson's River. Gorman saw the performance while hunting, collected a party, came upon the Indians while they were asleep, and after several of the latter were killed, the maiden was rescued to become in due season the wfe of the rescuer. But Cornelius, the first of the Vanstaverns in Bath, was born in Delaware in 1756, and his daughter Katharine married Joseph Carson in 1822, a date much too recent to fit into any Indian raid into the valley of Jackson's River.

Jacob Persinger is thought to have been born at the mouth of Potts Creek. When about twelve years old, he was taken with thirty other captives to the Shawnee towns and adopted by a squaw who had two boys. Boards were tied to their backs to make them straight, and every morning all three had to take a plunge bath, after which they ran about nude until their skins were dry. As a consequence of the treaty of 1764, the boy was brought in that year to Jackson's River. No one claiming him he went back to his foster mother, who was greatly pleased. The chief insisted that it was not right for him to stay with the red men, and three braves returned him to the settlement, but he escaped from them. This time the squaw concealed him, but he was at length seen by the chief, who said he must go back to the whites. The boy thought the Indians were no longer willing for him to be among them, and he made no further attempt to return. This time he was claimed by a German woman who had lost a son, although he did not have a scar from the bite of a rattlesnake, such as was on the foot of her own child. The returned captive was six feet four inches tall, while she was but four feet six inches. But she adopted him and he lived in her home a while. He went to school, but every day carried his rifle, knife, and tomahawk to the schoolroom. After some time, he built a cabin on Stony Mountain and lived the life of a hunter. He married Mary Kimberlin, who, on finding he had no bed except the floor and two bearskins, insisted that he adopt a more civilized way, and she carried her point. He became a good famer and reared his large family well. He was a scout in the Dunmore War and a soldier in the Revolution. This story is probably correct in the main, although an older Jacob Persinger was the pioneer of that name on Potts Creek.

XXV

THE FAMILIES OF GREATER BATH

IN THIS book the spelling of proper names ordinarily follows the style now in common use. It is very true that present usage is not always the same as that of the colonial time. It is also true that these ancient spellings are a part of history. But in those days, each person who wielded a pen spelled a surname according to the way it sounded to him, and sometimes wrote it several different ways in the same document. How are we to choose in such a case as that? And how can we be sure of those instances where the deviation from modern usage is simply the work of a poor speller? Nevertheless, we give below some of the more conspicuous divergencies:

Abercrombie—Abercromby
Benson—Benston
Bourland—Borland, Boreland
Byrd—Bird
Byrnside—Burnside, Burnsides
Carlile—Carlyle, Carlisle, Carolile
Clements—Clemons
Clendennin—Clendening
Daugherty—Doharty, Docharty
Dickenson—Dickerson
Eddy—Edde
Feamster—Feemster, Fimster
Gay—Guy
Gillespie—Galaspy
Given—Givens
Graham—Grymes
Hughart—Hogarth
Kincaid—Kinkead
Knox—Nox
Lockridge—Loughridge
Mayse—Mays, Maze, Mais
McCay—McKay
McClintic—McClintock
McDannald—McDonel, McDonald
McFarland—McFarlin
Millroy—McElroy
Montgomery—McGummery
Moore—Moor
Muldrock—Muldrough
Rhea—Reah, Reagh
Wanless—Wandless

According to C. K. Bolton, the following Ulster immigrants came from County Antrim: the Arbuckles, Campbells, Clarks, Crawfords, Givens, Harpers, Jacksons, Jamesons, McCays; from Derry, the Grahams, Lockridges, Pattons, Rheas; from Down, the Carliles, Dunlaps, Mathewses, Steuarts; from Donegal, the Brattons, Hamiltons; from Londonderry, the Kincaids; from Tyrone, the Burnsides, Knoxes, and Walkups.

THE FAMILIES OF GREATER BATH 187

Certain of the families who have migrated from this county include names of considerable prominence. Thus James B. McCreary and his kinsmen, Thomas C. McCreery of Kentucky, are descendents of John McCreery, of the Cowpasture. Both these men have served in the United States Senate, and the former has twice been governor of his state. Dr. Charles McCreery, the first physician to remove the collar-bone in a surgical operation, which was done in 1813, is also of the same family. By way of North Carolina, we are told that Zebulon B., Robert B., and Robert E. Vance of North Carolina, are of the Vance family of Back Creek. All three served in Congress. The first was also governor of North Carolina, and the second was a brigadier general in the Confederate army. Meigs County, Tennessee, is named for Return Jonathan Meigs, a descendant of the Clendennins. C. C. O'Hara, an eminent geologist, appears to be a descendant of the O'Hara who once lived on the Cowpasture. William Bratton, one of the picked men of the Lewis and Clark expedition of 1803, was a grandson of Robert Bratton, of the Calfpasture. A monument stands over his grave in Indiana giving his services in that famous expedition. Colonels Robert and John McFarland, early pioneers of Jefferson County, Tennessee, are descendents of Duncan McFarland, as was also William McFarland, a congressman from that state.

The remainder of this chapter is devoted to paragraphic mention, in alphabetic order, of a large number of the families which are more or less associated with the history of this county. The list includes names belonging to the Alleghany area and the Calfpasture. Names belonging quite particularly to that portion of the old Bath which now lies in Highland are discussed in the author's history of that county. And as there is a History of Pocahontas, written by Reverend Mr. Price, there is no attempt in this chapter to cover that part of the old county that lies beyond the Alleghany Front.

The list does not assume to be exhaustive. In the case of Bath, as in the case of all counties once a part of the American frontier, there has all the while been coming and going. Names once prominent are now virtually forgotten. Some other names that were once here, yet never seem to have made more than a slight impress, are likewise all but forgotten. Certain names, especially those occurring in our mention of surveys and patents are given no place here, because our genealogic knowledge of them is too slight.

But some of the names still occurring in Bath would either appear, or would have more space, if we had been given the necessary information.

Some further explanation, bearing upon this chapter, will be found in the preface to this book.

* * * * * * * * *

Robert Abercrombie was a man of enterprise and more than ordinary education. He took up several large surveys, and seems to have lived several years on the stream named for him; Cromby's Run, otherwise Molly Moore's Run, but now called Thompson's Creek. He was one of the persons who followed Craighead to North Carolina.

James Anglin lived until about 1756 at the mouth of Benson's Creek, which at first was called Anglin's Creek. Like so many other settlers he became embarrassed by debt. The Indians may have had something to do with his leaving, although he seems to have made a new home beyond the Alleghany. We read of Isaac and other Anglins in that quarter, and there is an Anglin's Run near the western line of Greenbrier. Anglin's Ferry, now Philippi, was named for William Anglin.

Robert Armstrong, of Jackson's River, is mentioned by Doctor Walker in 1750. Another Robert Armstrong was living at the same time near Churchville, and so we cannot always tell which man is referred to in the records. There even seems to have been a third Robert. The one in Bath moved to Kentucky about 1793, but his son of the same name lived here several years longer, and was often foreman of the grand jury. He gave much attention to raising horses. Archibald Armstrong was a neighbor and probably kinsman, who finally removed to Augusta. An Archibald who died here in 1800 had children named Robert, Ann, Thomas, Isabella, William, and Jean. Ann was the wife of James Elliot.

John Baxter came to Back Creek with the Vances and removed to Pocahontas before 1800.

In 1755 the mother of James Beard made oath that her boy's ear had been bitted off by a horse. In those days the human ear was liable to get its owner into trouble. It was sometimes chewed off by animals, whether wild, or domestic, and also by the human animal in the brutal fights of the time. And as slicing off the lobe of the ear was then a mode of punishment, it was not desirable to be under suspicion as a convict. This James was probably a son of an older James. It was doubtless the one or the other who purchased the Crockett place on the Cowpasture in 1776. A James Beard had removed to Tennessee by 1794.

George Benson, a maternal ancestor to the late Joseph Benson Foraker, of Ohio, died near Williamsville about 1809. Several sons of his brother Matthias, went to Monroe.

Alexander Black, the first owner of the Byrd farm near Williamsville, died in 1764, leaving sons named William and Alexander. The latter and probably the former also, went to Kentucky with the McCreerys and settled in the same county. The James Black who owned Fassifern in 1794 seems of another family.

William Blanton, whose wife was Christina Gwin, lived a while somewhere near Williamsville. He moved to the vicinity of Union in Monroe County, where he was a prosperous and well known citizen, as well as a member of the first Methodist congregation west of the Alleghanies.

John Bollar, whom tradition styles a fearless soldier, was a planter on Jackson's River in 1762. His daughter Elizabeth, wedded a Lewis. The John who married a granddaughter of William Wilson and gave his name to Bolar Spring, was a son or grandson.

William Bonner, a veteran of the Revolution, was born in Pennsylvania, in 1759.

James Bourland came from Pennsylvania in 1752, and was murdered nine years later. One Thomas Murray was committed for the crime. Archibald seems to be a brother. His wife was Jean Jackson. James left a son named Andrew, and there were probably other sons.

Robert Bratton was one of four brothers. Samuel remained in Pennsylvania, James settled in Montgomery county, and the sons of the fourth went to South Carolina. Robert married the widow of Alexander Dunlap. His sons, James and Adam, remained here, two sons going to Kentucky. Adam, who married Agnes, a sister to William Given, settled on Jackson's River. James purchased in 1779 the farm and mill of James Rhea. Robert, son of Adam, married Susannah Feamster, daughter, of William. Elizabeth, a daughter of Robert Bratton, married Samuel Craig.

John Brown, born in Ireland in 1743, settled at Ebbing Spring. He was a major in the Revolution and a justice of Bath for 33 years. His adult children were Joseph, Margaret, John, and Rosanna.

Joseph and John Burns, brothers, settled in the Red Holes about 1792, Peter, a third brother, going to Tennessee. Joseph married Kate Keiffer, and John married Margaret Monroe. John died in the Red Holes in 1805. Of his seven children, Peter, who married Elizabeth C. Monroe, in 1817, was the only son to leave posterity in this county. The hamlet of Burnsville takes its name from this family.

James Burnside was a stepson to Archibald Clendennin, who willed him 300 acres in the "New Found Land." Burnside lived quite a while on the Bullpasture. He moved to Monroe, was burned out by Indians in 1763, and returned for about six more years. He died at Union in 1812. He was arbitrary and contentious, but an energetic trader and land operator. He had a sister Rachel. His descendants changed the spelling to Byrnside.

John Byrd, a brother-in-law to John and William Dean, was killed by Indians two years after his purchase on Jackson's River in 1754. Of the wife and six children who were carried away, John, Jr., is the only one we know to have returned. The family were trying to escape to Fort Dinwiddie. The son became so Indianized that it was quite a while before he could reconcile himself to the ways of his own people. He was a favorite with the red men, and made at least one attempt to go back to them. His wife was a Hamilton. There were seven children, but Andrew H., whose wife was Elizabeth Capito, was the only son to stay in Bath. He was twice its sheriff. A sister two years older than John, Jr., remained with the Indians. Another sister was Sarah, born in 1743. She does not seem to have been carried away, and chose John Dean as guardian.

James Callison came from Albemarle about 1749.

Charles Edward Cameron, born precisely twenty years later than Washington, was a soldier at Point Pleasant, where his only brother was killed. General Lafayette, who esteemed him as a personal friend, presented him with a gold-headed cane in 1781. He became a colonel. About 1790 he settled at Fassifern, which he named after his ancestral home in the Scottish Highlands. He died here in 1829. His wife was Rachel P., daughter of Jacob Warwick. The only son to grow to maturity was Andrew W., grandfather to Mrs. Tate

Sterrett. But Colonel Cameron reared Andrew Gatewood, and also Charles L. Francisco, son of his half-sister, Mary, and afterward county clerk. Colonel Cameron was of very estimable character.

James Carlile died on the Calfpasture about 1752, where he had for several years been living on a farm of 578 acres. He told the Lewises he did not want the land on account of the "barrens" in it, but would complete the purchase if he could have the portion of the survey east of the river. Otherwise he would leave, but asked payment for his improvements. These—on 400 acres—were sold to William Hamilton for $87.50, against whom James, Jr., and the widow, Elizabeth, brought suit for the $25 still due. Robert and John Carlile, of the Bullpasture were undoubtedly other sons. The late John G. Carlisle, of Kentucky, was a grandson of Robert.

Joseph Carpenter came from New York in 1746, and took a large river-bottom survey a little below Covington. Tradition states that a first visit was in the spring and that he started a crop of corn. On his return in the fall, he found that a young buffalo had broken through the fence and was trying to relieve the owner of the trouble of harvesting. The poacher was promptly converted into steak. Carpenter came with a large family nearly grown, and he wished them to settle around him. He seems to have been living in 1776. Close by was another Carpenter family, that of a brother, the name of the pioneer appearing to be Solomon. John and Joseph were sons of Joseph, Sr., and Thomas and Jeremiah of Solomon. Two daughters of Joseph Sr., married Jeremiah Seely and John Mann. Of a later generation was Samuel, who died in 1842, leaving six chldren.

The Joseph Carpenter who came from England as an indentured servant, and lived about seven years with Loftus Pullin, was not related to the other families. He settled in Little Valley about 1790, and reared twelve children.

The father of John Cartmill came to the vicinity of Winchester during the infancy of settlement, and a part of the family homestead is still in the family, being owned by T. C. Cartmill, historian of the lower Shenandoah Valley. John was one of eleven children. His own sons were John, James, Samuel, and Thomas.

Jacob Cleek seems to have come from Rockbridge. He died in 1813, and his sons were David, Josiah, John, and Benjamin.

Jacob Clements died in 1759. His children were nine daughters.

Archibald Clendennin lived on the John Walker survey, and was buried there in 1749. He left half the farm to his son, John, then about five years old, who later went to East Tennessee. The boy had a sister, Margaret, and James Burnside was a half brother. Archibald, Jr., a son by the first wife, moved to Greenbrier and was murdered by Indians in 1763. His wife was a Ewing. Five of his six children were also killed, but the wife escaped to the Cowpasture. George and Charles seem to have been other sons. The latter gave his name to the capital of West Virginia.

Hugh Coffey went to South Carolina about 1756.

John Cowardin, who married a Lewis, rented the Fort Lewis plantation after the death of Colonel Charles Lewis.

Alexander Crawford, Sr., lost his life in one of the massacres on Kerr's Creek. The son seems to have lived on the Cowpasture till after the Revolution, when he returned to Rockbridge. There were other Crawfords in Bath.

Captain Robert Crockett came to America in 1740, and died in Beverly Manor in 1746, leaving nine sons and a daughter. John and Archibald inherited the Cowpasture land, but moved to Mecklenburg County, North Carolina. John and James sold the Calfpasture property. Samuel, who inherited the place on Jackson's River, was a sergeant at Fort Dickenson in 1763. Robert, Jr., was killed in Tennessee, in 1769, where he was a member of a company of hunters. Whether the celebrated Davy Crockett sprang from this family we do not know. There were other Crocketts in Augusta in pioneer times.

William Daugherty was a blacksmith. The family was in Kentucky in 1791.

Patrick Davis, who was living near Windy Cove in 1750, removed to Greenbrier.

William Dean was a minister on the Brandywine in Pennsylvania. Shortly before his death, which took place in 1748, he purchased land in the Borden grant and on Jackson's River. The latter place fell to William, Jr., who sold it to his brother, John. The latter, who was also a minister, and in 1794 sheriff of Bath, died in 1811, aged about ninety. His daughters, Mary, Margaret, Alice, Elizabeth, Nancy, Sarah, and Jean, married, respectively, William Bourland, William Crawford, John Kincaid, James Kincaid, James

Anderson, James Venable, and Andrew McClung. There was also a son William.

John Donally died before 1772, and his farm seems to have fallen to John Clark, a son-in-law. Charles, who died on Stuart's Creek in 1733, was probably a brother. His children were Andrew, Charles Ann, and Catharine. Captain Andrew Donally moved to Greenbrier about 1769, and his stockade withstood a heavy attack by the Indians in 1778. A few years later he moved on to Kanawha County, of which he was one of the first justices.

Alexander Dunlap came from near Philadelphia and is said to have been the first settler on Great River. He became a captain of horse in 1743, but died the following year, leaving personality to the then considerable value of $811.48. His house stood near the spot now occupied by the Alleghany Inn at Goshen. His wife was Jean McFarland, and his children were John, Alexander, and Elizabeth. The first lived in Rockbridge. The other two went to Kentucky. Goshen Pass was first known as Dunlap Pass, and Bratton's Run was first Dunlap's Run. It was another Dunlap who gave his name to Dunlap's Creek.

John Eddy moved to Botetourt before 1797.

Thomas Feamster, a wheelwright, came from Pennsylvania and lived a while in Hampshire. In 1743 he was an appraiser of the estate of Christopher Graham. He died in 1797 on the farm near Williamsville where he had been living about half a century. His personality amounted to almost $4,400. A daughter hid his will and the estate was not settled for fifteen years. The document was at length found by a grandson, Thomas Sitlington, who burned it. The daughters of Thomas Feamster were Martha, Rachael, Elizabeth, Susanna, and Sarah, who married, respectively, John McCreery John Carlile, Adam Bratton, Joseph Wallace, and Hugh Brown. The only daughter of Sarah Brown married Matthew Wallace. The sons of Thomas Feamster were William and John, who moved away, the first settling in Greenbrier before his father's death. William was three times married. The second wife was a Black, the third was Mary Fulton. The three daughters by the first wife married and went to Indiana. The one son by the second was Thomas, who married Polly McClung, 1796, and has descendants in Tennessee. The sons by the third marriage are the ancestors of the Feamsters of Greenbrier.

Conrad Fudge, who died in Alleghany about 1849, married a daughter of Jacob Persinger, by whom he had fourteen children. He owned lands then worth $7,000, and left $1,000 to each of five sons.

David Frame was the oldest son of John Frame, who came from Pennsylvania. The son purchased the Benjamin Lewis farm and lived on it some years, but moved to Greenbrier about 1797.

John Fulton was a pioneer of the Calfpasture. The Fulton Spring on Mill Creek seems to be associated with James or with a son. James died in 1753, leaving eight children.

James, Henry, John, Robert, and William Gay, whose names appear in the Pastures between 1745 and 1755, were brothers. Their sister, Eleanor, married William Kinkead. James died in 1776, leaving eight children. Several of the later Gays went to Kentucky.

Samuel Given purchased in Beverly Manor in 1738 and was one of the early justices of Augusta. His son William seems identical with the William Given of the Wilson settlement, who died in 1793, leaving ten children.

Christopher Graham, who died in 1748, was probably the father of John, who lived until 1771, and had eight children. One of these was Jean, who married Andrew Lockridge. Robert inherited a half-interest in his father's gristmill. Florence married her cousin, James Graham, a pioneer on the Greenbrier. It may have been her brother James, who was owning the Mitchell patent at his death in 1829. That he owned silver tableware besides a bed and curtains inventoried at $45, indicates that he was comfortably situated.

Naphthalim Gregory was a soldier of the Indian war and must have died at an early age. His widow, Mary, continued to occupy the farm on Back Creek.

James Hall died about 1764, a date which suggests that he may have been a victim of the Indian raid in 1763. His appraisers were Thomas Feamster and George and John Lewis. His son Robert was in North Carolina in 1737, but as he purchased one-half of a Jackson survey five years later, he must have been one of the number who preferred the Augusta highlands to the Southern lowlands.

We are in some doubt as to who was the first Hamilton on Jackson's River and Back Creek, and there may have been more than a single pioneer in that quarter. Tradition relates that the first Hamilton family on Back Creek used for a while an Indian camping hut.

It is said that trees from which bark had been stripped to cover such shelters continued to stand until a recent day. Charles, Osborn, and Robert seem to be sons of this family. Major Andrew Hamilton moved to Greenbrier, where he was a wealthy resident, owning much property in lands and slaves. He had a brother William. Two sisters married James McCay and William Mann, and a third married a Bowen.

Hugh Hicklin, who lived some years on the Millroy patent, was the oldest son of Thomas, of the Bullpasture, and he moved to Kentucky about 1797. Sonora Hicklin, who married the late William M. Boggs, of Napa, California, may have been a descendant. Mrs. Boggs left the statement that her great-grandfather Hicklin was in Kentucky before Daniel Boone.

Samuel Hodge died in 1773. His sons were John and James. The latter was born 1747. His daughters, Sarah, Agnes, Margaret, Catharine, and Elizabeth, married in order, a McDonald, a Martin, a McIlvaine, a Kelly, and a McCutchen. Another daugrter was Eleanor.

John Henry Insminger, a blacksmith, lived a while on the Cowpasture and then went to Monroe, where he remained.

Captain William Jameson died about 1753. To John, his oldest son, he left his land on Jackson's River and his best suit of "close." Other sons were George, Andrew, and William, of whom the last named had the Calfpasture homestead. John left Augusta.

James Kelso was a servant in 1759. He married a daughter of John Sitlington, lived nearly opposite Laverty, and was a prominent citizen.

William Keyser purchased land on the west side of Warm Springs Mountain in 1797.

Even in the infancy of Augusta the Kincaids were many. The John who bought land on the Calfpasture lived at New London, in Pennsylvania, and at once conveyed the place to David Kincaid, of Albemarle.

James Knox, who died in 1772, lived a mile northeast of Williamsville. His children were James, John, Robert, Jean, Abigail, Elizabeth, and Mary. The wife's name was Jean. It is stated on very good authority that James, Jr., an officer in Washington's army, was the man who gave his name to Knoxville, Tennessee, and not

General Henry Knox, as is the usual claim. Jane, the mother of President Polk, was a daughter of one James Knox. That the latter was a kinsman is very probable.

The LaRue family is derived from Isaac, who settled near Winchester in 1738. Abraham, a son, moved to Augusta County.

Ralph Laverty died in 1792 at the mouth of Stuart's Creek, where he had lived near half a century. He was a person of some means and prestige, and until the Revolution his name often occurs in the Augusta records. But he operated a still, and on one occasion he was fined for being too drunk to give testimony. His second wife, whom he married in 1764, was Jean, widow of Robert Graham. His sons, William and Steele, settled on New River at the mouth of Indian Creek. The latter was killed by Indians. The former, who died a natural death in 1818, was the parent of fourteen children. The daughters of Ralph were Elizabeth, Agnes, Sarah, and Martha. To the first, who married James Hamilton, of Rockbridge, he left his homestead. The otrers married, in order, a Haddon, a Clark, and a Meek. In 1800, a slave named Chainey, belonging to the widow Laverty, murdered her own child. The people of Bath were not willing to see the woman hanged, and she was sent out of the county.

Captain John Lewis, of Warm Springs, was a son of Thomas and a nephew of Charles. He commanded a company at Point Pleasant, and was also an officer under Washington. He died in 1788, leaving four children, Thomas L., Elizabeth S., Charles A., and John B.

George Lewis was unrelated to the other connection. He came from Lancaster County, Pennsylvania. He seems to have been illiterate. His sons, John and Benjamin, between whom he divided his homestead, went to Greenbrier. Yet the father may have been the George Lewis who was exempted from head-tax in 1785 because of age.

James Lockridge seems to have come to the Calfpasture in 1753. He sold his purchase to his son Andrew and went to North Carolina. Andrew built a mill soon after his arrival, but in 1774 he removed to a large purchase north of Burnsville and died there in 1791. James and Lancelot were his brothers, and there was probably also a Robert. His own sons were John, Andrew, James, William, and Robert. Rev. Andrew Y. Lockridge, a Presbyterian missionary to the

Cherokee Indians, is a descendant. Sarah, a daughter of the first James, married John Gay, son of James, and went to Kentucky. The celebrated Colonel Lockridge, of Texas, killed in Walker's filibustering expedition to Nicaraugue, is believed to have been another descendant.

Humphrey Madison was a deputy sheriff in 1753 and was killed by Indians three years later. He must have lived on the Cowpasture, as his estate was appraised by four men of the Dickenson settlement.

Michael Mallow seems to be identical with the Michael whose father of the same name settled near Upper Tract in Pendleton County. The son was born about 1755 and carried off by Indians in childhood, but was restored. He was identified by a scar on the thumb. Michael, of Alleghany, died in 1830, leaving seven children.

Moses Mann, an early settler in Beverly Manor, died about 1758, and seems to be the father of John, William, and Thomas, of whom the first was the administrator. The brothers William and Thomas settled on Jackson's River. William died about 1778. His first habitation was a saltpeter cave, in which a son was born. His children were Moses, Thomas, William, John, Jenny, and Sarah. The sons were given land in Bath and Monroe. Thomas, brother of William Sr., traded with the Indians and lived until 1794.

Thomas Massie came from Frederick County.

James Mayse, a cooper, was the first pioneer in Bath to hold a civil office. He was killed by Indians, leaving personalty worth about $150. His sons were William, Joseph, anad Richard. The third, whose administrator was William Douglas, died in 1809. Joseph Mayse, of the Fort Lewis settlement, may have been a brother, yet we are not certain that there was an entire identity of surname. His son Joseph died in 1840 at the age of eighty-four. His brief captivity among the Indians is elsewhere mentioned. A severe wound in the battle of Point Pleasant induced his mother to ride there on horse-back with only a negro attendant. She nursed him back to recovery, yet at a much later time amputation of the injured leg became necessary. He had a brother Isaac.

James McAvoy was kidnapped from Ireland when a youth and sold to Robert Carlile.

Thomas and John McAllister, of Ugly Creek, died about

the same time—1829. The sons of the former were William and Reese; of the latter, James and Samuel.

JamesMcCay moved to Greenbrier.

John McClung, Jr., came from Rockbridge to Thompson's Creek in 1751, when only eighteen years old. His wife was Sarah McCutchen, and his sons were Robert, John, and William.

William McClintic purchased a part of the Bourland place in 1774, and lived there till his death in 1801. His sons were Alexander, William, Joseph, and Robert. Two daughters married Milhollens. A brother to William was so desperately wounded at Guilford that he only partially recovered. In 1786 the court of Botetourt recommended him for a pension. He died soon afterward, leaving a son.

John McCreery, a carpenter, was a settler of some means and enterprise. He died on his homestead in 1768, after dividing it between his sons John and Robert, both of whom were prominent in both civil and military life in this county before moving to Kentucky. The pioneer McCreery had also several daughters. Elizabeth married Colonel George Wilson in 1750. Wilson is mentioned in another paragraph. Jane married Major Andrew Donally, a pioneer of Greenbrier and Kanawha, and whose fort near Lewisburg was the scene of a battle with the Indians in 1778. Nancy—named for her mother, Nancy Crawford, of Dublin, Ireland—married James Huston, who went to Kentucky in 1783 and died at his home near Covington in 1818, at the age of ninety-five. The wife of John McCreery, Jr., was a daughter of Wallace Estill.

The children of John McDannald, who seems to have been a physician, were Samuel, John, Elizabeth, James, Mary, Rebecca, and William. Samuel was living on Mill Creek in 1790. John went to Ohio and James to Kentucky. Elizabeth was several years a captive among the Indians. As the widow of Robert Sitlington she gave $1,000 to Windy Cove church.

Duncan McFarland seems to have come from Lunenburg County. Alexander and William were sons. The first was a soldier of the Revolution. He sold to Jacob Cleek and went to North Carolina. The other absconded about 1775, leaving his father-in-law to care for the wife and her seven children.

Robert McGuffin came from Rockingham and purchased land below Falling Spring in 1795.

Alexander Millroy seems to have moved to Rockbridge about 1762.

John Mitchell was living in North Carolina in 1766. But a John who may have been the same died in Augusta in 1771. His children were Thomas, Robert, John, James, Eleanor, Mary, and Elizabeth. One John Mitchell died a natural death in 1783 at David Frame's stillhouse; according to the verdict of the coroner's jury.

John Moore, who settled near the mouth of Thompson's Creek, was a victim of the Indians. According to tradition, his widow Molly accepted a brave as her second husband, and her son, Joseph, fought on the side of the red men, thereby arousing great indignation among the white people who had known him in boyhood. This legend may be confused as to names and details. Moore is not one of the rare names and it was not rare in pioneer Augusta. At all events the Moore name was not blotted out in Bath, and a Joseph Moore was living in this county in 1797.

Richard Morris died on Jackson's River in 1805. His nine children seem mostly to have gone to Ohio. Isabella and Frances married, respectively, William Elliot and Archibald Armstrong.

Andrew Muldrock died in 1758 or 1759, leaving a will which was not put on record. The widow, Jean, seems to have moved to the mouth of the Cowpasture.

Anthony Mustoe came to Warm Springs Valley about 1790. He was associated with William Chambers in some land operations.

In 1762 Michael O'Hara was a ward of Alexander Millroy.

John Oliver, a large landholder and a prominent citizen, died in 1791, leaving a son of the same name.

Jacob Persinger was one of the earliest pioneers of Potts Creek and had a numerous posterity. His son Jacob died in 1841, leaving eleven children. To his brother Henry, who preceded him seventeen years, there were born ten.

Adam Porter settled on Porter's Mill Creek shortly after the Revolution, and built a gristmill. Three son were Robert, Reese, and Adam.

John Putnam was born in Massachusetts in 1764, and came to Stuart's Creek at the age of thirty. As Jeptha Putnam he was a fifer in the Revolution when a boy of thirteen.

Michael Rainey moved from the upper Cowpasture to Indian

Creek and ended his days there. He seems to have had no children.

John Ramsey, who married the widow of Robert Gay, purchased the Coffey place.

William Renick owned the Benson farm for seven years before moving to Greenbrier, and may have lived on it.

William Rhea died on Mill Creek in 1801, after having lived there at least thirty years. His sons were William and John. To a grandson he left a copy of "Whitefield's Sermons."

James and William Scott apear to be brothers. The latter died in 1751, and the widow married Joseph Carpenter, the guardian of his children. Elizabeth Scott, who died in 1841, was an aged widow who left $200 to the Presbyterian church at Covington.

Andrew Sitlington, who came to America before 1760, and to the Cowpasture soon after 1766, lived chiefly on the Craighead farm till his death in 1804 . To relatives and friends he left sums amounting to $3,000. Like his brother Robert he had no children. A third Sitlington was John, who lived at the mouth of Stuart's Creek. William and James were his sons. The latter was killed in the battle of Falling Spring, though not, it is said, until he had slain two of the foe. His scalp, identified by its yellow hair, was recovered. William, who died in 1772, has many descendants, although the surname has for several decades been extinct both in Bath and Highland. The Sitlingtons were people of much thrift and prominence.

James Sloan, a neighbor, to the McClungs, married a daughter of John Sitlington.

James Stuart gave his name to the stream first known as Stuart's Mill Creek. He was probably a brother-in-law to Ralph Laverty, and was killed by Indians in 1757. James, Ralph, and John were then minor children. James and Ralph went to Tygart's Valley, where the former died in 1777, probably while in militia service. Robert, who was living on the patent in 1789 and keeping a store, was probably the oldest son.

Van and Leonard Swearingen, living on Mill Creek in 1790, seem to be descendants of the Van who was living in Berkeley County in 1738.

Thomas Thompson came from Delaware about 1749, and settled on the stream which now bears his name. He was guardian of James Stuart, Jr. He died about 1760, perhaps another victim of the red man. Edward, the administrator, seems to be a brother. There were a William and a younger Thomas. Robert, a soldier at Point Pleasant, was born in 1758. Joseph, living in 1781 on the Botetourt section of Jackson's River, was probably of a distinct family.

The surname Usher calls up a romance, of which our knowledge is all too fragmentary. One Edward Usher wedded the only daughter and sole heir of a member of the English aristocracy. After a few years she was left a widow and sought a reconciliation with her father. She was walking toward his mansion, leading her children, when he drove by. The parent merely tossed her a coin with the remark that that was all the brats should have of his property. In some unknown manner, the three daughters came to the Dickenson settlement. In 1745, James Knox, as guardian of Ann Jenny Usher, executed the first fiduciary bond on record in Augusta County. She married Loftus Pullin, of the Bullpasture. Martha married Colonel John Dickenson, and Margaret married William Steuart of the upper Cowpasture. Steuart, an educated Scotchman, came to America when about twenty years old, but the ship he took passage with was captured by pirates and he was set ashore with nothing at all but a piece of canvas. All three had families. There was almost certainly a brother, who must have emigrated from this region. The aristocratic grandparent finally relented and sent an agent to America, but the sisters did not know of it till afterward, and do not seem to have been much interested in the matter.

Samuel Vance came to Mountain Grove by 1765, and lived there till his death in 1807. His children were James, Benjamin, Ally, Allen, Patsy, Nancy, Sarah, and Elizabeth. John would appear to be a brother to Samuel.

James Waddell bargained for his survey on the Cowpasture in 1743. He fell into debt to a number of people and betook himself to Pennsylvania in 1747. Robert Bratton attached a mare. Laverty was his security to John Scott on a note of $21.86. Scott brought suit, and Laverty petitioned that he might be allowed to patent Waddell's survey, the face of the note and the purchase price of the land being nearly the same. This was granted, and a valuation of the improvements was made by McCay, Cartmill, Stuart, and Adam Dickenson.

Thomas Wallace came from Deleware in 1781, purchased the upper half of the McCreery homestead, and died on it in 1799. His children were Matthew, David, Josiah, John, Benjamin, Joseph, Thomas, Polly, and Nancy. Matthew, born in 1772, is the ancestor of the Wallaces of Bath. General W. H. L. Wallace, killed in the Battle of Shiloh in 1862, sprang from another branch.

James Ward, born about 1727, lived some years at Warm Springs where he kept a tavern. He was a lieutenant, and was a brother-in-law to Sampson Mathews and Matthew Arbuckle. He removed to Anthony's Creek in 1769. John Ward, excused from poll tax in 1768, seems to have been his father and to have lived with him at Warm Springs. Colonel William Ward, the oldest of the seven children of James, was taken by Indians near Fort Dinwiddie, but was restored. He was a justice of Greenbrier and otherwise a leading man there. He finally removed to Ohio, where he founded the city of Urbana in 1805. Captain James Ward, the second son, was killed at Point Pleasant.

William Warwick came from Williamsburg and married Elizabeth Dunlap. His sons were Charles and John. The latter was a scout in the Indian war and went to Kentucky in 1789. Captain Jacob Warrick, a son, was killed at Tippecanoe, and Warrick County, in Indiana, is named for him. General Harrison complimented his company by saying he had never seen a finer body of men. Major Jacob Warwick owned for a while the Fort Dinwiddie farm. He moved to Pocahontas about 1800. Three sons-in-law were Charles E. Cameron, Sampson Mathews, and William Gatewood.

Joseph Watson died in the spring of 1747, and the widow married John McCapen. In the inventory of Watson's effects is the first mention in Augusta of knives and forks, their value being fifty-eight cents.

Elisha Williams came from Frederick County. Hazel Williams, whose wife was Rachel Cauley, was a miller on Lick Run in 1792.

William Wilson, of Bolar Run, came from Brandywine Creek in Pennsylvania about 1749. Stephen Wilson was a neighbor and kinsman.

George Wilson seems to have been a man of much energy and influence and to have had some enemies. He acquired several widely-separated surveys, but appears to have lived at Green Valley. During the Indian war he commanded a company of militia. About 1763 he removed to the west of Pennsylvania and settled near where he had campaigned in the Braddock war. After the Revolution began he was lieutenant colonel of the Eighth Pennsylvania, but died in that service in 1777.

Archibald Withrow was born in 1773 and died at the age of seventy.

Peter Wright settled on the site of Covington and had a gristmill. Fort Young was built on his homestead. He died about 1758, and his son of the same name was his executor.

ERRATA

Page 7, line 14:   Read *were,* not *are.*

Page 16, line 25:   Read *Alexander* not *William.*

Page 35, line 1:   Read *purchases,* not *purchasers.*

Page 40, line 27:   Read *Thomas C. McCreary,* not *McCreery.*

Page 41, line 5:   According to very recent information, these McFarlands were not discended from Duncan.

Page 72, line 1:   Read $7.84, not $5.00.

Page 92, line 32:   Omit *the*

Page 93, line 10:   Read $50, not $30.

Page 100, line 18:   Read *"Deficalty,"* not *"Deficasy."*

Page 102, line 36:   Read *principles,* not *principals.*

Page 195, line 7:   Read *John Byrd, Jr.,* not *Bowen.*

A few other errors are quite slight and therefore are not mentioned here.

GENERAL INDEX

NOTE: The topics beginning on pages 27, 36, 106, 111, 128, 153, 168, and 170, contain numerous proper names arranged with one exception in alphabetic order. These names are not repeated in the present index.

Abercrombie, Robert..........188
Act of Assembly, 1790.......107
Alleghany, Naming of........176
Alleghany, Formation of......176
Alleghany, Physical Geography 176
Alleghany, Statistical 177
Alleghany, Industrial 177
Alleghany, Scenic Features ..178
Alleghany, Organization of...180
Alleghany in War of 1861....182
Alleghany, Justices, 1823-1852.180
Alleghany, Early History of 181, 182, 184
Anglin, James 188
Animals and Plants.......... 6
Armstrong, Robert 188
Augusta County 15
Augusta in 1783.............. 78

Bailey, Ann.................. 99
Bath Alum 49
Bath, Form and Size 1
Bath, Boundaries 1
Bath, Organization of 108
Bath, Curtailments 134
Bath, Magisterial Districts ...138
Bath, Valuation, 1860 138
Bath, Progress, 1790-1860 139
Bath, Squadron 146
Bath, Modern 172
Bath, Tourists 172
Bath, Statistical 174
Bath, Pioneer Families 186
Bath, Soldiers in Revolution 95, 98

Bath, Officers in Revolution 95, 96, 97
Bath-Pendleton line, 1793....134
Baxter, John 188
Beard, James 188
Benson, George 189
Black, Alexander 189
Blanton, William 189
Blowing Cave 9
Bolar Spring 45
Bollar, John 189
Bonner, William 189
Botetourt County, Formation of 54
Bourland, James 189
Bratton, Robert 41, 189
Brown, John 190
Burns Family 190
Burnside, James 190
Byrd, John 190

Calfpasture, Position of......167
Calfpasture, Early Officials...167
Calfpasture, Lewis and Patton Survey 167
Calfpasture, Pioneer Settlers 168-170
Calfpasture, Emigrants from..169
Callison, James 190
Cameron, Charles E. 190
Carlile, James 191
Carpenter, Families 191
Cartmill, John 191
Chesapeake & Ohio R. R.....179
Church Buildings, 1860.......138
Cleek, Jacob 191
Clements, Jacob 191

Clendennin, Archibald ...40, 192
Clifton Forge 180
Climate 6
Cloverdale 162
Coffey, Hugh 192
Confederate Soldiers, Roster of 152
County Government, Colonial. 52
Courthouses 136
Covington 179, 181
Cowardin, John 192
Craighead, Alexander 67
Crawford, Alexander 192
Crockett, Robert 192

Daugherty, William 192
Davis, Patrick 192
Dean, William 192
Dickenson, Adam and John... 38
Donally Family 193
Dunlap, Alexander 193

Ebbing Spring 9
Eddy, John 193

Feamster, Thomas 193
Flag Rock, View From 8
Fort Lewis Settlement 19
Frame, Daniel 194
French and Indian War 79
Fort Dinwiddie 96
Fudge, Conrad 194
Fulton, John 194

Geology 4
Given, William 194
Gregory, Naphthalim 194
Graham, James 194

Hall, James 194
Hamilton Family 194
Healing Springs 45, 49
Hicklin, Hugh 195
Hodge, Samuel 195
Hot Springs 44
Hot Springs, Town of 47
Hot Springs, Walker's Visit to
                       62, 78

Immigrants, Ulster Homes of .40
Incidents, 1790-1860 .....135, 139
Indian Names 14
Indian Legend 45
Indian Raids, 1756-59 82
Indian Raid, 1763 ....84, 85
Indians, Relations with 79
Indians, Defense against 80

Jackson Family 39
James River and Kanawha Canal 179
Jameson, William 195
Justices, 1791-1823 136

Kelso, James 195
Keyser, William 195
Kincaid Family 195
Knox, James 195

LaRue Family 196
Laverty, Ralph 196
Law and Order 69
Legal Documents 71
Letter by Andrew Lewis 86
Letter by Andrew Sittlington . 87
Letter by Charles Lewis 88
Letter by John Dickenson ...100
Letter by W. Chambers 138
Letter by Robert Bratton 142
Lewis Family 196
Lewis, John 14, 15
Lewis, Charles 92
Lewis Land Grant 15, 23
Litigation 69
Liquor, Petition against 140
Lockridge, Andrew 196

Madison, Humphrey 197
Mallow, Michael 197
Mann Family 197
Mann's Fort, attack upon ... 84
Marriage Bonds, list of 128
Marriage Formalities 127
Massie, Thomas 197
Mathews, Sampson and Geo..162
Mayse Family 197

GENERAL INDEX

Mayse, Captivity of Joseph... 85
McAvoy, James 197
McCallister Family 197
McCay, James 198
McClung, John 198
McClintic Family 198
McCrary, John 40, 198
McDonnald, John 198
McFarland, Duncan 198
McGuffin, Robert 198
Meadow Lake 9
Millboro Springs 49
Militia System 69
Millroy, Alexander 199
Mineral Waters, Nature of... 42
Mineral Springs of Cowpasture 49
Mitchell, John 199
Money in Colonial Times ... 71
Moore, John 199
Moravian Missionaries 76
Morris, Richard 199
Mountain Ranges 2
Mountain Passes 3
Muldrock, Andrew 199
Muster Roll, Wilson's Company 86
Mustoe, Anthony 199

O'Hara, Michael 40, 199
Oliver, John 199

Paths, aboriginal 56
Pennsylvania Road 62
Pensioners of Revolution 98
Persinger Family 184, 199
Petition of 1727 18
Petition of 1779, Signers of...106
Petitions of 1779-1788 104
Pioneer Settlement Areas 36
Pioneer Conditions 62
Pioneer Houses 66
Pioneer Costume 63
Pioneer Taverns 51
Pioneer Occupations 66
Pioneer Stores 52
Pioneer Farming 66

Pioneer Mills 52
Pioneer Prices 73
Pioneer Postal Service 76
Pioneer Forts 81
Pioneer Schools 69, 170
Plantations 71
Point Pleasant Expedition ... 89
Point Pleasant, Battle of 90
Pontiac War 83, 85
Population Figures 135, 174
Porter, Adam 199
Powder Mills 75
Presbyterianism 67
Prices, 1781 97
Processioning 65
Public Land, Methods of Obtaining 22, 23
Putnam, John 199

Rainey, Michael 199
Ramsey, John 200
Rangers, Dickenson's 86
Renick, William 200
Revolution, Three Stages of
                          94, 96
Revolution, Local Events 96
Revolution, Bath Soldiers in . 94
Rhea, William 200
Rivers of the Pastures 13
Roads, Pioneer 56
Road Overseers, 1748-88 ... 60
Rocky Springs Church 170
Rubino Spring 45

Scenery 7
Schools, Petition on 140
Scotch-Irish Settlers 11
Scott Family 200
Selim, the Algerine 101
Sheriffs, 1823-61 137
Sittlington Family 200
Slavery 139
Sloan, James 200
Society, Grades of 64
Society, State of 67, 69, 76

Soils 57	War of 1861, War Justices ..143
Spottsylvania County 15	War of 1861, Local Document-
Spottswood's Expedition 10	ary History 144, 182
Stranger, A Mysterious 141	War of 1861, Jones' Raid ...149
Stuart, James 200	Ward, James 202
Suit, Mayse vs. Lewis 26	Warm Springs 44, 49
Surnames, 1782-3 111	Warm Springs, Town of 48
Surnames, 1791 118	Warm Springs Valley, Settle-
Surnames, 1913 122	ment of 46
Surveys and Patents, Lists of . 27	Warm Springs, Description of 50
	Warm Springs, Strother's Eu-
Terrill Brothers 143	logy 50
Trompson, Thomas 200	Warwick, William 202
Toryism 98	Water-courses 4
Usher, Edward 201	Watson, Joseph 202
	Whiskey War 133
Vance Family 40, 201	Williams, Elisha 202
Vanstavern Story 184	Wilson, William 202
	Wilson, George 202
Waddell, James 201	Windy Cave Church 67
Wallace, Thomas 202	Withrow, Archibald 203
War of 1861, local incidents of	Wright, Peter 203
143, 147	

www.ingramcontent.com/pod-product-compliance
Lightning Source LLC
Chambersburg PA
CBHW051059230426
43667CB00013B/2362